Environmental Inequalities Beyond Borders

Urban and Industrial Environments

Series editor: Robert Gottlieb, Henry R. Luce Professor of Urban and Environmental Policy, Occidental College

For a complete list of books published in this series, please see the back of the book.

Environmental Inequalities Beyond Borders

Local Perspectives on Global Injustices

edited by JoAnn Carmin and Julian Agyeman

The MIT Press
Cambridge, Massachusetts
London, England

For information about special quantity discounts, please e-mail special_sales@ mitpress.mit.edu

This book was set in Sabon by Toppan Best-set Premedia Limited. Printed and bound in the United States of America.

Library of Congress Cataloging-in-Publication Data

Environmental inequalities beyond borders : local perspectives on global injustices / edited by JoAnn Carmin and Julian Agyeman.
    p.   cm. — (Urban and industrial environments)
Includes bibliographical references and index.
ISBN 978-0-262-01551-6 (hardcover : alk. paper) — ISBN 978-0-262-51587-0 (pbk. : alk. paper)
1. Environmental justice. 2. Environmental degradation. 3. Globalization—Environmental aspects. I. Carmin, JoAnn. II. Agyeman, Julian.
GE220.E575   2011
363.7—dc22
                                                              2010038606

10 9 8 7 6 5 4 3 2 1

Contents

Acknowledgments

This project emerged out of informal monthly discussions we had on environmental justice research and teaching. Through the course of these exchanges, we came to recognize the distinct perspectives we each bring to the field based on our respective training in geography and sociology, as well as our shared views as scholars and educators in the field of urban and environmental planning. Ultimately, we came to the conclusion that there was a need for a volume that engaged the spatial and institutional dimensions of environmental justice scholarship, one that would spark debates among scholars and support the courses we teach on this topic. While we had a particular vision in mind at the outset, our exchanges and engagements with the chapter authors expanded our perspectives and enhanced our thinking and understanding of the dynamics of the field.

We are grateful to the authors of the chapters, because each brought a unique perspective to this project that ensured that multiple vantage points were conveyed and that the boundaries of our knowledge of the field of environmental justice were expanded. Special thanks go to Andrea Alejandra Betancourt, Eric Mackres, and Amanda Martin for providing detailed comments on early versions of chapters they read in the context of a graduate environmental justice seminar held at MIT. We also thank Sue Delaney for providing administrative support as well as faculty colleagues in the Department of Urban Studies and Planning at MIT and the Department of Urban and Environmental Policy and Planning at Tufts for their encouragement as we worked on this book. Finally, we are grateful to Clay Morgan of The MIT Press and Robert Gottlieb, series editor, for their ongoing guidance and enthusiasm and to the anonymous peer reviewers who provided insightful comments on how the chapters and overall manuscript could be improved.

1

Introduction: Environmental Injustice Beyond Borders

Julian Agyeman and JoAnn Carmin

As we upgrade at an ever faster rate, campaigners are calling for action to prevent toxic, electronic or "e" waste being dumped on poor countries. The United Nations believes we generate between 20m and 50m tonnes of e-waste around the world each year. Agbobloshie dump site in Ghana's capital, Accra, is a computer graveyard. But PCs are not given a decent, safe burial—they are dumped on this expanding, toxic treasure trove. Many of the well-known brands are there: Compaq, Dell, Gateway, Philips, Canon, Hewlett Packard. Labels give away the fact that many lived their useful lives in the UK: "Richmond upon Thames College," "Southampton City Council," "Kent County Council," are just a few.

—"Computers Pile Up in Ghana Dump" 2008

The deepening of globalization is fundamentally reshaping, and perhaps even redrawing, the environmental justice terrain. Over the past thirty years, many influential texts on environmental justice, especially those from the United States, have revealed heroic struggles. These have taken place from Warren County, North Carolina, to Kettleman City, California, and from Altgeld Gardens, Chicago, to Dudley Street, Boston, as low-income and minority communities have mobilized to fight off unwanted land uses or gain access to appropriate and adequate public goods and services. While inequalities like these and countless others become visible at the local level as communities seek to "speak for themselves," an often-overlooked scalar dynamic is that many of the perpetrators of injustices are situated in distant locations.

As the example at the outset of this chapter suggests, when European educational and government institutions use and then dispose of their computers, these computers often turn up in waste sites in countries such as Ghana. This is happening despite the 1989 Basel Convention on the Transboundary Movement of Hazardous Wastes and the European Union's (EU) 2002 Restrictions on Hazardous Substances (RoHS) and Waste Electrical and Electronic Equipment (WEEE) Directives. The WEEE directive is based on the principle of extended producer responsibility, which states that manufacturers are legally responsible for safe and environmentally friendly product disposal or, failing this, they must contract with a government-approved waste-handling firm to undertake disposal. However, according to the Basel Action Network, a transnational social movement organization, approximately three-quarters of the e-waste generated in the European Union is unaccounted for (Basel Action Network 2008). To make the situation worse, many of the shipments to Ghana and other developing countries are placed in containers labeled "secondhand goods" since EU law allows reusable electronic goods to be exported (Greenpeace 2008). EU guidelines state that electronics can only be considered secondhand, reusable goods if they are tested for use and properly packed and labeled. However, estimates suggest that 25 to 75 percent of the secondhand electronic goods exported to Africa are broken beyond repair. The altruistic intent of bridging the digital divide by shipping electronics to other countries is having the unintended consequence of developed nations "dumping on the poor" (Greenpeace 2008, 10).

The act of disposing of e-waste, whether for altruistic reasons or not, highlights a critical aspect of a global environmental inequality that has emerged over the years—namely, the presence of a spatial disconnect between public consumption and the desire for profitability by multinational corporations in one part of the world, and the environmental and human rights burdens these drivers of action can and do impose on others. In some instances, global supply chains are a source of inequities as corporations respond to remote demand by seeking to extract resources or site facilities in ways that pose threats to human and ecological health. In other instances, governments, consumers, and consumptive patterns are driving the movement of waste, toxics, and other hazardous materials to distant locations and, in the process, are having negative impacts on natural resources, environmental quality, public health, and local social and cultural dynamics.

Shipments of e-waste to Ghana, as well as to other developing countries, are an example of a global spatial inequality that is having significant environmental and health impacts. For instance, after the waste arrives at its destination, it often is manually dismantled by workers or scavengers, many of whom are children and teenagers. The workers are given no protective gear and use rudimentary tools such as stones to break the products apart in order to salvage scrap metals. The remaining waste materials, including plastic and cables, are either burned or dumped into unprotected sites. Samples of soil, ash, and sediments from these waste sites reveal the presence of a wide variety of hazardous substances such as lead, cadmium, phthalates, and chlorinated dioxins. These substances are known to have neurological impacts as well as to promote cancer (Brigden et al. 2008; Greenpeace 2008). The result is that those who have direct contact with the materials are exposed to hazardous substances, as are residents of surrounding communities, because of toxins being disbursed into the air and leaching into groundwater. The case of e-waste is just one instance among many where poor communities and individuals trying to earn a subsistence wage are faced with significant environmental and health impacts as a consequence of consumption and "business as usual" in other parts of the world.

Drawing on diverse international case studies, this book illustrates how an increasingly globalizing world is altering the environmental justice terrain. Injustice, in this context, refers to the presence of inequalities that result when particular groups, values, or views are given privilege over others (Young 1990, 1996). According to the U.S. Environmental Protection Agency, an environmental injustice is present when communities, groups, or individuals must contend with an environmental burden that is not of their making and does not reflect their preferences, or when the acceptance of a hazard fails to provide significant and meaningful benefits to all of the affected parties. Most studies of environmental justice focus on how local, regional, and nationally initiated hazards affect domestic communities and groups. While domestic environmental injustice(s) will continue to remain important in specific locations around the world, this book examines how globalization is changing the scalar dynamics of inequities by increasing the distance between those who benefit and those who must cope with the social, economic, and environmental inequalities resulting from corporate behaviors and governmental indifference (Kurtz 2003).

Changing Environmental Justice Scholarship

Since the 1970s, academic and community activists in the United States have focused on the ways in which environmental "bads," such as the siting of hazardous waste facilities and the emission of toxic chemicals into the air and water, and environmental "goods," such as parks and open spaces, are unequally distributed among the general population. Such proximity and distributional analyses were part of the "first wave" of environmental justice scholarship (Williams 1999). For example, in 1982, the U.S. General Accountability Office (GAO)[1] examined the location of four landfills containing hazardous wastes in the Southeast portion of the country. While the racial minority population in the region averaged 20 percent, the four facilities were located in communities where they made up 38, 52, 66, and 90 percent of the population. Based on the trends, the GAO concluded that there was enough evidence to be concerned about decision making regarding the location of facility siting (General Accounting Office 1983).

The relationship between race[2] and environmental exposure has been confirmed in numerous studies (e.g., Adeola 1994; Bryant and Mohai 1992; Bullard 1990; Mohai and Bryant 1992; Goldman 1993). A widely cited study conducted by the United Church of Christ showed that, independent of class, communities of color in the United States are at disproportionate risk from commercial toxic waste (United Church of Christ Commission for Racial Justice 1987). It also led to the coining of the term *environmental racism* by Benjamin Chavis. Based on these findings, he maintained that the practice of targeting communities of color as places to locate toxic waste sites and allowing these residents to be exposed to pollutants represented a form of discrimination.

Growing awareness and anger about environmental racism in the location of toxic facilities contributed to the emergence of an environmental justice movement that mobilized to bring attention to these issues and to alter decisions and actions (Cole and Foster 2001; Gottlieb 1993). While the concept of environmental racism points to the presence and location of the problem, environmental justice often is associated with a more positive outlook because it emphasizes a desired outcome (Bryant 1995). The integration of a justice perspective into the claims and vision of the environmental movement fosters greater appreciation for and understanding of the relationship between humans and the environment (Bullard 1993). From this perspective, environmental concerns are not limited to nature and natural resources, but extend to ways the natural environment sustains and affects human health and well-being. In other words, people are entitled to equal access to environmental goods such as clean air, parks, and water as well as to equal protection from environmental threats (Bullard 1993; Agyeman, Bullard, and Evans 2003).

The centrality of race as the driving factor in the location of toxic waste and facility sitings has been challenged by scholars who argue that socioeconomic status and market forces are at the root of these decisions (e.g., Been 1994). For more than two decades, the debate has ensued over the relative roles of race versus class as predictors of exposure to disproportionate levels of environmental risk (e.g., Pulido 1996; Mohai and Saha 2006, 2007). Assessments of race and socioeconomic status associated with facility sitings remain central to the field. However, scholars have demonstrated that environmental exposures extend to a variety of issues, such as workplace safety and subsistence lifestyles (e.g., Perfecto and Velasquez 1992; Pellow and Park 2002; Corburn 2005), and that environmental inequalities can be attributed to a diverse array of factors, including gender (Krauss 1993), disability (Charles and Thomas 2007), and immigration status (Pellow and Park 2002), among others.

As many scholars were expanding their understanding of environmental inequalities and coming to recognize that a broader range of subpopulations are affected by deeply entrenched patterns of inequity, others were developing increasingly robust quantitative models to examine proximity to and the distribution of environmental hazards among the general population. While this research originated in the United States, parallel investigations and analyses have been conducted in Canada (Agyeman et al. 2009; Gosine and Teelucksingh 2008), South Africa (McDonald 2002; Jacobs 2003), Latin America (Carruthers 2008), the former Soviet Union (Agyeman and Ogneva-Himmelberger 2009), Nigeria (Agbola and Alabi 2003), India (Williams and Mawdsley 2006), France (Laurian 2008), The Netherlands (Kruize et al. 2007), and the United Kingdom (Stephens, Bullock, and Scott 2001; Agyeman and Evans 2004). Collectively, these studies demonstrate that vulnerable groups throughout the world are not only shouldering a disproportionate share of both environmental burdens and opportunities, but also lack recognition and voice in the many decisions that affect their lives (Schlosberg 2007; Schrader-Frechette 2002; Young 1990, 1996).

In recent years, environmental justice scholarship has taken a new turn. In an effort to develop more robust theories, an emerging wave of scholarship builds on the understanding of inequitable distribution, but takes a cross-disciplinary perspective to explaining the roots of inequity as well as offering potential solutions. Rather than focus on distribution and proximity per se, these studies explore the multiple spatialities of environmental injustice (Walker 2010; Holifield, Porter, and Walker 2010) while anchoring their analyses in social theory (e.g., Pellow 2000; Sze and London 2008), theories of the racial state (Kurtz 2010), urban political ecology (Swyngedouw and Heynen 2003), and gender studies (Buckingham and Kulcur 2010). In addition to offering a critical perspective on spatial dynamics associated with environmental injustice, these works also are pointing to the ways multilevel institutions give rise to and reinforce unequal exposure to environmental inequalities and differential access to environmental goods (Holifield, Porter, and Walker 2010; Walker and Bulkeley 2006; Pellow 2000).

The Globalization of Environmental Inequalities

The rise of transnational practices associated with resource depletion and manufacturing and the increasing movement of pollutants and waste across borders have created multiple spaces for new, critical understandings of the relations between a globalized economy, environment, and society. Indeed, as Szasz and Meuser (1997, 111) argue, "Environmental inequality is a global phenomenon routinely generated by the normal workings of international political economy." For many years, as academics and activists from the global South have shown (e.g., Bello 1992; Escobar 1996; Khor 1993; Shiva 1997), transnational corporations have located their facilities in remote locations to obtain cheap labor and supply chains have reached into the far corners of the earth to obtain the raw materials that sustain global production and consumption. These practices have given rise to countless examples of how communities that rely on these enterprises for their livelihoods and resources for their subsistence are exposed to unhealthy, unsustainable, and inequitable forms of development (Byrne, Glover, and Martinez 2002; Sachs 2002; Agyeman, Bullard, and Evans 2003; Newell 2005).

Inequalities stemming from foreign exploration, exploitation, and investment have been taking place for many years and in many nations. However, technological advances have made it possible for the perpetrators of degradation and injustice to never set foot on foreign soil and, in some instances, to not even be aware that they are causing harm in other parts of the world. While emissions have long been recognized as transcending international boundaries, issues such as the movement of e-waste to developing countries or the impacts of climate change have shifted the scale and spatial nature of the problem. The result is that in addition to placing groups and communities at risk, in some instances entire nations and continents are coping with threats as a consequence of consumption patterns in distant lands (Adger et al. 2006; Roberts and Parks 2007). The impacts of climate change, for instance, are exacerbating existing global inequalities as less developed countries are faced with attending to a problem that is not primarily of their making and that they are ill equipped to address (Adger et al. 2006; Anguelovski and Roberts, chapter 2, this volume).

The increasing distance between those who benefit and those who must contend with the environmental, health, economic, and social impacts of remote demand is intertwined with the rise of spatial inequities due to global economic, social, and political institutions. Over the years, science and technology have resulted in innovations that have improved and become synonymous with a desired quality of human life. Despite the advances they offer, many new products and processes have been accompanied by a host of new environmental and health risks that can be attributed to the exportation of production, the transport of products, and the disposal of toxic wastes to remote locations (Beck 1992).

Environmental inequalities tend to be understood and addressed in ways that reflect one of two distinct theoretical views. The proactive efforts of corporations, as well as those of many governments and some nongovernmental organizations, often are rooted in the view that economic growth and ecological conservation are compatible. From this perspective, known as *ecological modernization* (Mol 1995), environmental reforms through advances in science and technology make it possible to address risks, and therefore to continue to pursue economic development without altering consumption and other forms of demand (Mol and Sonnenfeld 2000). In this way, some states and corporations have taken the initiative to engage in what they believe to be more environmentally and socially responsible behavior. However, as the view known as the *treadmill of production* suggests, the desire for profitability and the aims of economic and political elites often take precedence over social and environmental considerations (Schnaiberg 1980; Gould, Schnaiberg, and Weinberg 1996).

Rather than seek to explain consumption and demand, and its relationship to production and risk, much environmental justice scholarship places equity and equality, as well as community capacity, connectivity, and resilience, at the heart of its analysis (e.g., Blowers 2003; Pellow 2007). However, the presence of the global spatial disconnect, which is a manifestation of spatial injustice, also gives rise to a new set of questions and issues that form our point of departure in this book. In particular, we consider the ways that global production and consumption entrench existing wealth and power dynamics, whether international institutions and emerging governance structures live up to their promise of promoting equity, and the types of institutions, networks, and governance measures that provide recognition, voice, and capacity to populations and groups most at risk (see Adger et al. 2006). Addressing questions such as these provides a means for understanding and fostering environmental and social change. While they may not alter demand or break the cycle associated with the treadmill of production, the answers to these questions provide new insights into how vulnerable individuals and communities might come together alongside key transnational social movement and nongovernmental organizations such as the Basel Action Network and Greenpeace International, to develop what Faber (2008) and Pellow (2007) characterize as an emergent transnational movement for environmental justice.

Chapter Overview

The chapters in this book demonstrate how spatial and multilevel institutional dynamics interact to shape the ways global inequalities play out in local contexts. In particular, they integrate spatial and institutional perspectives to examine how social and environmental inequalities propagated by remote demand and consumption are constructed, understood, experienced, and addressed. Toward this end, they are organized into three thematic sections. Part I, "Consumption and the Rise of Inequalities beyond Borders," examines how consumption and production in distant locales can undermine and threaten local environmental quality and human rights. In chapter 2, Anguelovski and Roberts take consumption and the emission of greenhouse gases in the global North as a starting point for understanding the presence of environmental and social burdens in Durban, South Africa. While they echo themes in the literature about how climate change is contributing to inequities across countries, they provide an in-depth assessment of how climate impacts further entrench disparities within countries. In particular, they demonstrate the climate inequalities faced by poorer and fragile residents in Durban and examine how climate change is affecting the municipal goals of infrastructure development, tourism expansion, poverty reduction, and sustainable development. They conclude by discussing how Durban is responding to spatial inequity through climate adaptation planning and implementation.

Inequities stemming from foreign demand for oil and gas form the basis of chapter 3, by Stephenson and Schweitzer, who focus on the environmental justice claims of the Ogoni peoples in response to petroleum extraction in the Niger River Delta. While many accounts of environmental degradation in the Delta are attributed to multinational firms, the authors suggest there are far more interdependencies than are often acknowledged and that achieving environmental equity is contingent on accountability across multiple scales of governance. Chapter 4, by Ali and Ackley, examines the impact that investments are having in Fiji and the pros and cons of economic diversification for local populations. Extending arguments initiated in the previous chapter, they maintain that justice will only be achieved when it is accompanied by environmental policies and systems of accountability that foster communication and coordination across industrial sectors and levels of government.

Part II, "The Amplification of Inequality through International Donors and Institutions," consists of three chapters, each of which examines how global institutions and protocols—often designed to foster justice—can inadvertently promote and further entrench inequities. In chapter 5, Lewis picks up on the theme of foreign investment. However, her focus is on how funding for environmental projects from foreign foundations has shaped environmental agendas in Ecuador. She observes that many donors target their support for biodiversity projects rather than issues such as pollution reduction, workplace safety, and natural resource protection. She argues that the promotion of these agendas has, in turn, marginalized the growth and activism of organizations that focus on issues related to environmental justice.

Vermeylen and Walker take a different starting point in their investigation in chapter 6 by examining how international conventions designed to protect the rights of indigenous[3] peoples and communities from exploitation do not always achieve their stated intent. More specifically, they examine how extraction of Hoodia, a plant that has medicinal properties, has undermined environmental quality and the rights of the San tribes in Namibia and South Africa. They maintain that because conventions are based on values and views imposed by external parties, they are unable to achieve outcomes that are regarded as just and fair in indigenous communities; these outcomes may even contribute to the rise of internal dissent. Caniglia also considers international protocols in chapter 7, but focuses on the structure and processes of committees and organizations rather than the outcomes of their decisions. Through an assessment of the Committee on Sustainable Development and the United Nations Convention on Climate Change, she finds that treaty organizations are unable to be as responsive to the claims of nonstate actors, and therefore are less likely to engage and support issues of environmental justice. As with other chapters in this section, her chapter points to the ways in which international institutions designed to promote equitable outcomes can have unintended and paradoxical effects.

The first two sections of the book illustrate the ways inequalities are perpetrated and often amplified through remote demand and the activities of international organizations. While all of the chapters consider how equitable outcomes can be achieved, those in Part III, "Networked Responses to Global Inequality," place at the heart of their analysis the ways governments and civil society actors have dealt with global pressures. In chapter 8, Weidner examines the expansion of Chinese oil extraction into the global South and how the patterns of human rights abuses, labor injustices, and ecological destruction have varied across regions. She maintains that the practices of operators in all parts of the world are below acceptable standards, but finds that the presence and impact of transnational networks in Latin America have resulted in the formation of standards that all operators are required to meet. In contrast, the advocacy vacuum in Africa and Asia, has few activists, NGOs, scholars or journalists monitoring, challenging, and calling attention to the practices of operators. This has resulted in Chinese firms being able to employ a lower standard of environmental protection measures.

In chapter 9, Alkon also contributes to the argument that transnational mobilization can affect change through her assessment of the effects of the Green Revolution and subsequent World Bank and International Monetary Fund policies of demand privatization in Latin America. Drawing on cases of Cuban organic and low-input agriculture and the Brazilian city of Belo Horizonte's declaration of food as a human right, Alkon demonstrates that some national and local governments have countered the domination of market-driven forms of agriculture by increasing food access and local control of the food system. She continues, using the demands for "food sovereignty" among organizations such as Brazil's Landless Workers Movement and movements such as *La Via Campesina*, to demonstrate the impacts of structural adjustment and to illustrate ways the U.S. food justice movement can strengthen its opposition to existing policies by drawing on transnational network ties to expand the movement globally.

In chapter 10, Hicks expands on discussions of transnational networks by showing that there are times when local groups trying to address undesired corporate practices and unwanted land uses need to bypass the state to achieve equitable outcomes. Using examples of mining disputes in Bulgaria, she suggests that in countries with weak norms of participation and inconsistencies in the rule of law, local groups are more effective when they enlist the support and tap the strengths of national and transnational environmental and human rights organizations.

The final chapter in the section—chapter 11—is by Pellow, who further explores the rise of a transnational movement for environmental justice. Drawing on the case of toxic waste disposal in Mozambique, Pellow demonstrates how transnational inequalities can affect vulnerable and privileged populations alike and how transnational activists can effectively work to leverage power across borders.

Part IV, "Conclusion," brings the book to a close. In chapter 12, "Reflections on Environmental Equality beyond Borders," Carmin and Agyeman summarize major trends revealed by the previous chapters. While many individual chapters affirm classical views and arguments present in the environmental justice literature, together they offer a richer, more nuanced perspective on how global forces affect localities and how they can further entrench existing inequalities. At the same time, they point to the ways networks and mobilization can foster institutional change and promote social equality and environmental justice.

Notes

1. At the time, the GAO was called the General Accounting Office.

2. We are aware of the contested nature of the concept of "race" (see, for instance, Omi and Winant 1994). While race may not stand scientific scrutiny as a robust categorization of humans, we use it in this introduction since it is a powerful and widely used construct among the public and in the environmental justice literature.

3. The term *indigenous peoples* is less specific and strict than some terms such as First Peoples or First Nations. However, we adopt this term because it is commonly used by organizations such as the United Nations, the International Labour Organization, and the World Bank.

References

Adeola, Francis. 1994. Environmental hazards, health and racial inequity in hazardous waste distribution. *Environment and Behavior* 26(1):99–126.

Adger, Neil, Jouni Paavola, Saleemul Huq, and M. J. Mace. 2006. *Fairness in Adaptation to Climate Change.* Cambridge, MA: MIT Press.

Agbola, Tunde, and Moruf Alabi. 2003. Political economy of petroleum resources development, environmental justice and selective victimization: A case study of the Niger Delta region of Nigeria. In J. Agyeman, R. Bullard, and B. Evans, eds., *Just Sustainabilities: Development in an Unequal World.* Cambridge, MA: MIT Press.

Agyeman, Julian, Robert Bullard, and Bob Evans. 2003. *Just Sustainabilities: Development in an Unequal World*. Cambridge, MA: MIT Press.

Agyeman, Julian, Peter Cole, Randolph Haluza-DeLay, and Pat O'Riley. 2009. *Speaking for Ourselves: Environmental Justice in Canada*. Vancouver: University of British Columbia Press.

Agyeman, Julian, and Bob Evans. 2004. Just sustainability: The emerging discourse of environmental justice in Britain? *Geographical Journal* 170(2): 155–164.

Agyeman, Julian, and Yelena Ogneva-Himmelberger. 2009. *Environmental Justice and Sustainability in the Former Soviet Union*. Cambridge, MA: MIT Press.

Basel Action Network. 2008. UK investigates e-waste dumping in Ghana. http://www.ban.org/BAN_NEWS/2008/081018_uk_investigates_e-waste_dumping_in _ghana.html.

Beck, U. 1992. *Risk Society: Towards a New Modernity*. London: Sage.

Been, Vickie. 1994. Locally undesirable land uses in minority neighborhoods: Disproportionate siting or market dynamics? *Yale Law Journal* 10:1383–1422.

Bello, Walden. 1992. *People and Power in the Pacific: The Struggle for the Post Cold War Order*. San Francisco: Food First Books.

Blowers, Andrew. 2003. Inequality and community and the challenge to modernization: Evidence from the nuclear oases. In J. Agyeman, R. Bullard, and B. Evans, eds., *Just Sustainabilities: Development in an Unequal World*. Cambridge, MA: MIT Press.

Brigden, Kevin, Iryna Labunska, David Santillo, and Paul Johnston. 2008. *Chemical Contamination at E-Waste Recycling and Disposal Sites in Accra and Korforidua, Ghana*. Amsterdam: Greenpeace International.

Bryant, Bunyan. 1995. *Environmental Justice: Issues, Policies, and Solutions*. Washington, DC: Island Press.

Bryant, Bunyan, and Paul Mohai, eds. 1992. *Race and the Incidence of Environmental Hazards*. Boulder, CO: Westview Press.

Buckingham, Susan and Rakibe Kulcur. 2010. Gendered geographies of environmental injustice. In R. Holifield, M. Porter, and G. Walker, eds., *Spaces of Environmental Justice*, 70–94. West Sussex: Wiley-Blackwell.

Bullard, Robert D. 1990. *Dumping in Dixie*. Boulder, CO: Westview Press.

Bullard, Robert D. 1993. Anatomy of environmental racism and the environmental justice movement. In R. D. Bullard, ed., *Confronting Environmental Racism: Voices from the Grassroots*, 15–40. Boston: South End Press.

Byrne, John, Leigh Glover, and Cecllia Martinez. 2002. *Environmental Justice: Discourses in International Political Economy*. New Brunswick, NJ: Transaction Books.

Carruthers, David. 2008. *Environmental Justice in Latin America: Problems, Promise, and Practice*. Cambridge, MA: MIT Press.

Charles, Andrew, and Huw Thomas. 2007. Deafness and disability—forgotten components of environmental justice: Illustrated by the case of Local Agenda 21 in Wales. *Local Environment: The International Journal of Justice and Sustainability* 12(3):209–221.

Cole, Luke W., and Shelia R. Foster. 2001. *From the Ground Up: Environmental Racism and the Rise of the Environmental Justice Movement*. New York: New York University Press.

Computers pile up in Ghana dump. 2008. BBC News, August 5. http://news.bbc.co.uk/2/hi/africa/7543489.stm.

Corburn, Jason. 2005. *Street Science: Community Knowledge and Environmental Health Justice*. Cambridge, MA: MIT Press.

Escobar, Arturo. 1996. Constructing nature: Elements for a poststructural political ecology. In R. Peet and M. Watts, eds., *Liberation Ecologies: Environment, Development, Social Movement*. London: Routledge.

Faber, Daniel. 2008. *Capitalizing on Environmental Injustice: The Polluter-Industrial Complex in the Age of Globalization*. Lanham, MD: Rowman & Littlefield.

General Accounting Office. 1983. *Siting of Hazardous Waste Landfills and their Correlation with Racial and Economic Status of Surrounding Communities*. Washington, DC: Government Printing Office.

Goldman, Benjamin A. 1993. *Not Just Prosperity: Achieving Sustainability with Environmental Justice*. Washington, DC: National Wildlife Federation.

Gosine, Andil, and Cheryl Teelucksingh. 2008. *Environmental Justice and Racism in Canada*. Toronto: Emond Montgomery Publications.

Gottlieb, Robert. 1993. *Forcing the Spring: The Transformation of the American Environmental Movement*. Washington, DC: Island Press.

Gould, Kenneth, Alan Schnaiberg, and Adam Weinberg. 1996. *Local Environmental Struggles: Citizen Activism in the Treadmill of Production*. New York: Cambridge University Press.

Greenpeace. 2008. *Poisoning the Poor: Electronic Waste in Ghana*. Amsterdam: Greenpeace International.

Holifield, Ryan, Michael Porter, and Gordon Walker. 2010. Introduction: Spaces of environmental justice—frameworks for critical engagement. In R. Holifield, M. Porter, and G. Walker, eds., *Spaces of Environmental Justice*, 1–23. West Sussex: Wiley-Blackwell.

Jacobs, Nancy. 2003. *Environment, Power, and Injustice: A South African History*. New York: Cambridge University Press.

Khor, Martin. 1993. Economics and environmental justice: Rethinking North-South relations. In Richard Hofrichter, ed., *Toxic Struggles: The Theory and Practice of Environmental Justice*. Philadelphia: New Society Publishers.

Krauss, Celene. 1993. Women and toxic waste protests: Race, class and gender as resources of resistance. *Qualitative Sociology* 16(3):247–262.

Kruize, Hanneke, Peter P. J. Driessen, Pieter Glasbergen, and Klaas van Egmond. 2007. Environmental equity and the role of public policy: Experiences in the Rijnmond region. *Environmental Management* 40:578–595.

Kurtz, Hilda. 2003. Scale frames and counter scale frames: Constructing the social grievance of environmental justice. *Political Geography* 22:887–916.

Kurtz, Hilda. 2010. Acknowledging the racial state: An agenda for environmental justice research. In R. Holifield, M. Porter, and G. Walker, eds., *Spaces of Environmental Justice*, 95–115. West Sussex: Wiley-Blackwell.

Laurian, Lucie. 2008. Environmental injustice in France. *Journal of Environmental Planning and Management* 51(1):55–79.

McDonald, David. 2002. *Environmental Justice in South Africa*. Athens: Ohio University Press.

Mohai, Paul, and Bunyan Bryant. 1992. Environmental injustice: Weighing race and class as factors in the distribution of environmental hazards. *University of Colorado Law Review* 63:921–932.

Mohai, Paul, and Robin Saha. 2006. Reassessing race and socioeconomic disparities in environmental justice research. *Demography* 43(2):383–389.

Mohai, Paul, and Robin Saha. 2007. Racial inequality in the distribution of hazardous waste: A national-level reassessment. *Social Problems* 54(3): 343–370.

Mol, Arthur. 1995. *The Refinement of Production: Ecological Modernization Theory and the Dutch Chemical Industry*. Utrecht: Jan van Arkel Books.

Mol, Arthur, and D. A. Sonnenfeld. 2000. Ecological modernisation around the world. *Environmental Politics* 9(1):3–14.

Newell, Peter. 2005. Race, class and the global politics of environmental inequality. *Global Environmental Politics* 5:70–94.

Omi, Michael, and Howard Winant. 1994. *Racial Formation in the United States: From the 1960s to the 1990s*. London: Routledge.

Pellow, David N. 2000. Environmental inequality formation. *American Behavioral Scientist* 43:581–601.

Pellow, David N. 2007. *Resisting Global Toxics: Transnational Movements for Environmental Justice*. Cambridge, MA: MIT Press.

Pellow, David N., and Lisa S. Park. 2002. *The Silicon Valley of Dreams: Environmental Injustice, Immigrant Workers, and the High-Tech Global Economy*. New York: New York University Press.

Perfecto, Ivette, and Baldemar Velasquez. 1992. Farm workers: Among the least protected. *EPA Journal* 18:13–14.

Pulido, Laura. 1996. A critical review of the methodology of environmental racism research. *Antipode* 28(2):142–159.

Roberts, J. Timmons, and Bradley Parks. 2007. *A Climate of Injustice: Global Inequality, North-South Politics, and Climate Policy*. Cambridge, MA: MIT Press.

Sachs, Wolfgang. 2002. Ecology, justice, and the end of development. In J. Byrne, L. Glover, and C. Martinez, eds., *Environmental Justice: Discourses in International Political Economy*. New Brunswick, NJ: Transaction Books.

Schlosberg, David. 2007. *Defining Environmental Justice: Theories, Movements and Nature*. Oxford: Oxford University Press.

Schnaiberg, Alan. 1980. *The Environment: From Surplus to Scarcity*. New York: Oxford University Press.

Schrader-Frechette, Kristen. 2002. *Environmental Justice: Creating Equality, Reclaiming Democracy*. New York: Oxford University Press.

Shiva, Vandana. 1997. *Biopiracy: The Plunder of Nature and Knowledge*. Boston: South End Press.

Stephens, Carolyn, Simon Bullock, and Alister Scott. 2001. *Environmental Justice: Rights and Means to a Healthy Environment for All*. Special Briefing No. 7. London: ESRC Global Environmental Change Programme.

Swyngedouw, Eric, and Nik Heynen. 2003. Urban political ecology, justice and the politics of scale. *Antipode* 35:898–918.

Szasz, Andrew, and Michael Meuser. 1997. Environmental inequalities: Literature review and proposals for new directions in research and theory. *Current Sociology* 45(3):99–120.

Sze, Julie, and Jonathan K. London. 2008. Environmental justice at the crossroads. *Social Compass* 2(4):1331–1354.

United Church of Christ Commission for Racial Justice. 1987. *Toxic Wastes and Race in the United States: A National Report on the Racial and Socio-Economic Characteristics of Communities with Hazardous Waste Sites*. New York: United Church of Christ Commission for Racial Justice.

Walker, Gordon. 2010. Beyond distribution and proximity: Exploring the multiple spatialities of environmental justice. In R. Holifield, M. Porter, and G. Walker, eds., *Spaces of Environmental Justice*, 24–46. West Sussex: Wiley-Blackwell.

Walker, Gordon, and Harriet Bulkeley. 2006. Editorial—geographies of environmental justice. *Geoforum* 37(5):655–659.

Williams, Glyn, and Emma Mawdsley. 2006. Postcolonial environmental justice: Government and governance in India. *Geoforum* 37:660–670.

Williams, Robert. 1999. Environmental justice in America and its politics of scale. *Political Geography* 18:49–73.

Young, Iris Marion. 1990. *Justice and the Politics of Difference*. Princeton, NJ: Princeton University Press.

Young, Iris Marion. 1996. Communication and the Other. In S. Benhabib, ed., *Democracy and Difference: Contesting the Boundaries of the Political*. Princeton, NJ: Princeton University Press.

I

Consumption and the Rise of Inequalities Beyond Borders

2

Spatial Justice and Climate Change: Multiscale Impacts and Local Development in Durban, South Africa

Isabelle Anguelovski and Debra Roberts

In recent years, the phrase "think globally, act locally" has become something of an environmental cliché. It nevertheless serves to highlight the fundamental truth that without some level of local action and on-the-ground understanding of impacts, global environmental challenges cannot be dealt with in an equitable and sustainable way. Among all of the prevailing global environmental challenges, climate change is undoubtedly the most significant. It threatens our future development and, in some people's minds, puts at risk the continued existence of our own species and the global ecosystems on which we depend. Furthermore, addressing the issue of "dangerous climate change" is becoming sociopolitically explosive as the glacial progress of negotiations around the United Nations Framework Convention on Climate Change (UNFCCC) increasingly contrasts with the immediate and severe consequences of climate change in specific locales.

During the COP-15 negotiations in December 2009, core disagreements between Northern and Southern countries on the relative levels of responsibility for climatic changes, the increased vulnerability of certain regions, and the development of impact mitigation strategies amplified feelings among Southern nations that they were being once again marginalized in the global political arena and that inequities between countries were being further reinforced. Today, many scientists, academics, and NGOs maintain that a profound unfairness exists between the countries that contribute the most to climate change through the production and consumption of fossil fuels and those most at risk from its effects (for instance IPCC 2007a; Parks and Roberts 2006; Oxfam 2007). Many nations facing rising oceans, increased droughts, or extreme disasters are those least responsible for the problem and with the lowest levels of resources available to cope with the resultant challenges (Huq et al. 2007; Parks and Roberts 2006; Adger et al. 2006). The vulnerability of countries that will be hardest hit by climate impacts has been intensified by the global division of labor and the political economy of production of goods and resources (Parks and Roberts 2006). Current global funding mechanisms do little to remedy this imbalance since there is limited provision to support governments, and poorer governments in particular, to adapt to climate change impacts (Huq et al. 2007).

The outlook is particularly somber for Africa, because recent studies demonstrate that the extreme vulnerability of the continent to climatic changes is aggravated by the interaction of "multiple stresses" occurring at various levels and by a low adaptive capacity. This vulnerability is also exacerbated by developmental challenges, fragile institutions, limited access to capital, weak infrastructure and technology, ecosystem degradation, and complex disasters and conflicts (IPCC 2007a). A further challenge for Africa is that the political and scientific debate around climate change has primarily focused on characterizing the global nature, extent, and impact of anthropogenic influences leading to climate change. By comparison, relatively little effort has been spent on understanding how climate change will impact locales and the costs these communities will need to bear. The tendency to talk about impacts in generalities obscures the developmental price that local communities in the South will have to pay in servicing the global carbon debt.

Environmental and climate inequities, and the related impacts on marginalized communities, manifest themselves most obviously and immediately at the regional and local levels. In this chapter, we examine how climate change is creating inequities between Northern and Southern countries and how climate impacts are projected to intensify patterns of vulnerability, relations of dependence and domination, and sociospatial injustice in cities in the global South. More specifically, we draw on the spatial and climate injustice literatures to understand how climate change and climate politics are further entrenching local sociospatial inequities in the multiethnic and global South African city of Durban. We conclude the chapter with a discussion of how Durban is responding to these multiscale inequities through climate adaptation planning and implementation.

Spatial Dimensions of Climate Justice

Traditionally, justice refers to the appropriate division of social advantages between people over time (Rawls 1971). Beyond questions of fair or unfair distribution, justice scholars are concerned with issues of identity and difference between groups and individuals, because conceptions of justice tend to differ according to individual and collective values and preferences (Walzer 1983; Young 1990; Honneth 1992). In that sense, achieving justice not only requires determining how people and agencies deny rights and ways of life to specific groups and communities, and addressing deeper relations of domination and oppression in society, but doing so in ways that account for difference (Young 1990).

The concept of spatial justice offers a means for understanding the presence of climate inequalities between and within countries, as well as the claims of governments and activists for climate justice. Spatial justice is defined as the equitable allocation of socially valued resources such as the jobs, political power, income, social services, and environmental goods in space, and the presence of equal opportunities to make use of these resources over time (Soja 2009; Marcuse 2009). While their emphasis remains on achieving justice, most spatial justice scholars investigate the ways geographic determinants and differentials shape diverse forms of inequities, including those related to environmental, urban, and regional inequalities.

A dialectical dynamic is present at the center of spatial injustices since social and human processes shape spatial patterns as much as spatial patterns shape social processes (Soja 2009). On the one hand, for instance, social exclusion and poverty often result in rural–urban migration and the subsequent growth of slums on the outskirts of cities. In cities such as Quito and Rio, this process has resulted in entire fragile hillsides and slopes slowly being transformed into *favelas*. On the other hand, when government agencies situate public housing structures in floodplains and on other types of marginal lands, local residents are placed at risk in the case of extreme weather events. While a dialectical relationship may be present, national, regional, and urban spatial injustices typically are produced and reproduced by relatively stable institutions and norms that are contained within geographic areas (Dikeç 2001).

Spatial injustices occur at a variety of scales. At the global scale, the capitalist model of growth and profit maximization, and the related goal of protecting capital and lower labor costs, often is viewed as being at the root of injustices that emerge between countries (Harvey 1996; Merrifield and Swyngedouw 1997; Soja 2000). Capitalist growth and cycles of investments and devalorization also are influential at the local level. For instance, patterns of urban renewal and growth force the poor to live in marginalized neighborhoods with poor living conditions

(Merrifield and Swyngedouw 1997; Soja 2000). The social organization of urban space often is reflected in local politics because wealthier communities tend to have greater access to political power, and subsequently achieve better services and infrastructure for their neighborhoods (Soja 2009; Fainstein 2006).

One of the ways that spatial injustices manifest themselves in urban areas is in local environmental inequities. Traditionally, deprived urban neighborhoods and communities of color have been victims of greater contamination than well-off and white communities (Bullard 1990; Pellow 2000). For instance, incinerators, landfills, or refineries have historically been located in poor and powerless communities rather than in affluent suburbs (Bullard 1990; Pellow 2000). Such communities also are prone to receiving fewer environmental services, from street cleaning to maintenance of open space to solid waste management (Harvey 1973; Hastings 2007).

Global Dimensions of Climate Injustices

Spatial injustices are reflected in inequalities that exist within and between locales (Merrifield and Swyngedouw 1997). Just as geographic inequities are present in the environmental, urban, and labor arenas, they also are prevalent in the climate domain. Climate injustice traditionally refers to the inequities that exist between countries and regions in their climate responsibility, vulnerability, and mitigation. It also refers to the weaker ability of poor nations to negotiate effectively in global climate conferences (Roberts and Parks 2007a).

In terms of responsibility for climate change, Europe and the United States have contributed over 50 percent of total greenhouse gas emissions, while developing nations in Africa, Latin America, and Asia have only contributed 15 percent (Borchert 2007). Although China's emission levels have recently outstripped emissions from the United States, emissions of fast-growing countries such as China and India are still relatively low if measured per capita. However, emissions are increasing sharply in developing countries as rich nations "offshore" the energy- and natural resource–intensive stages of production (Roberts and Parks 2007b). Industrialized nations are thus in a situation of "carbon debt" or "ecological debt" relative to the remainder of the globe (Martinez Alier 2002; Roberts and Parks 2007b). They have greatly exceeded their share of equitable, global per capita carbon emissions, and have already used up most of the "space" available for greenhouse gas emissions in the atmosphere (Simms 2005).

By way of comparison, developing countries are in a state of carbon credit, without having derived equal economic benefits from the burning of fossil fuels, as has been the case in richer nations (Roberts and Parks 2007b). Despite this gap in carbon emissions, the developing world is coming under increasing pressure to reduce its emissions. And, to date, global climate change negotiations have led to little success in addressing inequities between Northern and Southern nations. In fact, because social understandings of fairness are contingent on a country's position in the global hierarchy, opposing perceptions of "climate justice" pose a serious threat to a political resolution of climate change (Roberts and Parks 2007b; Parks and Roberts 2006; Roberts and Parks 2007a). Developing countries are politically weak due to their economic dependence vis-à-vis richer nations. More often than not, developing countries are unable to have meaningful participation and constructive input in global policy dialogs (Adger et al. 2006; Roberts and Parks 2007a), let alone influence outcomes (Anand 2004). The result is that many of their concerns tend to be marginalized in final decisions (Adger et al. 2006). Nowhere is this more evident than in the participation of the so-called BASIC countries (i.e., Brazil, South Africa, India, and China) in the development of the Copenhagen Accord in December 2009.

Prior to COP 15, it would have been unthinkable that a country such as South Africa would compromise on its demands for a legally binding emission reduction agreement for the sake of what has been referred to in some circles as "climate structural adjustment." However, instead of the deep emission cuts required of the developed world, the divide-and-coerce tactics of Copenhagen saw the richest of the poor countries (i.e., the BASIC countries) complicit in instituting a new form of inequality, and sacrificing effective action for financial resources. Ironically, these countries were also the ones that made the most significant commitments to emission reductions—in South Africa's case, a deviation below the current emission baseline of 34 percent by 2020 and 42 percent by 2025. As noted by the Sudanese negotiator in the G7/ Lumumba Di-Aping on the last day of the Copenhagen meeting, "This deal will definitely result in massive devastation in Africa and small island nations. . . . The architecture of this deal is extraordinarily flawed. What has happened today has confirmed what we have been suspicious of—that a deal will be superimposed by the United States . . . on all nations of the world." As this quote suggests, is not surprising that developing countries perceive that they have to forgo economic growth to help address a complex problem that they did not create in the first place (Pearce 2007).

In many Southern nations, the need to mitigate immediate and extreme climate impacts on the ground compromises poverty alleviation and development projects. For instance, the need for infrastructure repair after storms and hurricanes can jeopardize the financial ability of municipalities to build new roads or bridges in poor areas that need to be better connected to the city. Addressing flooding in slums and repairing damaged buildings and houses requires financial resources that could be put toward new housing developments. Therefore, in order to be adequately tackled, climate change must be confronted "in an integral way with the problems of poverty and exclusion in the South and over-consumption of fuel dependence in the North" (Pettit 2004, 105).

In terms of vulnerability to climatic changes, countries in the weakest economic position are often most vulnerable to climate impacts and susceptible to damages and disasters, especially when they are faced with multiple stresses (IPCC 2007a). For example, nations facing rising oceans and drought such as Mozambique and Honduras have made minimal contributions to emissions and have limited resources to protect their populations, natural resource base, and infrastructure (Huq et al. 2007; Parks and Roberts 2006; Adger et al. 2006). Furthermore, developing countries are not equipped with the resilient risk-management capacity to mitigate extreme weather impacts, nor with the financial resources to adapt to and recover from climate effects. Thus, ultimately, addressing environmental inequities will require targeting the imbalances between the ability of rich and poor nations to cope with climate impacts (Yohe 2000).

Local Views on Climate Inequities

A closer look at nations within the global South reveals that the remote emission of greenhouse gases and the political economy of production and consumption have significant impacts on individuals, communities, and policy goals and plans. While impacts play out at these different scales, climate injustices often exacerbate existing local inequities, as marginalized individuals, vulnerable communities, and policies of livability and equity are being sacrificed, and long-term poverty alleviation and sustainability goals become marginalized by the need to attend to immediate priorities.

At the individual scale, within developing countries and cities in particular, spatial injustices related to climate change manifest themselves through the acute vulnerability of the urban poor to environmental hazards and extreme weather events in comparison with richer and dominant groups. Their vulnerability to extreme events is derived from their socioeconomic conditions, their higher exposure to climate risks, a lower preparedness, as well as a weaker recovery capacity. The range of predicted impacts of climatic changes on fragile urban populations is broad and includes an increase in the frequency of extreme weather events (i.e., flooding, storms, droughts, sea-level rise), decreased water availability and food security, infrastructural damage, spread of water- and vector-borne diseases, biodiversity loss, and increased heat-related mortality (IPCC 2007b).

At the community scale, the exposure of urban populations to climate impacts is more deeply structured by the sociospatial segregation by which poor communities in cities are less able to cope with disaster. In fact, the urban poor face more difficult access to safe land, infrastructure, sustainable economic activity, and risk-management resources. For instance, low-income communities tend to be more dependent on traditional farming activities in and around cities, which are severely impacted by floods or droughts. Poor residents are also forced to live in areas exposed to unstable climate, such as floodplains, fragile coastlines, or hillsides, and they cannot easily change residence, activities, and ways of life (Carmin, Roberts, and Anguelovski 2009). In short, the main victims of climate disasters are those with the smallest roles in creating "climate destabilization"—coastal communities, small islanders, farming and pastoral communities (Shiva 2002). Poor populations have also historically been excluded from decision making on their land and lack opportunities for true engagement with policymakers (Pellow and Brulle 2005). This absence of spaces for participation further entrenches relations of domination between groups who have access to power and others who remain marginalized. Eventually, poor communities are caught in a cycle of deeper poverty and isolation while stronger and well-off communities can more easily adapt to and recover from climatic impacts.

At the policy level, in the mid- and long term, climate injustices further threaten the ability of developing countries to meet their broad sustainable development goals (Pettit 2004). Cities in particular are confronted with climate risks, fragile infrastructure, and extreme weather events, and have to push back long-term equity and sustainability goals in order to tackle more immediate priorities. Here again, the victims are low-income and fragile individuals and communities faced with structural development problems and poverty alleviation needs. The inequities in the impacts and benefits of carbon emissions have thus led many planners and community organizations to advocate for an increase attention to adaptation needs, rather than simply mitigation.

Climate Inequities in the African Context: The Case of Durban

Poor and vulnerable individuals and communities in cities will predominantly depend on local-level action in their quest for justice and survival in a climatically changed future. South Africa is one of Africa's most developed countries, and, yet, the end of apartheid in South Africa "left in its wake a population with great poverty and income inequities, largely defined by racial groups" (Department of Environmental Affairs and Tourism 2006, 31). Apartheid also created substantial environmental problems and inequities (International Mission on Environmental Policy 1995), which still pose significant developmental and political challenges to the country sixteen years after the first national democratic elections in 1994. The net result is that, even before the impacts of climate change are considered, South Africa enters the developmental race with a significant environmental handicap. Climate change merely ups the ante on who will cross the finish line and who will not.

The scale of the climate-related problems faced by a country such as South Africa is best exemplified by examining climate impacts at the local level. Durban is an illuminating case for understanding how a South Africa city is coping with climate change. The city of Durban, located in the province of Kwa-Zulu Natal, is the largest port on the east coast of Africa with a municipal area of 2,297 km^2. While only 35 percent of the municipal area is considered urban, over 80 percent of the city's residents live in these more developed areas. The city has a total population of 3.7 million people, and is composed of a mix of races, cultures, and classes, with strong African, Indian, and European influences (Corporate Policy Unit, *Quality of Life*, n.d.). From an economic perspective, manufacturing, finance and business services, transport and communication, and tourism are the motors of local economic development (Economic Development Unit 2008).

The local government body responsible for planning and managing the city is eThekwini Municipality. The vision for Durban is that, "by 2020, eThekwini Municipality will be Africa's most caring and livable city" (Corporate Policy Unit, *Integrated Development Plan,* n.d., 10). However, Durban faces a complex mix of social, economic, environmental and governance challenges. Such challenges include low economic growth, high unemployment (34.4 percent), and an increase in extreme poverty (28 percent between 2001 and 2006), especially among women and racial minorities. In addition, the municipality is working to address the presence of limited access to basic household and community services, low levels of literacy and skill development, the highest HIV infection rate in South Africa, and the persistence of both petty and violent crime. Further, the city has a history of unsustainable development practices and a lack of adequate protection and conservation of its globally significant biodiversity.

Climate protection planning in Durban has confirmed that climate change brings with it new environmental inequities. Experience and assessments in Durban have demonstrated that the city is faced with a situation whereby the harm associated with climate-driven change falls disproportionately on poorer communities and deepens existing inequities. Poor and vulnerable communities stand to lose their livelihoods and lives, while wealthier communities are better able to find protection from climate events and more likely to lose or reduce their wealth as a consequence of climate impacts. However, given the significant range of local developmental and environmental challenges that Durban faces, global climate change has been a relatively recent addition to the city's planning and management agenda. Work on the development of a Municipal Climate Protection Program (MCPP) began in 2004 and has been undertaken under the auspices of the city's Environmental Planning and Climate Protection Department (EPCPD).

From the outset, the EPCPD acknowledged that local decision makers and stakeholders were more likely to be concerned about the local impacts of climate change, particularly those that affected or reinforced local development needs and pressures, rather than being interested in more generalized changes in global climate. As a result, the first step in the development of the MCPP was the initiation of a research project with the help of local consultants and staff from eThekwini Municipality aimed at understanding the local impacts of climate change in Durban. This resulted in the preparation of the *Climatic Future for Durban* report in 2006, which summarizes a number of critical changes and impacts expected to affect the city (CSIR NRE 2006).

The key findings of the climate projections for the period 2070–2100 indicate that both the maximum and minimum temperatures in the city will increase, as will the number of days with temperatures exceeding 30°C. An increase in the total amount of rainfall will be combined with a change in distribution, resulting in longer drought periods and more intense flooding. In the coastal zone, a number of economic and tourist areas may be affected by sea-level rise, which will be worsened by extreme events such as flooding and storm surges. Given these predicted changes, the city is vulnerable at a number of levels, including increases in vector- and waterborne diseases and increases in the frequency and intensity of floods and droughts. Climate impacts also encompass projected extinction and changes in the distribution of plant and animal species, infrastructure damage due to extreme weather events, threats to human safety, increased insurance costs, erosion of coastal areas, heat stress, changes in energy consumption, economic losses due to property damage, as well as decreases in tourism revenue, food security, and water availability.

In sum, these trends suggest that climate change will pose a significant threat to Durban and to the municipality's long-term objective of ensuring broad-based, sustainable, and equitable development. This vision is outlined in the Integrated Development Plan (IDP). The IDP is a central strategic planning document for local policymakers and is meant to guide and inform all planning, budgeting, management, and decision making in the municipality. Reflecting the long-term goals of eThekwini Municipality, the IDP also seeks to outline an integrated vision by balancing social, economic, and ecological pillars of sustainability without compromising the institutional capacity required in the implementation, and by coordinating actions across sectors and spheres of government. The IDP is organized around eight core plans: (1) sustaining the natural and built environment; (2) economic development and job creation; (3) quality living environments; a (4) safe, healthy, and secure environment; (5) empowering citizens; (6) celebrating cultural diversity; (7) good governance; and (8) financial viability and sustainability.

Climate impacts in Durban pose a significant threat to achieving the goals outlined for the city in the eight IDP plans. In the following sections, we examine the IDP plans that best exemplify how climate impacts are further exacerbating sociospatial inequities and exclusion in Durban by looking at how they play out across three different scales: individuals, communities, and municipal policies and goals.

Individual Sociospatial Inequities

The IDP outlines the need to sustain and protect ecosystem services (Plan 1), and secure good health systems and conditions (Plan 4) for Durban's residents. However, at the individual level, disappearing ecosystem services due to climatic changes, as well as more acute health and humanitarian emergencies, will impact the living conditions of poorer residents and their families. In the near future, such impacts will likely amplify already existing sociospatial inequities in Durban and pose new challenges for local institutions and planners.

Climate Impacts on Ecosystem Services   Durban is unusual among local governments in South Africa because it puts a strong emphasis on the value of the natural resource base of the city and the role it plays in ensuring urban sustainability and meeting people's basic needs. In fact, the IDP stipulates that eThekwini Municipality must "direct and manage the use of the built and natural environment to ensure sustainable and integrated growth and development" (EThekwini Municipality 2008, 10). This positioning of the natural resource base within the local development debate reflects the fact that it has been conceptualized and promoted as green infrastructure, providing a range of developmentally critical ecosystem services.

These ecosystem services include "clean air, climate stabilization, rainfall, flood attenuation, marine resources, leisure and recreation areas, fertile soils, food, building materials, amenity and heritage" (EThekwini Municipality 2008,10). It is also acknowledged within the IDP that these services would be impossible, or extremely costly, to replace if they were to be lost to inappropriate and unsustainable development, and that residents depend fundamentally on the flow of theses goods and services for their survival (McCray, Hammill, and Bradley 2007).

In Durban, urban and periurban low-income communities are most dependent on ecosystem services for meeting their basic needs, and climatic impacts threaten their reliance on such services. For example, in former townships and in rural wards where there are no water taps, people often extract water from rivers. In areas where there is no electricity, people collect wood from forests and woodlands. Meeting basic needs and combating poverty in Durban are therefore closely associated with the ability to ensure and sustain the quality and integrity of the local natural resource base. This task is made more difficult by the fact that poor people in the city tend to live in already fragile or degraded environments and therefore have fewer natural resources from which to draw during periods of stress or crisis. As a result, these communities are more vulnerable to the observed or predicted effects of climate change than other sectors of society.

The magnitude and impact of the potential loss can be understood if one considers that the replacement value of the ecosystem services provided by the city's open-space system has been estimated at approximately $387 million. Climate change therefore poses a serious threat to the future sustainability of the city, because it contributes (along with other factors such as population growth, urbanization, and land-use change) to the degradation of ecosystems and the services they deliver.

This in turn creates potential problems, such as declines in freshwater availability; decrease in crop yields; drought and flooding; shifts in optimal areas for forest growth; sea-level rise; and negative effects on high conservation-value ecosystems and biodiversity (McCray, Hammill, and Bradley 2007). Impacts in these different areas will be felt again more acutely by the urban poor, who are directly dependent on ecosystem services for their survival.

Climate Impacts on Health and Humanitarian Emergencies   Climate change also affects the ability of eThekwini Municipality to protect the health of vulnerable residents in Durban and, as the IDP states, "to promote and create a safe, healthy and secure environment" (Ethekwini Municipality 2008, 46). The IDP underlines key strategic interventions in this area, including the promotion of the safety, health, and security of citizens, and the safety of municipal assets. These interventions are more challenging for the city to realize while navigating climate impacts.

As was highlighted previously, the potential impacts of climate change in Durban will affect the protection of people, property, and public health. Greater incidences of extreme weather events could mean more frequent humanitarian emergencies and increased loss of secure shelters, assets, and infrastructure. Under these conditions, the poor are the most vulnerable because they often live in high-risk areas (floodplains, unstable slopes, etc.) and in the weakest housing structures. A coastal city like Durban is particularly vulnerable to the impacts of sea-level rise and to the associated loss of and damage to homes and livelihoods along the extended coastline.

Climate change will also trigger public health impacts, especially in a city with a high level of HIV/AIDS infection such as Durban. This situation has resulted in a large number of immunocompromised individuals who are more susceptible to disease and physical stresses, such as those experienced during heat waves, floods, or severe storms. Adequate protection from these stressors will depend on access to services such as sanitation, adequate housing conditions, safe drinking water, and proper healthcare services—themselves under threat from climate change.

Other groups vulnerable to climate impacts on health include the elderly, because their fragile health is often accompanied by chronic illnesses that may increase susceptibility to infectious diseases or extreme environmental conditions (e.g., weather events, smog, and water contamination). Children and young people are also exposed to increased temperature and smog, water contamination, and infectious diseases, which is to be taken seriously in a city where nearly half the population is under the age of twenty-five (Corporate Policy Unit, *Quality of Life*, n.d.). In sum, the city's fragile residents are already highly vulnerable, and their vulnerability will increase under climate change conditions.

Ongoing studies analyzing the impacts of the projected climatic changes in Durban suggest that the associated potential health-related risks may include heat stress as well as vector- and waterborne diseases (such as malaria and cholera). For instance, heat stress is exacerbated by factors of age (people above sixty-five years of age and children under four years are more susceptible), lower income, informal housing, and lack of electricity. The most at-risk residents within the city—those who live in peripheral areas of the city without easy access to public services, infrastructure, and health centers—will be most significantly affected by climate change–induced health impacts (Golder Associates 2008). Similarly, an analysis of the vulnerability of the wards within the municipality to cholera indicates that the poorest and most rural wards are most at risk to outbreaks because they are often dependent on a non-piped water supply, nonflush toilets, low incomes, informal housing, no formal refuse system, and education below grade 7 (Golder Associates 2008). On the contrary, well-off residents tend to be more resilient and have greater access to formal health and service structures.

The distribution, transmission, intensity, and seasonality of malaria are also affected by environmental factors, most notably temperature, rainfall, and humidity. Control measures aimed at both the malaria vector and parasites have eliminated malaria from the city. The maintenance of an effective and sustainable malaria control program is therefore critical in a climate-changed future (Golder Associates 2008). Increasing economic hardship may make it difficult for such systems to sustain themselves, which raises the possibility of malaria reinvading areas from which it has been previously eradicated. Here again, the poor and marginalized residents would be most vulnerable should government institutions be unable to deliver a suitable malaria control service, while well-off residents would tend to be more resilient and have greater access to formal health and service structures.

Community Sociospatial Inequities

The IDP emphasizes the importance of protecting local biodiversity, agricultural crops, and fish resources (Plan 1); creating food security (Plan 4); and promoting and strengthening cultural diversity (Plan 6). However, as Durban faces climatic changes, impacts at the community scale will likely affect the ability of vulnerable communities to secure traditional livelihoods, meet their food needs, and protect their cultural identities. In the long term, such impacts will likely entrench already existing relations of dependence, domination, and exclusion in the city, and intensify sociospatial inequities between groups.

Climate Impacts on Traditional Livelihoods   The IDP notes the need for eThekwini to promote social development programs through the "implementation and promotion of food security," and through the protection of food resources for vulnerable communities (EThekwini Municipality 2008, 52). At the baseline, sub-Saharan Africa already has significant environmental handicaps in the arena of food production, such as limited water resources and nutrient-deficient soils. These environmental conditions are likely to be intensified by climate change. In Durban, declining crop yields and reduced food production can be expected as temperatures change, water availability decreases, and seasonal droughts become more common. In turn, such declines will have an impact on the food supply chain in terms of the availability and distribution of food for the whole Durban population.

Over time, all of these factors will combine to impact the ability of traditional farming communities to secure sustainable livelihoods as they depend on agricultural activities to meet their nutritional and food security needs (Golder Associates 2008. This is especially true in the periurban and rural wards of Durban. Today, farming communities in Durban grow seventeen different types of vegetables and fourteen different types of fruit. Of particular concern in terms of climatic impacts is the future viability of maize, given its importance as the predominant subsistence crop. Currently the majority of the city shows a moderate potential for the production of maize under subsistence management conditions (from 1.5 to 3.1 tons/ha/annum). However, the situation changes rapidly with an increase in temperature of one degree Celsius, with the majority of the area becoming unsuitable, and only a few small patches retaining their original predicted yield. With an additional degree, almost the entire area becomes unsuitable, and with an increase of three degrees, the entire municipal area is unsuitable (Golder Associates 2008).

Such impacts will likely increase poverty, as communities see the productivity of staple crops decline. Eventually, poor communities might be unable to perform small-scale traditional agriculture because of shifts in agriculturally suitable zones and decreased water availability (CSIR NRE 2006). Municipal authorities will thus need to intervene to assist poor communities in moving to replacement food sources, such as sorghum, cassava, wheat, pumpkins, sweet potatoes, and madumbes, a wild taro. If they fail to do so, the existing structure of local livelihoods and reliance that many families have on subsistence farming may be destroyed.

Similarly, poor traditional fishing communities will likely see their way of life and sources of nutrition and income threatened by climate impacts on water conditions, fish stocks, and biodiversity. In Durban, the extent to which the aquatic environment will be affected by climate-induced changes such as sea-level rise is of particular concern because the city has 98 km of coastline, eighteen major river catchments, and sixteen estuaries. It is likely that changes in the sea level will result in increased coastal erosion, saltwater intrusion into estuaries and groundwater, raised groundwater tables, and increased vulnerability to storm events (Department of Environmental Affairs and Tourism 2006). Fluctuations in rainfall will also change the amount of freshwater runoff.

Such changes are significant in the marine environment, because any reduction in freshwater flow has direct impacts on estuaries and the marine biota that utilize these systems, such as estuarine-dependent fish species (Department of Environmental Affairs and Tourism 2006). Reduced freshwater flow also decreases the extent to which wastewater discharges are diluted before they reach estuaries, thereby increasing the concentration of pollutants in the coastal zone and limiting the capacity of estuarine systems to support natural biota (Department of Environmental Affairs and Tourism 2006).

In turn, variations in water conditions are highly problematic for maintaining existing fish stocks in Durban, with acute health and social consequences for the fishing communities engaged in and dependent on subsistence fishing. This situation is exacerbated by the fact that fish stocks have already been badly affected by offshore line fishing, rock and surf angling, and estuarine fishing (Environmental Management Department, n.d.). Many of these traditional communities have high levels of poverty and rely on local fisheries both for their livelihood and survival (Branch et al. 2002). Any danger to key ecosystems, such as estuarine and inshore marine environments, puts these subsistence-level communities at long-term risk of disappearing.

In sum, climate change pressures are likely to translate into local extinctions and range shifts for the surviving species, with species required to move into the more transformed landscapes of the city where habitat availability is restricted. The extent to which species in Durban can adapt and ecosystems will shift, disintegrate, or reorganize due to climate change will have significant implications for the poor and vulnerable communities in the city who rely directly on ecosystem services and natural resources for meeting their basic food and income needs.

Climate Impacts on Cultural Resources and Structures   The IDP under-lines the important of creating "conditions under which sport, recreation, arts and culture, and heritage opportunities can be realized for personal growth, community solidarity, and economic advantage" (EThekwini Municipality 2008, 67). In addition to providing recreational opportuni-ties, cultural activities often represent an occasion for celebrating community diversity and strengthening identity. From a social standpoint, cultural festivals, parades, sports events, and rallies constitute opportuni-ties for cultural groups and communities to gather and build greater social connections and social capital, strengthen support mechanisms, and attract political attention from decision makers. Threats from climate change to existing infrastructure, buildings, and community spaces will be a limiting factor for organizing events. Overall, these patterns suggest that climate impacts in Durban may undermine the goal of fostering cultural solidarity and identity for minority communities.

Climate change could also significantly affect traditional cultural structures in low-income wards around Durban. Recent studies show that climate impacts are likely to trigger rural-urban migration, social tension between the rich and poor due to differing access to resources, cultural dilution because of increased migration, loss of cultural heritage, and changes in lifestyles (CSIR NRE 2006). Such impacts could affect cultural leadership structures and have deep consequences for the urban poor, who may look to traditional cultural practices and leaders for help in adapting to climate change and its effects. While cultural leaders and the practices they promote do play a central support role for low-income vulnerable communities, migration might force traditional leadership structures to relocate and possibly leave entire communities without sources of mutual help and guidance.

All in all, in Durban, climatic impacts on traditional farming and fishing communities and on structures that communities rely on for support increase the vulnerability of such communities to climate change. They also strengthen their dependence on existing livelihoods, and increase the fragility of these livelihoods. Lastly, climate change is likely to intensify sociospatial inequities in the city between communities, because well-off and traditionally advantaged communities in Durban have more diverse source of food, activity, and income. They can also more easily move and recover from problems like extreme weather events, and are better geographically and politically connected to structures of power and social capital in the city.

Municipal Policies and Sociospatial Inequities

Last, the IDP emphasizes the need for policymakers in Durban to promote economic growth and poverty alleviation (Plan 2), implement good governance policies (Plan 7), and ensure quality living environments through adequate services such as housing, water, electricity, and sanitation (Plan 3). However, in Durban, climate change may have negative repercussions for policies of economic development such as infrastructure and tourism expansion, as well as participatory governance. In the mid-term, climatic impacts, coupled with financial resource scarcity in Southern cities, will likely affect the capacity of municipal authorities to achieve their objective of poverty reduction, economic growth, and good governance.

Climate Impacts on Economic Development   Durban's IDP identifies a range of strategic interventions essential to achieving long-term economic development. In the IDP, economic development and job creation involve "developing the economic wealth of the Durban region for the material well-being of all its citizens" through "strong economic growth, sustainable job creation and poverty alleviation" (EThekwini Municipality 2008, 23). Durban is basing its development plans on already existing strengths and opportunities: an extensive coastline, the busiest port in Africa, the second largest business hub in South Africa, a large tourism center, and a center for international events such as the 2010 Soccer World Cup and its buildup events (EThekwini Municipality 2008). The city is also the second largest manufacturing base in the country and is well poised to boost nonmanufacturing industries such as agriculture and agriprocessing, service industries (i.e., ICT), Business Process Outsourcing or "offshoring," and creative industries (EThekwini Municipality 2008).

A critical component of the city's current and future economic strategy is the tourism sector. In 2004, 1.1 million foreign tourists visited Durban, resulting in a foreign tourism market worth approximately $270 million (Economic Development Unit 2008). However, climatic changes are likely to decrease the potential for tourism in the city. This is a particularly significant impact given the importance assigned to tourism as a sector capable of providing significant employment opportunities through accelerated growth and broad-based economic empowerment for black residents (Economic Development Unit 2008). Climate change likely presents a strong obstacle to the implementation of poverty alleviation policies and to the reduction of social inequities because extreme weather events and sea-level rise might affect tourism infrastructures and local coastlines and beaches.

Building quality living environments is another critical long-term goal for Durban. EThekwini Municipality is working to "promote access to equitable, appropriate and sustainable levels of household infrastructure and community services, and facilitate access to housing" (EThekwini Municipality 2008, 36). Infrastructure development will, however, be put at risk by climate change due to sea-level rise and extreme weather, decreased water availability for human and industrial consumption, and the flooding of economically significant areas. These impacts, coupled with the need for municipal authorities to cope with immediate risks and disasters rather than planning and building new housing, roads, and bridges, create significant developmental and social problems for Durban.

Such challenges are likely to directly affect poor and vulnerable groups, and their ability to access well-connected infrastructure and municipal services, which will further strengthen existing sociospatial inequities in the city. The municipality currently has 140,000 urban and 65,000 rural households that lack access to adequate services such as housing, water, electricity, and sanitation (Department of Environmental Affairs and Tourism 2006). Not only will these existing backlogs be compromised by the negative impacts of climate change, but existing developments such as the low-cost housing projects in Durban—many of which have been constructed on steep slopes and adjacent to drainage lines—are likely to be increasingly vulnerable as the climate continues to change. The end result is that any developmental progress that has been achieved in South African cities under democracy could be significantly undermined by existing and future climate change.

Under these conditions, eThekwini Municipality is faced with increasing difficulties in meeting the financial goal of the IDP, which is to "maximize the utilization of the Municipality's financial resources to ensure long-term financial viability" (EThekwini Municipality 2008, 80). The economic implications of climate change will be significant for new infrastructure and housing developments, given the predicted damage to the infrastructure and the accompanying impacts of agricultural shifts and effects on human health. Climatic impacts will necessitate additional expenditure on food production and health care, as well as the search for additional sources of national and international funding, which could divert funds away from future development projects.

Climate change is therefore likely to create an impossibly high hurdle in terms of achieving financial viability and sustainability, particularly if adaptation and mitigation measures are not implemented in a timely manner. Funding mitigation and adaptation measures will, however, also affect the expenditures available for service delivery and infrastructure development. This could increase the costs of essential services such as electricity and water, which in turn could lower local, national, and foreign investment in the country.

Climate Impacts on Governance and Institutional Transparency   In the area of governance and institutional transparency, the IDP places an emphasis on making eThekwini Municipality a "strong and caring institution which promotes and supports a consultative and participatory local government" (EThekwini Municipality 2008, 71). Climate inequities, however, endanger transparency and participation opportunities in the city, especially for marginalized groups whose voice tends not to be heard by policymakers and public officials. This situation will further entrench sociospatiality inequities between groups in Durban. Given the cross-sector and broad-ranging impacts of climate change, and the resultant economic need and social stress, good governance is likely to become increasingly difficult to achieve as government institutions become less able to meet people's needs and concerns, especially poor populations isolated on the periphery of the city.

The only effective response to residents' expectations and demands will be to improve the independence and resiliency of local communities in the mid- and long term, which will require a fine texture of engagement and consultation around climate change issues (i.e., community-level rather than city-level). The existence of elected Ward Committees in each of the municipality's 100 wards provides a potential vehicle to achieve this goal. In two pilot communities, the local Councilor and Ward Committee have already engaged in information sharing around climate change as part of a process seeking approval for community involvement in pilot projects that will let community members participate in local-level climate change risk assessment and adaptation planning, as well as research into improved food security and water harvesting. This time- and resource-intensive engagement is likely to be critical in moving the situation from one of a "solely responsible government" to one of shared and participatory governance around climate change issues.

In sum, climate change has a deep and broad impact on municipal goals, policies, and institutions in Durban. In addition to threatening the capacity of officials and decision makers in Durban to achieve social equity and economic development, it also has broad implications for good-governance objectives. In a context in which international financial institutions and other donors condition their loans on progress around these goals, municipalities such as eThekwini appear politically and economically strangled. They need to search for innovative frameworks to continue the pursuit of their sustainable development policies and respond to multiscale sociospatial inequities. In this regard, Durban has made significant progress toward climate adaptation planning and implementation on the ground, as an inevitable priority and a response to inequities in climate politics and policies.

Addressing Sociospatial Inequities: Climate Action in Durban

The projected climatic changes in Durban highlight how climate impacts can pose a significant challenge to the developmental aspirations of local governments and decision makers. Climatic change will likely impede economic growth, threaten the natural resource base, jeopardize the health and well-being of poor and minority communities, and foster social isolation. Ultimately, local impacts will intensify relations of exclusion and dependence in the city and exacerbate inequities on the ground.

Using a climate lens to analyze some of the core IDP plans shows that three types of inequities are likely to emerge in Durban: (1) individual inequities arising from threats to ecosystem services, increased humanitarian crises, and aggravated health issues; (2) community inequities as a result of impacts on current traditional farming and fishing activities, as well as cultural resources; and (3) the inability to realize municipal goals of economic and infrastructure development, as well as good governance and participation. However, local environmental injustices in Durban are not limited to these distributional inequities. Climate change impacts and politics also further exacerbate existing relations of power between groups and individuals in Durban, intensify the isolation of certain communities, and increase their dependence on traditional fragile livelihoods that are at risk of climatic changes.

To address these challenges, eThekwini Municipality is engaged in local municipal planning to respond to climate change and climate impacts. For instance, the requirement for the development of a Municipal Climate Protection Programme has already been incorporated into the IDP (Plan 1, Programme 6). Durban's decision makers and planners are also increasingly realizing that the vulnerability of the poor and marginalized communities to climatic changes necessitates that adaptation be regarded as an urgent developmental and human rights priority in the city. This need to place adaptation at the forefront of municipal policies has been acknowledged through the preparation of a Headline Adaptation Strategy for key municipal sectors. As part of this process, eThekwini Municipality is developing detailed Municipal Adaptation Plans (MAPs) for high-risk sectors such as water, health, and disaster management.

Local action is also being undertaken to initiate community-level projects that will address the adaptation needs of poor, fragile communities in terms of risk management, improved food and water security, and protection of ecosystem services with potential positive additional spin-offs such as job creation and capacity building (Roberts 2008). For instance, working in collaboration with the NGO Wildlands Conservation Trust, eThekwini Municipality has been implementing the Indigenous Trees for Life (ITFL) program as a platform for the development and implementation of the Buffelsdraai Community Reforestation Project in the north of the city. The objective of ITFL is to establish sustainable livelihoods that contribute to the restoration of the region's forest ecosystems and the sequestration of carbon dioxide. The program draws on a network of "tree-preneurs," often orphaned and vulnerable children, who grow indigenous trees and then trade the trees for food, clothes, bicycles, and other necessities that the Trust secures through corporate donations. The trees are then replanted in urban greening projects or forest restoration carbon sinks (Diederichs 2008).

Climate adaptation projects that are sensitive to the needs of poor and vulnerable residents allow cities such as Durban to tackle the ethical dimensions of climate justice. As Adger et al. (2006, 6) suggest, "There are both ethical and instrumental reasons for ensuring that adaptation to climate change does not further amplify existing vulnerabilities. The ethical reason is that climate change justice requires the consideration of principles such as precaution and the protection of the most vulnerable because of the uncertainties and irreversibilities inherent in the climate system and climate science." However, despite all of the evidence of potential impacts, and inroads that representatives from municipal departments in Durban have made to ensure climate justice, in the recent Draft Risk Based Audit Plan, climate change was rated as a "low" risk because it is not seen as a threat in the short term. This is a clear indication of the significant amount of work that still needs to be done to mainstream an understanding of climate change and its risks to the city and its residents. This need is probably the greatest challenge that lies ahead for climate change practitioners working at the local level in South Africa and Southern countries in general. It is still simply too easy to avoid engaging with the climate change debate, when the other developmental needs are so pressing.

By the same token, climate change practitioners would be well advised not to ignore these developmental priorities when trying to refocus local government's attention onto this new challenge. The consequences of such oversights are plainly evident in the recent political changes in South Africa, where inadequate and unequal levels of development and economic growth have contributed to the "recalling" of political leadership. In Africa, as well as in most other parts of the global South, the climate change debate and the development debate are, and will continue to be, inextricably linked. The impacts of climate change at several scales within a municipality are not unique to Durban and pose similar changes to other developing cities.

This focus on adaptation policies at the local level is also critical given that national- and international-level policymakers have to date focused predominantly on mitigation, and adaptation funding is still less than adequate. However, recent shifts in international conferences and forums have highlighted that it is now clear that mitigation and adaptation policies are not alternatives; both need to be pursued actively and in parallel: "Mitigation is essential and adaptation in inevitable" (UNFCCC 2006). On the ground, this need to pursue urgent, goal-directed adaptation plans is complicated by the fact that municipal governments in the South tend to lack the competence and financial resources, and suffer from huge infrastructure backlogs as well as a shortage of skills and technology, to adapt to climate change. Therefore, achieving climate justice is ultimately contingent on the creation of a working and appropriately resourced global adaptation fund that can assist local governments in addressing the impacts of climate change. At the end of the day, while the causes of climate change are global, the impacts are local and need to be dealt with at the local level. Local people, using local knowledge and capacity, must decide on their priorities. Only in this way is climate justice possible.

References

Adger, Neil, Jouni Paavola, Saleemul Huq, and M. J. Mace, eds. 2006. *Fairness in Adaptation to Climate Change.* Cambridge, MA: MIT Press.

Anand, Rucchi. 2004. *International Environmental Justice: A North-South Dimension.* Burlington, VT: Ashgate.

Borchert, Peter. 2007. Who are the culprits? *Africa Geographic,* August, 48–52.

Branch, George Meredith, Julien May, Benjamin Roberts, Eddy Russell, and Barry Clark. 2002. Case studies on the socio-economic characteristics and lifestyles of subsistence and informal fishers in South Africa. *South African Journal of Marine Science* 24:439–462.

Bullard, Robert. 1990. *Dumping in Dixie: Race, Class, and Environmental Quality.* Boulder, CO: Westview Press.

Carmin, JoAnn, Debra Roberts, and Isabelle Anguelovski. 2009. Government institutions and innovations in governance for achieving climate adaptation in cities. Paper presented at the Urban Research Symposium "Cities and Climate Change: Responding to an Urgent Agenda," Marseille, France.

Corporate Policy Unit. n.d. *EThekwini Municipality Integrated Development Plan 2010 and beyond: 2007–2008 Review.* Durban: EThekwini Municipality.

Corporate Policy Unit. n.d. *The Quality of Life of Durban's People. Trends: 1998–2005.* Durban: EThekwini Municipality.

CSIR NRE. 2006. *Climatic Future for Durban.* Durban: CSIR.

Department of Environmental Affairs and Tourism. 2006. *South Africa Environment Outlook: A Report on the State of the Environment.* Pretoria: Department of Environmental Affairs and Tourism.

Diederichs, Nicci. 2008. *Community Reforestation Project Proposal.* Report prepared for eThekwini Municipality.

Dikeç, Mustafa. 2001. Justice and the spatial imagination. *Environment & Planning A* 33(10):1785–1805.

Economic Development Unit. 2008. *Economic Development Strategy 2008: Hands of Prosperity.* Durban: EThekwini Municipality.

Environmental Management Department. n.d. *State of the Environment Report: 2003/2004 Municipal Financial Year.* Durban: EThekwini Municipality.

Ethekwini Municipality. 2008. *EThekwini Municipality Integrated Development Plan 2010 and beyond: 2008–2009 Review.* Durban: EThekwini Municipality.

Fainstein, Susan. 2006. Planning and the just city. Presented at the Conference on Searching for the Just City, GSAPP, Columbia University, April 2006.

Golder Associates. 2008. *Progress Report on Preparation of an Urban Integrated Assessment Framework for Climate Change.* Unpublished report prepared for the Environmental Management Department, eThekwini Municipality.

Harvey, David. 1973. *Social Justice and the City.* Baltimore: Johns Hopkins University Press.

Harvey, David. 1996. *Justice, Nature and the Geography of Difference.* Cambridge, MA: Blackwell.

Hastings, Annette. 2007. Territorial justice and neighborhood environmental services: A comparison of provision to deprived and better-off neighborhoods in the UK. *Environment and Planning C* 25:896–917.

Honneth, Axel. 1992. Morality, politics, and human-beings, 1: Integrity and disrespect—principles of a conception of morality based on the theory of recognition. *Political Theory* 20(2):187–201.

Huq, Saleemul, Sari Kovats, Hannah Reid, and David Satterthwaite. 2007. Reducing risks to cities from disasters and climate change. *Environment and Urbanization* 19(1):3–15.

IPCC. 2007a. Climate Change 2007: Impacts, Adaptation and Vulnerability. Contribution of Working Group II to the *Fourth Assessment Report of the Intergovernmental Panel on Climate Change*, M. L. Parry, O. F. Canziani, J. P. Palutikof, P. J. van der Linden, and C. E. Hanson, eds. Cambridge, UK: Cambridge University Press.

IPCC. 2007b. Climate Change 2007: Synthesis Report. Contribution of Working Groups I, II, and III to the *Fourth Assessment Report of the Intergovernmental Panel on Climate Change*. Core Writing Team, R. K. Pachauriand A. Reisinger, eds. Geneva, Switzerland: IPCC.

International Mission on Environmental Policy. 1995. *Building a New South Africa: Environment, Reconstruction and Development*. Canada: International Development Research Center.

Marcuse, Peter. 2009. Spatial justice: Derivative but causal of social injustice. *Spatial Justice* 1:49–57.

Martinez-Alier, Joan. 2002. *The Environmentalism of the Poor: A Study of Ecological Conflicts and Valuation*. Cheltenham: Edward Elgar.

McCray, Heather, Anne Hammill, and Robert Bradley. 2007. *Weathering the Storm: Options for Framing Adaptation and Development*. Washington, DC: World Resources Institute.

Merrifield, Andy, and Erik Swyngedouw, eds. 1997. *The Urbanization of Injustice*. New York: New York University Press.

Oxfam. 2007. *Adapting to Climate Change: What's Needed in Poor Countries and Who Should Pay*. Oxford: Oxfam International.

Parks, Bradley, and J. Timmons Roberts. 2006. Globalization, vulnerability to climate change, and perceived injustice in the South. *Society & Natural Resources* 19(4):337–355.

Pearce, Fred. 2007. *The Last Generation: How Nature Will Take Her Revenge for Climate Change*. London: Transworld.

Pellow, David. 2000. Environmental inequality formation: Toward a theory of environmental injustice. *American Behavioral Scientist* 43(4):581–601.

Pellow, David, and Robert Brulle, eds. 2005. *Power, Justice and the Environment: A Critical Reappraisal of the Environmental Justice Movement*. Cambridge, MA: MIT Press.

Pettit, Jethro. 2004. Climate justice: A new social movement for atmospheric rights. *IDS Bulletin* 35(3):102–106.

Rawls, John. 1971. *A Theory of Justice*. Cambridge, MA: Belknap Press of Harvard University Press.

Roberts, Debra. 2008. Thinking globally, acting locally: Institutionalizing climate change at the local government level in Durban, South Africa. *Environment and Urbanization* 20(2):521–537.

Roberts, Timmons, and Bradley Parks. 2007a. *A Climate of Injustice: Global Inequality, North-South Politics, and Climate Policy*. Cambridge, MA: MIT Press.

Roberts, Timmons, and Bradley Parks. 2007b. Fueling injustice: Globalization, the ecological debt, and confronting responsibility for climate change. *Globalizations* 4(1):193–210.

Shiva, Vandana. 2002. *Water Wars: Privatization, Pollution, and Profit*. Boston: South End Press.

Simms, Andrew. 2005. *Ecological Debt: The Health of the Planet and the Wealth of Nations*. London: Pluto Press.

Soja, Edward. 2000. *Postmetropolis: Critical Studies of Cities and Regions*. Oxford: Blackwell.

Soja, Edward. 2009. The city and spatial justice. *Spatial Justice* 1:31–38.

United Nations Framework Convention on Climate Change. 2006. *Technologies for Adaptation to Climate Change*. Bonn: United Nations Framework Convention on Climate Change.

Walzer, Michael. 1983. *Spheres of Justice: A Defense of Pluralism and Equality*. New York: Basic Books.

Yohe, Gary. 2000. Assessing the role of adaptation in evaluating vulnerability to climate change. *Climatic Change* 46(3):371–390.

Young, Iris Marion. 1990. *Justice and the Politics of Difference*. Princeton, NJ: Princeton University Press.

3

Learning from the Quest for Environmental Justice in the Niger River Delta

Max Stephenson Jr. and Lisa A. Schweitzer

The peoples of the Niger River Delta have been engaged in ongoing struggles to secure some measure of genuine development from the continued oil production in their territory (Okonta and Douglas 2001) despite the ecological degradation that accompanies those processes (Moffatt and Linden 1995). Many analysts, who have examined the environmental pollution of the Delta and the role of petroleum exploration and production in that process, have concluded that more just outcomes could be achieved with more transparent and accountable governance in Nigeria itself. However, because this region accounts for a significant percentage of the world's oil production, a hefty share of the overall profits of one of the globe's largest corporations (Royal Dutch Shell), and much of the oil consumed in the United States, it is unlikely that current patterns of degradation and exploitation will be altered unless changes are also made in the patterns of transnational trade and economic globalization shaping these activities.

This chapter situates environmental justice claims used as surrogates for poverty and cultural marginalization in the Niger River Delta into two broader currents of theory building. First, we examine the unfolding Delta story through the lens of Ulrich Beck's cosmopolitan realist theory, particularly his concept of the double contingent character of the current international political order's changing contours. This perspective provides a means to understand better the claims and capacities of the institutional participants in the struggle (Beck 2005). Second, and equally important, we summarize widely held views concerning accountability claims appropriate to democratic governance and identify the primary alternate international and intranational accountabilities at play in the Delta. This second perspective is useful for distinguishing the role(s) of the Nigerian state and other relevant actors at multiple analytical scales. All levels of the Nigerian government have been complicit in the degradation of the Delta environment, although to varying degrees, for different reasons, and in dissimilar ways. Their roles have been shaped in part by internal national pressures and in part by domestic and international interdependencies. Together these forces have created a tragedy of global significance.

Globalization and the Changing Contours of International Politics

Beck (2005) examined the character of international politics resulting from the ongoing globalization of trade and other economic and cultural forms. He suggested that the meaning of state sovereignty, as a consequence of globalization, is now in flux and the roles of internationalizing capitalist and civil society institutions are similarly undergoing rapid change: "How might we conceptualize a world and a set of global dynamics in which the problematic consequences of radicalized modernization effectively eliminate the cornerstones of action—certain historically produced fundamental distinctions and basic institutions—of its nation-state order?" (p. xi).

The power game in this new global order is neither clear nor ordained by any one of its member actors alone. What is apparent is that states, even militarily and economically powerful ones, no longer possess the same measure of authority or power over the economic and political fortunes of their territories they once may have enjoyed. Instead, their purview and scope for discretionary action is challenged not only by other states as states or via international organizations, but also by the political-economic pressures and power of corporations that may be able to locate their operations virtually anywhere in the world and that command vast resources of their own. The essential characteristics of international politics and the role of states within it have changed, with nations becoming more susceptible to global capital flows and to the role(s) multinational corporations play in determining those capital flows. States are also increasingly subject to the claims of supralevel international organizations when these are supported by coalitions of other state actors willing to resource and enforce them.

Nonetheless, while ongoing globalization and the continued growth, however uneven, of transnational governance institutions have thus rendered states less determinative actors than they once were, they remain a vital organizing force in global politics. The primary result of a less-state-centered international politics is, as Beck (2005, xi) observes, "[a] game in which boundaries, basic rules and basic distinctions are now being renegotiated—not only those between the 'national' and 'international' spheres, but also those between global business and the state, transnational civil society movements, supranational organizations and national governments and societies." Not only, according to Beck, are the actors in international politics constantly adopting new strategies to maximize what they take to be their interests, but the rules of the game itself are subject to constant (re)negotiation. Beck (2005, 7) argues that this creates a double contingency situation for states as actors:

In the transition from one order to the next, politics is entering a peculiar twilight zone, the twilight zone of *double contingency*. Nothing remains fixed, neither the old basic institutions and systems of rules nor the specific organizational forms and actors; instead, they are disrupted, reformulated and renegotiated during the course of the game itself. Just how far this will go is unclear since it depends on contingent circumstances, like the goals and alternatives of politics in general.

In such a circumstance the analyst might be forgiven for imagining that international politics has now assumed the characteristics of the famous croquet match in *Alice in Wonderland* in which both the rules of the contest and the tools of the game (flamingos for mallets and hedgehogs for balls) were constantly moving and changing locations (Carroll 1982).

States doubtless still possess a variable measure of authority and power to mediate strong globalization-related constraints and pressures, but whatever the standing and reach of the nation involved, this capacity is circumscribed by the reality that no state by itself can control global capital flows or, indeed, secure itself and its population from the vagaries of those movements. Nor can many countries stand alone against the collective ire or combined pressure of other nations when these are willing to press their claims in a unified way. All of this said, Beck argues states are now but one participant in an extremely complicated international system and possess only limited capacity to overcome by themselves the realities of corporate power. As a result, any new form of international politics that hopes to be democratic will have to include ways and means to counter the growing power and influence of global capital.

Beyond individual states and their efforts to secure collective action and regulation of corporate action where appropriate, Beck looks to civil society organizations, especially those that can operate transnationally, to act along with states as counterweights to multinational firms when these threaten to close plants or move economic activities to alternate locations if specific conditions are not met by affected governments and communities (Beck 2005). We turn next to sketch an ideal model of the democratic accountabilities at play as the Niger Delta peoples have struggled to address the distributive conflicts unleashed by their oil resources.

Charting the Stakeholders and Accountabilities at Play: An Ideal Model

Five widely shared tenets of democratic governance appear to demand specific behaviors of the various stakeholders engaged in international environmental conflicts. First, democracy requires free and fair elections. Second, democracy demands politically accountable decision processes that are open to public scrutiny and debate. Third, democracy requires transparent decision making and resource allocation. Fourth, democracy must ensure ways and means for aggrieved citizens to secure an impartial hearing of their concerns. Last, democracy requires that elected governments make all reasonable efforts to secure the health and well-being of those citizens whose interests they are pledged to represent while in office (Held 2006). In context, these stipulations suggest that elected Nigerian governments at all levels (national, state, and local) owe it to their citizenry to engage in ongoing efforts to ensure effectiveness, transparency, and accountability in their decision processes and finances. The national government owes all the nation's citizens its best efforts to secure both improved conditions in their lives and development of economic and social possibilities for those of rising generations.

To claim the mantle of democracy, the federal government owes states and localities that share governance responsibilities for the nation such resources as its leaders determine to be reasonable and appropriate to serve their citizens' needs. Such choices should follow a period of open public debate and consideration. Because attaining this balance of competing claims over time will require a distribution of resources that will differentially affect a variety of constituencies, these resources should be shared via formulas or criteria that are themselves openly debated and justified with citizen involvement. As far as the environment is concerned, the central government owes all of its citizens its best professional efforts to ensure effective and equitable use of the nation's natural resources so these may be sustained across generations or, if the resources are not renewable (as with petroleum), so they can be exploited and the proceeds invested in such a way as to benefit the citizenry across a similar future time frame.

Under the same rationale, Nigerian state and local governments owe their citizens effective services in the health and education domains—over which they exercise primary responsibility under the Nigerian constitution. Like the national government, these entities should devise and offer open budgetary, accounting, and administrative systems by which their use of federally allocated resources may be judged. State officials should work to provide educational opportunities for citizens and for development in each of the state's communities. State actors should coordinate with national officials to secure the nation's environmental protection, regulation, and remediation. Localities owe their citizens the same transparency and determined efforts to secure program and project effectiveness for which the nation and states are responsible, including wise use and protection of natural resources. Like their state and national counterparts, they owe their citizens open choice-making processes and clear reporting concerning how public resources have been employed and why.

In the same vein, based on the normative ideal outlined above, the multinational oil corporations owe their host nation and its government(s) their best efforts to assist them in securing their people against unwanted or obnoxious external costs resulting from their operations, active compliance with relevant host-country and international law and norms, and fair dealing in contract development and business operations. Ethically, they owe their hosts due regard for the privilege of working in their territory and good-faith efforts to conduct their operations with appropriate accountability standards and in accord with relevant governmental and international requirements. To the extent that coexploitation of national resources may be considered a legitimate activity for both guests (such as multinationals) and hosts (Nigerians), multinational corporations have the ethical responsibility to be accountable to the mores and controls of the hosts in the sense of Derrida's ethics of hospitality (Derrida 2000).

This idealized model suggests the multiple and interrelated accountabilities governments face as custodians of the public interest both in terms of democratic processes and outcomes. There are obligations to deliver services—schools, medical care, environmental protection—that in fact rely on the governments' capacities to develop economically. In the case that follows, Beck's double contingencies help us understand how inequality lingers even as global and national actors begin to mature out of conflict into progressively more transparent and accountable actors.

Nigerian Development, Environmental Degradation, and Corporate Power

Figure 3.1 provides a map of the geography of Nigeria. The Niger River Delta region is located on the west coast of the country and contains urbanized port cities that grew rapidly during the slave trade era. That commerce deeply altered the existing sociopolitical structure of Africa's west coast as it worked to consolidate Britain's colonial control over the area by the 1910s (Gordon 2003). A number of authors have provided excellent histories of the Delta, including the varied impacts of oil exploration and the social movements that arose to address them (Naanen 1995; Ibrahim 2000; Boele, Fabig, and Wheeler 2001; Wheeler et al. 2001; Osha 2006). We cannot do justice here to the complex evolution of the region. Instead, we address several key concerns that lend context to our primary interest in theory building for governance and environmental justice.

Oil production in the Delta began in 1958 nearly concurrent with Nigeria's national independence from Britain in 1960. Thereafter, rapid corporate expansion in the region paralleled federal governmental

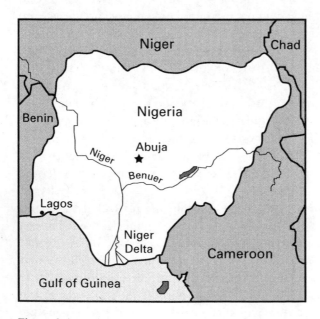

Figure 3.1
Nigeria and the Niger River Delta

instability for several decades. Nigeria's first leader, Prime Minister Sir Abubakar Tafawa Balewa, was assassinated in 1966 and his military successor, Major General Johnson Aguiyi-Ironsi, was himself murdered less than a year thereafter. Lieutenant Colonel Yakubu Gowon ruled next from 1966 to 1975, when he was overthrown and fled the country (Sklar 2004). His successor, Brigadier Murtala Ramat Mohammed, initiated the process of moving the country's national capital from Lagos, on Nigeria's western coast, to Abuja, centrally located inland (Moore 2008). This sad saga, which continues in less draconian form with the recent debilitating illness of the nation's elected president, Umaru Musa Yar'Adua, and his replacement by the country's vice president, is important here for what it suggests about the relative capacity of the national government vis-à-vis the multinational corporations active in petroleum production in Nigeria's Delta.

Organized calls for at least some measure of governance autonomy in the Delta began in the 1940s, even before Nigeria gained independence. Similarly, social opposition to the region's environmental despoliation grew in the decades following Nigeria's independence alongside the nation's continuing political turmoil (Haller, Blöchlinger, and John 2007). Many authors have described the connections between central government instability and the dominance of foreign corporate entities in forming the environmental, political, and social landscape of the Niger River Delta region (Naanen 1995; Ibrahim 2000; Boele, Fabig, and Wheeler 2001). As early as the 1970s, production and export of petroleum by foreign firms emerged as the principal driver of the Nigerian economy. The oil and the facilities needed to process it were (and are) located primarily in the Niger River Delta, which is populated by a number of minority ethnic groups who historically have farmed or fished as their way of life. The area's onshore and offshore operations constitute more than 90 percent of all petroleum-related activities in the country. Nigeria is now Africa's largest producer of oil at 2.7 million barrels per day as of 2006, with proven reserves estimated at 35.2 billion barrels (United States Energy Information Administration 2007).

Nevertheless, that economic bounty has not benefited the region that produces it by yielding strong development and increased wealth (International Crisis Group 2006). Instead, while the indigenous people have seen their home territories become host to over 600 oil wells along with major oil transport and processing facilities, their overall living situation has declined in real terms. Although estimates vary widely, reported spills from high-pressure pipelines and oil transfers annually number in the hundreds with perhaps 700,000 barrels escaping each year (Nwilo and Badejo 2006). Not all discharges are reported, and Shell, long one of the largest corporate actors in the region, has argued that as much as 70 percent of leaks and spillage have occurred through sabotage and theft, not mismanagement (Shell Oil, n.d.).

Whether the product of mismanagement or misguided ire, after two decades of increasingly serious oil spills, opposition to oil production in the Niger Delta coalesced in 1990 when tribal chiefs gathered to consider ways to demand change in living conditions in the Delta. One result of that meeting was the Ogoni Bill of Rights signed by leaders from the Ken-Khana, Nyo-Khana, Tai, Gokana, and Babbe communities. That Bill of Rights, presented to the Nigerian government, emphasized the Ogoni were a distinct people within the Delta who had not benefited from oil production in their traditional territories (The Ogoni People 1990).

Several developments in the justice movement in the Delta since 1990 bear directly on our discussion about the role of nation-state and subsidiary structures within the global-local conflict in the Delta. These include the coalescence of support for a change in political representation of area residents, a decision by the national government to suppress such dissent, and the unexpected salience of the controversy in the international media. The Movement for the Survival of the Ogoni People formed in 1992 following development of the Ogoni Bill of Rights. Movement leaders, especially including writer Ken Saro-Wiwa, were able to capture the attention of extraterritorial media outlets and nongovernmental organizations regarding the region's concerns about ongoing environmental degradation amid continuing penury (Bob 2005). General Sani Abacha sought to suppress such Delta protests after assuming control of the federal government in a coup in 1993. By 1994 regional activists were subject to increased levels of scrutiny and violence until finally a group of prominent opposition leaders were arrested, including Ken Saro-Wiwa, Baribor Bera, Saturday Dobee, Nordu Eawo, Daniel Gbooko, Barinem Kiobel, John Kpuine, Paul Levera, and Felix Nuate (Addo 1999). These men, subsequently called "the Ogoni Nine," were publically executed in November 1995. Thereafter, the Nigerian military further increased its presence in the Delta, and systematically sought to suppress Ogoni protest and dissent.

Far from stanching that protest, however, the violence directed at leaders and villages encouraged the groups that formed in the Delta to issue more strident ethnic sovereignty claims and undertake more virulent forms of opposition. The Movement for the Emancipation of the

Figure 3.2
Major Niger River Delta oil-related developments, 2000 to 2010

Niger Delta (MEND) went so far as to practice systematic hostage taking and oil-facility sabotage against Shell and other Western corporations in the 1990s. Figure 3.2 provides a timeline of major Delta-related events from 2000 to early 2010. As hostage taking continued from 2006 onward, the families of the executed "Ogoni Nine" sued Shell in 2009 for its alleged complicity in the Nigerian government's actions. The company settled the suit out of court for $15.5 million (Baldauf 2009). The decision among the parties not to pursue further action prevented any potential legal precedent concerning the liability of corporations in human rights violations. In any case, Shell Oil argued it was not complicit in the suppression or execution of Ogoni dissidents. The long saga of petroleum extraction in Nigeria took a new turn in late 2009 and early 2010 when Nigerian-owned companies began producing oil offshore (Salau 2009).

This hopeful new chapter, which at least potentially could allow increased native control over local extraction practices, followed a decade of intense levels of violence and unrest in the Delta, during which insurgents called increasingly for some form of home rule and just compensation to area residents for the environmental destruction of their homeland. Several interdependent factors linked to governance appear to have contributed to the continuing volatility of this situation: virtually complete Nigerian government reliance on oil revenues to sustain the public treasury; a lack of effective environmental regulation as a result of a continuing dearth of government capacity and political will at national, state, and local levels; unfettered corporate power and accompanying arrogance; intranational tensions over distribution of petroleum production-related receipts; and continued public corruption. We discuss each of these concerns briefly.

The Consequences of Oil as the Dominant Source of Public Revenue

The federal, or national, government in Nigeria has exclusive rights to the resources generated by oil within its territory. The nation collects all royalties and taxes in the country. This arrangement arose during a period of largely military rule from 1966 to 1999. During those roughly three decades the national government negotiated agreements with the multinational corporations that produce, refine, and export oil from the Delta, including Shell, Chevron, and British Petroleum, among others. The central government does not itself operate or own exploration, production, transport, or refining facilities. Instead, it has contracted with these and other corporations to bring its petroleum to the global market.

That arrangement makes Nigeria a rentier state, because oil accounts for an average of more than 90 percent of its exports by value and more than 70 percent of its revenues overall. The nation has not experienced much conflict over the contours of its agreements with the major oil firms operating in the Delta or offshore near it, although their negotiation has not always been easy. The nation's oil agreements have benefited Nigeria in the sense of providing growing revenues to the nation. In the 1970s, for example, the value of Nigerian oil production rose from $250 million to $11.2 billion in four years. The nation's petroleum revenues topped $45 billion in 2005. When the price of oil skyrocketed in 2008, the nation received a fresh revenue bonanza.

Recognizing the value of the revenues is not to argue that those assets have been well managed or used appropriately. Indeed, the reverse has often been true. While Nigeria's gross national product has risen to $86.9 billion, real per capita income now stands at one-third its 1980 level. Similarly, between 50 and 90 million Nigerians out of a national population of approximately140 million live in absolute poverty, surviving on average incomes of less than $1 per day. Nigeria now ranks 159th among 177 nations listed in the United Nations Development Program Human Development Index.

Unlike negotiations with the multinational firms, central-government distribution of oil revenues has been a lightning rod for conflict internal to the country. Because Nigeria is a federation, the national government determines how much petroleum-related revenue will be distributed to state and local governments around the country. On average, about 48.5 percent of oil receipts today remains with the national government, while 24 percent is allocated to states and about 20 percent flows to local governments (although generally such funds pass through the states). These percentages have increased in favor of state and local governments since the advent of civilian rule in 1999. Regardless of the specific sums received, state and local governments alike rely on shared oil receipts for the major portion of their budgets.

The oil-producing local governments of the Delta now receive approximately 13 percent of the revenues generated by oil production in their jurisdictions. This has recently translated into making these states among the richest jurisdictions in the nation. Yet, incomes, education, and health conditions in the Delta have not improved commensurately (Human Rights Watch 2007). The contrast of continuing penury amid growing receipts as a result of the willingness of national civilian governments since 1999 to return a larger share of oil revenues to Delta area states and communities raises the question of how such a situation can occur. The reasons suggest, in keeping with Beck's analysis, the intertwining of domestic and international factors.

As we noted, in the early 1990s, a popular movement arose in Ogoniland—an area within the Delta located near Port Harcourt, the refinery center for the region—demanding that the federal government return resources to the region proportionate to those its oil assets were producing for the nation. Ikporukpo has analyzed this protest movement (and armed insurrection) in some detail (Ikporukpo 2004). This movement reflected popular discontent, both with the slowness with which the oil majors responded to petroleum spills and leakage and with the companies' unwillingness to curtail flaring methane gas, a by-product of the refining process. For oil-community activists, environmental justice came to mean that all government rents received attributable to the area's resources be returned to the region's state and local governments.

Meanwhile, many citizens saw the oil companies, and not their state and local governments, as finally responsible for the conditions that troubled them. One Delta representative of Shell Oil Company put the point this way in 1999: "In many Delta communities, underdevelopment has led the people to perceive SPDC (Shell Oil in Nigeria) as the only 'form of government' they know. In recent years, this proximity to host communities has increased SPDC exposure to growing discontent with government" (Ikporukpo 2004, 338).

In the latter half of the 1990s, Delta-based environmental nongovernmental organizations (NGOs), including the Civil Liberties Organization, the Committee for the Defense of Human Rights, and the Constitutional Rights Project, advocated for the return of central government–controlled oil resources to the region to allow for remediation of environmental degradation and to secure increased development opportunities. International NGOs, such as Human Rights Watch, Amnesty International, and the World Council of Churches, also publicized the environmental and living conditions in the Delta and called for redistribution of resources as a partial means of securing resources for remediation. These organizations called on the corporations involved to take steps to help the communities in which they were working and to address pressing pollution abatement and cleanup needs. Ultimately, as noted above, the central government and corporations responded and provided more resources (International Crisis Group 2006). The national government shared increased revenues with state and local governments, while the oil companies began to provide specific development projects in tandem both with community groups and local governments within the areas of their operations. Human Rights Watch has formally acknowledged these developments, but has also suggested that these changes have done little to make changes in how Delta residents live (Human Rights Watch 2007). Paradoxically, while it seems clear that at least a share of the newfound willingness of the national government and petroleum companies alike to provide increased resources arose from the pressure applied by international NGOs, the citizenry at large continues to perceive these environmental groups as distant and untrustworthy elites (Okonta and Douglas 2001).

The Political Economy of Oil-Company Regulation

The tale of the specific arrangements by which the Nigerian government has overseen oil operations over the decades has been well told elsewhere. But to gain a perspective on what has occurred over the last four and a half decades, it may help to note that the multinationals have established an enormous infrastructure of machinery and facilities that necessarily has impacts on the limited land area and waters it occupies. Oil and its refined products cannot be produced without environmental effects. The issue was never whether the local ecology would be affected by such operations but rather, how that reality would be addressed, and when necessary, remediated (Onu 2003). The assortment of pipes, drilling machines, vent stacks, and other refining and transport equipment needed for petroleum exploration, processing, transport, and refining not only carried with it the potential for air and water pollution, but also brought population influxes and development stresses when the skilled workers necessary to operate and maintain the new infrastructure arrived. Likewise, and for similar reasons, oil exploration and production have placed upward pressure on local property values and the price of goods and services because firms and their employees can pay much more than local inhabitants for normally consumed items.

Relatedly, the state has been slow to establish effective regulation of multinational oil-firm operations. Nigeria did not create a Federal Environmental Protection Agency until December 1988 and its record of enforcement of relevant law in the Delta has been spotty at best. While environmental protection laws and regulations exist at federal, state, and local levels and have been encouraged by international attention since the Rio Earth Summit of 1992, these have been poorly enforced or are so difficult to access that the frequent result is that only elites may seek such redress (International Crisis Group 2006). And many elites, profiting from ongoing oil operations in one form or another, do not press to reduce pollution or to clean up existing degraded sites for fear the petroleum companies will reduce or eliminate the operations on which their own economic and social standing depends (Human Rights Watch 2007).

Pollution and environmental risk in the Niger Delta have taken many forms, including land degradation from crude oil piping and refined product tanker spills, gas flaring (largely of methane at the highest level of any refinery locations in the world), and frequent and largely unregulated discharge of effluents into creeks and estuaries (Ikporukpo 2004). For example, "4835 spillage incidents were recorded (in the Delta) between 1976 and 1996—an average of 440 a year" (Ikporukpo 2004, 329). Writing in 2003, Agbola and Alabi concluded: "Unfortunately and despite the haphazard collection of laws regulating the environment the Nigerian state, through its connivance with the operating companies, has blatantly violated the environmental laws and extracted its natural resources in the most unsustainable manner" (p. 273).

While the national government has a strong incentive to adopt policies to maximize oil revenues since the nation is so dependent on them, it is not clear that such a stance *necessarily* implies widespread tolerance of activities that may foment conflict with and among local populations or degrade all or portions of the nation's environment. Thus, if such tolerance is occurring and has transpired, it demands explanation. Such a situation could arise from corruption, from a dearth of qualified personnel, or as a result of too few resources overall dedicated to regulation. The state of affairs might also be tolerated as a result of discrimination against the peoples who live in the region. Indeed, all of these factors have been offered as potential explanations for government behavior. But the heart of the matter appears to be a culture of corruption that began in earnest during the nation's three decades of military rule and that has persisted and become institutionalized at all levels of governance to such a degree as to be labeled by one U.S. government announcement as a "kleptocracy" ("Fact Sheet" 2006). A sketch of the scale and institutionalization of corruption in government will suffice to illustrate its reach and portent.

Institutionalized Corruption

The World Bank and Transparency International define corruption as "the abuse of public office for private gain." The World Bank includes a range of practices under this rubric: extortion, bribes, patronage, nepotism, and theft of state assets and diversion of public revenues for private gain (World Bank 1997). The World Bank also distinguishes between state capture and administrative corruption. The first involves altering law and rules to favor specific groups or outcomes by illicit means, while the second involves illicitly directing public processes to ensure private gain to public officials. Nigeria has suffered from both forms of corruption. Nigeria's Economic and Financial Crimes Commission has estimated that more than $380 billion was stolen or squandered by public officials during the period of military rule from 1966 to 1999. General Ibrahim Babangida, who ruled from 1985 to 1993, allegedly stole some $12.2 billion of oil revenues for his personal use. The general was widely accused of systematically seeking to institutionalize corruption as a tool of political control and to have largely succeeded in doing so. Similarly, General Sani Abacha is believed to have stolen between $1 and $3 billion for his personal use during his four-year rule.

Even now, under a democratic national regime, local government budgets are not published routinely and it is difficult to gain an accounting of their revenues and expenditures. Elected officials often treat state government budgets as secret documents. Human Rights Watch and other INGOs have reported that these practices obscure widespread diversion of public funds for personal purposes. These examples illustrate the scope and scale of corruption in the nation's governments over the years. This intranational problem has proven to be both deep and relatively intractable.

Evaluating Stakeholder Actions

If the accountabilities envisioned in an ideal or model state represent a reasonable synopsis of what democratic processes would demand of responsible officials in Nigeria, governments at all levels should be working assiduously to ensure that resources are allocated by criteria that are subject to vigorous and open popular debate and that may be changed by suitable accountable government action. But the principal actors are not yet meeting these criteria. The national government is now elected in free (but not yet violence-free) elections and is making efforts to conduct its operations in a more transparent and accountable fashion, but it is still fighting corruption in its own ranks and has not succeeded thus far in addressing the rampant corruption in its state and local governments (Aluko 2006). It is now transferring larger sums to the state and local governments of oil communities than ever before, but citizens of the Delta are benefiting little from these resources owing to government corruption.

Indeed, a recent Human Rights Watch study revealed that Niger Delta states and localities are failing their citizens on a shocking scale. Corruption and ineffectiveness are epidemic and transparency and accountability for public funds is not a part of the behavior of relevant officials. Large sums simply "disappear" as projects are not completed and schools fall into such disrepair and so completely lack books and materials that they become both physically unusable and educationally untenable (Human Rights Watch 2007).

For their part, the major multinational corporations have begun to expend resources to support development projects in the communities near their facilities. The efficacy of these projects is hotly debated and the pace of improvement in environmentally relevant practices and initiatives is uneven. Shell Nigeria, in particular, has obliged itself to upgrade its pipelines and facilities to standards it meets at other locations, including those in the United States and Europe, and to sharply curtail its use of flaring. But the changes will take some years to complete due to their cost.

As helpful as our discussion may be in contextualizing the prospects of Delta communities for securing environmental improvements and more sustainable economies and thereby some measure of justice, we have not yet treated the significance of one factor that serves as a major driver in Nigeria's oil-production region: the role of international non-governmental organizations in securing worldwide salience for the Delta peoples' plight. Human rights and environmental INGOs have pressed vigorously for improvements in Nigerian governance and for improved living conditions in the Delta. These groups have succeeded in focusing major international media attention on the needs and issues of the Delta and have kept pressure on the Nigerian national government to secure changes in existing environmental regulatory policies and practices as well as resource distribution formulas. In short, these international actors have worked to serve as counterweights to the market-related power of the oil multinationals, whose standing the Nigerian government was ill-equipped to address alone.

Beck's "Double Contingency" and Environmental Justice in the Delta

Ulrich Beck's double contingency formulation is helpful in understanding the political-economic situation in the Delta and its consequences for environmental remediation and improved prospects for sustainable development. Like the international politics and global trade in which it is ensconced, the region and the agents with power to affect its destiny are in a state of flux. As Beck argued should occur, transnational civil society organizations have pushed for changes in how the Nigerian federal government distributes its oil revenues to Delta-area governments as well as improvements in the overall transparency and fiscal and political accountability of all levels of governmental budgeting and administration. Human Rights Watch, Amnesty International, and other INGOs have advocated publicizing the continuing venality and corruption of Delta state and local governments. Similarly, the same organizations and a variety of environmental INGOs, including World Wildlife Fund–UK and the International Union for the Conservation of Nature (World Conservation Union), have publicized the ecological damage evident across the region and have demanded the Nigerian governments at all levels address it (Brown 2006). These groups also have placed pressure on the oil companies to change their pollution-contributing practices.

Even as transnational NGOs sought to secure greater accountability on the part of the various levels of the Nigerian government as well as the multinationals, they also called on international organizations and especially leading Western states, such as the United States and Great Britain, home to many of the primary multinationals operating in the Delta, to influence these entities to change their behavior. These governments proved reluctant allies until the local protest movement, begun in Ogoniland in the early 1990s, gained salience (Ikelegbe 2001).

The combination of international media attention generated by local and INGO-generated efforts as well as continuing violence have prompted changes in petroleum-company attitudes and operations. And the years of community protest, ongoing NGO and INGO advocacy efforts, and finally, new behavior within the national Nigerian government with the advent of civilian rule, have brought changes to the Delta region. These changes, however, have not yet overcome the inertia represented by entrenched corruption in state and local governments in the Delta region. Accordingly, the area's citizens remain poor and continue to live in ecologically bereft conditions.

This situation highlights the fragility of the nation-state as actor in globalized scenarios and paradoxically, its continuing significance. Given Nigeria's relative dependence on oil revenues, it perhaps should have been expected that the national government would not advocate controlling the behavior of the international oil companies—"the geese laying their golden eggs." Nonetheless, there is little evidence that the companies would have shut down operations with the imposition of more vigorous federal government regulation to prevent pollution, given the quality of Nigerian crude, the profitability of Delta operations, and the relative reliance of the company's home governments on the region's oil and the political pressures implicit in that reality. Contrary to many types of conflicts between communities and corporations, multinationals engaged in resource-extraction industries cannot simply move their capital to wherever labor is most desperate and accommodating. The oil is where it is and as such it provides owner states like Nigeria with the power to negotiate.

What is clearer is that vigorous regulation did not occur, whether the product of powerful state disinterest, Nigerian governmental fear, federal officials' willingness to discriminate against the minorities in the region, or corruption. Despite sustained efforts by local and transnational civil society organizations, changes in national government policy, and disposition and shifts in petroleum-company behavior, the overall political and economic situation in the Delta has changed only slowly. As Beck might contend, the rules that would create new opportunities and improved lives for residents have evolved gradually and remain incomplete. Little additional progress seems likely without changes in the behavior of state and local public officials, especially.

International salience, born of NGO and INGO advocacy efforts, has created some change in oil-company attitudes and programs. These have also caused changes in major state willingness to countenance Nigerian government corruption and multinational corporation arrogance and environmentally reckless practices. But, thus far, none of these developments has resulted in less deprivation for the Delta's residents. Environmental justice for them, understood even so narrowly as remediation of only the most egregious forms of pollution, is unlikely if this condition continues.

Conclusions

Much of the conflict around environmental justice in the Delta since the early 1990s, particularly as framed by arguments advanced by local civil society groups, has cast the oil companies as perpetrators in creating the region's woes. It is easy to agree and to recoil from the fact that multinationals have degraded the Delta for too many years. But they did not do so without the active complicity of the nation's government for three decades and that of the region's state and local officials to this day. The multinationals, despicable though a share of their behavior may have been, cannot be held responsible alone for the penury and environmental catastrophe that the nation's citizens now confront.

Similarly, local activists in the Delta, as well as many who would support them from around the globe, have argued that Delta residents may be made whole. That is, they may achieve appropriate or just compensation for the environmental and development ills that have occurred in their homeland, by receiving either all or a greater portion of the revenues arising from oil production in the Delta. But the analysis provided here suggests at least two important difficulties with this view. First, it overlooks the fact that the federal government of Nigeria is responsible for serving all of that state's citizens and that the largest share of its revenues arise from oil produced in a geographically limited portion of the country. It cannot simply allocate those proceeds to only the Delta without thereby ill serving the remainder of the citizens of the nation and violating other principles of accountability. On the other hand, how much revenue should be shared with each state in the country and on what basis those sums should be determined and distributed, are reasonable questions for ongoing democratic public debate. Second, while the central government receives oil-related revenue from the multinationals, it is not itself the primary provider of health and primary education services to which a large share of those sums is dedicated. As a federal nation, these responsibilities rest squarely with the state and local governments. And these, as we have argued, have received markedly increased allocations from the federal government during the last decade, even as services to Delta residents have continued to decline. A change in allocated sums to the region from the national government alone is unlikely to remediate environmental problems or secure improved employment prospects and living conditions for the Delta's population.

Instead, we have suggested that the Nigerian national government (and interested states around the world) must continue to develop the capacity to ensure greater transparency and accountability in the use of public funds and must devise effective ways and means to secure that same result in the nation's (and especially the Delta region's) state and local governments. The national government must also regulate the oil producers in its midst more rigorously and devise cleanup strategies and enlist the support of oil producers and major state governments as well as international organizations and NGOs for its plans.

Outlining these realities underscores both the interdependent and multiscale character of the strategic environment in which environmental justice will or will not be attained for the Delta. It suggests clearly that a dynamic array of conditions and factors must all be influenced if positive change is to occur for the area's residents. It also demonstrates that increased accountability among some stakeholders, while perhaps indicative of progress toward more just end states, can still be eroded by failures of accountability among stakeholders that receive less scrutiny on the international stage.

Globalized trade came to the Delta long ago and its various impacts, for good and ill, have been profound. But economic globalization does not occur in a vacuum. Its worst effects demand a political response and a change in the accepted rules of the game. It seems clear to us that Beck was correct: multinationals will exploit their economic power to the extent they are permitted to do so. There are hopeful signs that other important local, national, and international actors with roles in shaping the political economy of the Delta have now embarked on a trajectory to change the conditions that have allowed corporations to exercise that power in an almost unfettered way for several decades. Whether these efforts will succeed is contingent, as Beck suggested, on whether these actors develop and sustain the political wherewithal to establish different rules for the corporate and governmental actors that promoted degradation and demand their compliance. It is only when transformations in the rules of the game are achieved, and stakeholders are held accountable for their actions, that environmental justice will be achieved.

Notes

The authors sincerely thank Christine George, an associate of the Virginia Tech Institute for Policy and Governance, for her research support and many insights as we prepared this chapter.

References

Addo, Michael K. 1999. *Human Rights Standards and the Responsibility of Transnational Corporations*. The Hague, Boston: Nijhoff.

Agbola, Tinde, and Moruf Alabi. 2003. Political economy of petroleum resources development, environmental injustice and selective victimization: A case study of the Niger Delta region of Nigeria. In Julian Agyeman, Robert Bullard, and Bob Evans, *Just Sustainabilities: Development in an Unequal World*. Cambridge, MA: MIT Press.

Aluko, Jones. 2006. *Corruption in the Local Government System in Nigeria*. Ibadan, Nigeria: Bookbuilders Editions Africa.

Baldauf, Scott. 2009. Shell hands over $15.5 million to settle lawsuit. *Christian Science Monitor*, September 6.

Beck, Ulrich. 2005. *Power in the Global Age*. Cambridge: Polity Press.

Bob, Clifford. 2005. *The Marketing of Rebellion: Insurgents, Media, and International Activism*. Cambridge: Cambridge University Press.

Boele, Richard, Heike Fabig, and David Wheeler. 2001. Shell, Nigeria and the Ogoni. A study in unsustainable development, II: Corporate social responsibility and stakeholder management versus a rights-based approach to sustainable development. *Sustainable Development* 9(3):121–135.

Brown, Jonathan. 2006. Niger Delta bears brunt after 50 years of oil spills. *The Independent*, October 26.

Carroll, Lewis. 1982. *Alice's Adventures in Wonderland*. Berkeley: University of California Press.

Derrida, Jacques. 2000. Hospitality. *Angelaki: Journal of the Theoretical Humanities* 5:3.

Fact sheet: National strategy to internationalize efforts against kleptocracy. 2006. George W. Bush White House online archives, August 10. http://www.whitehouse.gov/news/releases/2006/08/20060810-1.html.

Gordon, April A. 2003. *Nigeria's Diverse Peoples: A Reference Sourcebook*. Santa Barbara, CA: ABC-CLIO.

Haller, Tobias, Annja Blöchlinger, and Markus John. 2007. *Fossil Fuels, Oil Companies, and Indigenous Peoples: Strategies of Multinational Oil Companies, States, and Ethnic Minorities: Impact on Environment, Livelihoods, and Cultural Change.* Berlin: LIT Verlag.

Held, David. 2006. *Models of Democracy.* 3rd ed. Palo Alto, CA: Stanford University Press.

Human Rights Watch. 2007. *Chop Fine: Impact of Local Government Corruption and Mismanagement in Rivers State, Nigeria.* January. http://www.hrw.org/en/node/11042/section.

Ibrahim, Jibrin. 2000. The transformation of ethno-regional identities in Nigeria. In Attahiru Jaga, ed. *Identity Transformation and Identity Politics under Structural Adjustment in Nigeria,* 41–60. Uppsala: Nordic Africa Institute.

Ikelegbe, Augustine. 2001. Civil society, oil and conflict in the Niger River Delta region of Nigeria: Ramifications of civil society for a regional resource struggle. *Journal of Modern African Studies* 39(3):437–469.

Ikporukpo, Chris. 2004. Petroleum, fiscal federalism and environmental justice in Nigeria. *Space and Polity* 8(3):321–354.

International Crisis Group. 2006. Nigeria: Want in the midst of plenty. *Africa Report* 113:7. http://www.crisisgroup.org/home/index.cfm?id+4274&1=1.

Moffatt, David, and Olof Linden. 1995. Perception and reality: Assessing priorities for sustainable development in the Niger River Delta. *AMBIO: A Journal of the Human Environment* 24(7–8):527–538.

Moore, J. 2008. The political history of Nigeria's new capital. *Journal of Modern African Studies* 22(01):167–175.

Naanen, Ben. 1995. Oil-producing minorities and the restructuring of Nigerian federalism: The case of the Ogoni people. *Journal of Commonwealth Political Studies* 33(1):46–78.

Nwilo, Peter, and Olusegun Badejo. 2006. Impacts and management of oil spill pollution along the Nigerian coastal areas. In Adam Greenland and Paul van der Molen, eds. *Administering Marine Spaces: International Issues,* 119–133. Copenhagen: Fédéral International des Géomètres.

The Ogoni People. 1990. The Ogoni Bill of Rights. http://www.waado.org/nigerdelta/RightsDeclaration/Ogoni.html#_jmp0_.

Okonta, Ike, and Oronto Douglas. 2001. *Where Vultures Feast: Shell, Human Rights, and Oil in the Niger Delta.* New York: Random House.

Onu, N. Chukumeka Hemanachi. 2003. The oil rich Niger Delta region: A framework for improved performance of the Nigerian regulatory process. *AMBIO: A Journal of the Human Environment* 32(4):325–326.

Osha, Sanya. 2006. Birth of the Ogoni protest movement. *Journal of Asian and African Studies* 41(1–2):13–38.

Salau, Sulaimon. 2009. Agip buoys Nigeria's oil production by 25,000 bpd. *The Guardian,* December 16. http://www.ngrguardiannews.com/business/article01//indexn2_html?pdate=161209&ptitle=Agip%20buoys%20Nigeria's%20oil%20production%20by%2025,000bpd.

Shell Oil. n.d. Remediation issues in the Niger Delta. http://www.shell.com/home/content/nga/responsible_energy/respecting_the_environment/remediation/#_jmp0_.

Sklar, Richard L. 2004. *Nigerian Political Parties: Power in an Emergent African Nation*. Africa World Press.

United States Energy Information Administration. 2007. Country Analysis Briefs: Nigeria. http://www.eia.doe.gov/emeu/cabs/Nigeria/Oil.html.

Wheeler, D., R. Rechtman, H. Fabig, and R. Boele. 2001. Shell, Nigeria and the Ogoni. A study in unsustainable development, III: Analysis and implications of Royal Dutch/Shell group strategy. *Sustainable Development* 9(4):177–196.

World Bank. 1997. *Helping Countries Combat Corruption*. Washington, DC: World Bank.

4

Foreign Investment and Environmental Justice in an Island Economy: Mining, Bottled Water, and Corporate Social Responsibility in Fiji

Saleem H. Ali and Mary A. Ackley

Global inequality necessitates some transfer of resources from developed countries to developing economies, and foreign investment in various business sectors is a potentially viable conduit for this purpose. Globalization as manifest through responsible trade and accountable investment is likely to improve development indicators. However, without appropriate structures in place to manage the form and function of such investment, the larger goal of sustainable development for developing economies can be impaired, even if the investments are diversified. Small island economies are largely dependent on external investment as they move away from subsistence livelihoods and become part of the global economic system. The potential for environmental harm from external agents that are only remotely connected to the culture and have little to lose in this context becomes magnified. Such cases thus allow for social scientists to more acutely study the structural challenges of diversifying and making economies sustainable in economic, environmental, and social terms.

This chapter presents some survey findings and observational analysis of a mining region in the island nation of Fiji, which also has the potential for greater tourism development and is home to one of the country's most celebrated international brands, FIJI Water. Investment in all economic sectors has largely been from foreign interests with minimal government intervention. While diversification can theoretically provide an opportunity for a sustainable and more just economy and may be a necessary ingredient in "dependent development" (Evans 1979), the chapter will argue that such diversification is not a sufficient means of achieving these goals. Environmental planning processes and appropriate systems of accountability that allow different industrial sectors to intersect with each other at temporal and spatial levels are essential to make diversification effective. Such efforts need to be coordinated at the international level since many of the countries that are affected by such development are reliant on foreign investment in most sectors of the economy.

Our findings point to the need for a more integrated regulatory strategy that considers various industrial and service sectors in terms of their contribution to development. Furthermore, our study shows that it is essential to refine the granularity of policy analysis in the field to show how individual projects are affecting communities rather than relying on aggregate data, which can obfuscate environmental and social impact. Although rapid globalization may be a cause for some of the concerns that communities encounter at the behest of multinational companies, many solutions to these challenges also rely on the power of global networks. Systems of accountability that have emerged out of such networks of influence such as corporate social responsibility hold promise despite their potential for being misused as a source of shallow legitimacy or "greenwash." To be effective, these global networks of knowledge and exchange of "best practices" must be coupled with systems of enforcement through international norms. As our case analysis shows, there is still a great need for such networks of enforcement. Novel governance structures are evolving at the global level that are hybrids of state and civil society components and have growing influence at the national level. Such networks appear to be the most promising signs that foreign investment will be less likely to become a conduit for exploitation of developing economies.

Dependence, Justice, and the Race to the Bottom

Much of the environmental discourse on globalization has considered the dependence of developing countries on other countries and international institutions as a negative force that might hinder long-term prospects for development. However, the dependence of economies on multinational investment can also provide access to resources and accelerate development. This acceleration can often be asymmetric as businesses follow paths of least resistance and choose sectors or locations that are most unregulated in terms of environmental and social compliance costs. Such a "race to the bottom" is often attributed to globalization without appropriate institutional structures to ensure social and environmental justice. Asymmetries in development within countries can raise concerns of environmental and social injustice, because inequality can rise alongside aggregate economic indicators.

However, networks of globalization also have an intrinsic positive momentum of their own, once they are established to draw people in. The asymmetries that are created by rapid multinational investment can potentially be resolved through the agents of globalization as well. This is partly owing to human propensities for conformity and partly the result of inherent interdependence that multiple connections necessitate. Each intersection of threads that gives strength to a net is dependent on subsequent connections of threads. It is often easier to have knots and interfaces between threads if there is some common tensile strength and other properties of the threads—hence the tendency to build networks with some common dominant properties. This insight about human societal connections is revealed in a book by David Singh Grewal, *Network Power: The Social Dynamics of Globalization* (2008). The narrative presents the potential of networks in wielding power but also exposes the darker side of such power as it inexorably moves to a collectively self-inflicted conformity that can constrain choice. Grewal is particularly concerned about globalization in this context since he believes that "everything is being globalized except politics." By this he is referring to our tendency to move toward common norms on language usage, dress, and other harmonizing influences of globalization.

Thus through globalization, we are moving toward a set of common norms but individual choice in terms of choosing development paths and environmental priorities may be more limited as a result. Might such a subversion of genuine "choice" still be a positive development in the grander scheme of race relations? Grewal gives examples of the historical dominance of the gold standard, the growing dominance of English as a language to make his point. He also considers other areas where network power has encountered difficulties such as the failure of global trade talks in 2008. He does not have much sympathy for the collapse of the Doha Round of Trade talks because the network power generated by this kind of system would have required a "suppression of democratic politics at a national level." However, Grewal is perhaps too sanguine about the triumph of national politics, given various other challenges that confront us on a planetary scale. Environmental governance necessitates making connections across intrinsic ecological networks that are endowed by nature and often influenced negatively by anarchic human behavior. This is where making as many connections between individuals and societies in a systems-oriented approach to politics is so consequential.

In order to fully appreciate the linkage between globalization and environmental justice, particularly in the context of developing economies, it is essential to deconstruct "choice." What is the range of options available to a community and how might pluralism at the local level affect planetary health and hence limit the choice of others in the global system? Justice in the context of local politics and short-term impacts may well be in conflict with justice at a global scale and at longer temporal intervals. Globalization may be appropriately configured to reconcile some aspects of these conflicts, but this is only likely through some regulatory regimes that can operate at a transnational level.

Global environmental governance structures need to mature in order to allow for such contested frames of justice to be reconciled. This would inevitably require us to consider transcending the concept of state sovereignty to some extent through the emergence of novel global institutions. Globalization that is conceptualized as economic and political liberalization along with rapid technological change has spurred greater degrees of market integration but has also undermined the regulatory capacities of states. As a result, a set of operational gaps in governance have emerged: (1) between the territorial basis of the state system and the transborder nature of many if not most problems; (2) between the need to take speedy actions and while preparing for long periods of election cycles (3) between the complexities of cross-border problems and the knowledge possessed by governmental and intergovernmental actors that is needed to address them; and (4) between growing social expectations and global market expansion. In addition, a twofold participatory gap has emerged between those that are benefiting from the processes of globalization and those that are not, and between the demands for and the available opportunities for participation in authoritative decision making (Khagram and Ali 2008).

This chapter explores how two very distinct kinds of multinational investment in an island economy have raised concerns about the negative aspects of globalization and international investment. At the same time, the case analysis also considers how some of these challenges can be addressed by nascent institutional changes that are underway in public and private sectors of the global economy.

Fiji's Development Path and Environmental Justice beyond Borders

The Fijian archipelago of 330 islands lies along the edge of the Pacific Ring of Fire, a volatile zone of frequent volcanic and seismic activity known for its rich array of precious metal deposits. The country has achieved a modest level of economic diversification and is one of the

Table 4.1
Relative contribution to GDP by activity in 2007 at constant price [1995] and factor cost

Activity	% GDP in 2006
Wholesale and retail trade, hotel, and restaurants	18
Community, social, and personal services	18
Manufacturing	15
Agriculture, forestry, fishing, and subsistence	14
Financial, insurance, real estate, and business Services	14
Transport and communications	13
Construction	5
Electricity and water	4
Mining and quarrying	0.5

Note: Fiji Islands Bureau of Statistics 2007.

most developed Pacific Island economies. Agriculture and tourism are the primary sources of foreign exchange for Fiji, but gold mining, mineral water exports, garment manufacturing, and fisheries are also of considerable economic importance (Fiji Islands Bureau of Statistics 2008). The gross domestic product (GDP) of Fiji grew on average at a rate of 2.04 percent[1] between 2000 and 2006.

Agriculture and tourism are the country's two major sources of foreign exchange. Sugar exports accounted for over 22 percent of the total value of Fiji's domestic exports in 2007, while more than 539,000 tourists visited Fiji in the same year (Fiji Islands Bureau of Statistics 2008).

Although the contribution of the mining sector has declined from its early high in the 1930s and 1940s, mining remained a dependable source of employment for over three generations of miners and their families. The Vatukoula gold mine was started during British colonial times and has continued to be owned and operated by foreign corporations from Australia and South Africa. The ethnically diverse and culturally rich mining town of Vatukoula, which literally means "rock of gold," is situated in the collapsed caldera of an extinct volcano, near the edge of the Nakauvadra mountain range on Viti Levu, the largest Fijian island. Throughout its history the mine has attracted hopeful workers from around the country, including even the most remote outer islands. In the past, securing a position as a miner meant a steady income and potentially even training and advancement opportunities for the lucky few who were able to move into upper-level positions. Despite the efforts of this hardworking labor force, visitors to Vatukoula today will not find a prosperous and healthy economy or environment. Instead, the community of Vatukoula has experienced little economic growth at the expense of decades of environmental degradation.

On the morning of December 5, 2006, Emperor Mines Ltd. (EML) announced the sudden closure the Vatukoula gold mine, which had operated continuously for 73 years. Following an internal three-month review, the company indicated that the mine was no longer economically viable (Emperor Mines Limited, 2007). That day, 1,760 mine employees, their families, local businesses, and government officials were shocked to learn that their source of livelihoods for over seven decades had suddenly disappeared. After months of uncertainty and economic hardship, the mine was purchased by Westech Gold Pty Ltd. (Westech), an Australian-based company that began the process of resuming operations at Vatukoula on a smaller scale in August 2007. The unanticipated closure of the mine left Fiji's citizens questioning whether the income from this mineral resource was utilized effectively. Although the event caused hardship to many, it may also serve as an important opportunity for reflection on the sustainability of mining as a means of development, and the risks and benefits that accompany such development activities.

Throughout the history of the mine, Vatukoula residents have repeatedly expressed concern over the environmental contamination of surface waters, drinking water, and sulfur dioxide emissions. The case has all the characteristics that are highlighted in many of the early environmental justice studies in developed countries such as the United States (Bullard 2002), but with the added multinational dimension of the mine's operations. In February 1991, over 400 mine workers went on strike to protest alleged low wages, unsafe working conditions, health concerns, poor housing, and poor environmental standards (Macdonald 2004). The case was eventually dismissed based on a technicality; however, in the eyes of the strikers, the dispute remains unresolved. After more than sixteen years, a core group of former miners continue to sit in protest outside the mine on a daily basis. The community's primary water source, the Nasivi River, has been severely impacted by sewage and mine wastes (Fiji Geochemical Laboratory 2005; Fiji Geochemical Laboratory 2006). Despite this contamination, Vatukoula residents have been forced to drink untreated water from the river for decades. The major cause of illness at the local school is the consumption of contaminated water, because there is limited treated water available to students (Anjali,

Jikowale, and Lata 2007). Respiratory problems are also widespread in the Vatukoula community, and many believe that these symptoms are related to the air pollution that, prior to the mine's closure in 2006, regularly emanated from the mine's roaster stack for decades.

Our 2007 study conducted firsthand empirical research into the perception of environmental and health risks in the communities surrounding the Vatukoula mine. Primary data were obtained through a survey questionnaire designed to quantify and evaluate perceived risks ($n = 340$, representing approximately 24 percent of the target population). Concurrently, environmental samples were collected to assess the extent of environmental impacts at the study site. The study revealed that over 80 percent of all Vatukoula residents feel it is likely that air pollution has harmed their health, and more than 60 percent of all residents experienced severe respiratory symptoms at least once during the previous month. The head teacher at Vatukoula Primary School, which is located within sight of the mine's roaster stack, explained that when the mine was operating, the children and teachers were also affected by sulfur dioxide emissions. Teachers were often forced to close all the school windows from 8 a.m. until the early afternoon to avoid exposure to emissions, and several teachers requested transfers to different locations because of their environmental concerns (Head Teacher, personal communication, July 30, 2007). The pollution of rivers and streams and drinking-water pollution were also of great concern to most residents, with 88.6 percent of the people "somewhat" or "very" worried about the former and 86.7 percent "somewhat" or "very" worried about the latter.

The transportation, storage, and disposal of mining waste pose additional environmental risks for the Vatukoula community. Six large tailings dams are located in the region. These dams are designed to store industrial waste, or tailings, which are produced during mineral processing. Some residents live only meters away from the dam walls. Releases and failures of similar tailing dams have been documented across the globe. The majority of major mining-related environmental incidents worldwide have been the result of dam overtopping, breaching, geotechnical failure, or earthquakes (Akcil, 2006). In 2000, the Aural gold mine in Romania experienced a dam failure that caused leaching of mine wastes into the Danube river system. In 1988, the Kumtor mine in Kyrgyzstan recorded a spill of 100 tons of cyanide (Stenson 2006). While many developed countries maintain strict regulations on the storage and disposal of wastes from gold mines, mining corporations in the developing world often operate under much less scrutiny. According to the EML 2006 Annual Report, there was a major environmental incident involving a pipeline failure along a section of the Toko tailings dam pipeline. This incident resulted in the coverage of a 30 meter by 30 meter residential compound with industrial waste (Emperor Mines Ltd. 2006). During our study, one resident explained his concern about the lack of community knowledge of the risks posed by mining wastes: "At times we have cyanide spillages into the river. Because of the lack of knowledge in the community, at these times that the fish are dead in the river, we go out there and bring it and cook it and eat it, because we are not aware of that" (Romeo Kivi, personal communication, July 6, 2007).

As early as 1981, a United Nations Environmental and Social Commission for Asia and the Pacific (ESCAP) report recommended that until the mining company at the time, EML, could develop a "satisfactory program for monitoring their environmental impact," their lease should not be renewed (Macdonald 2004). Later, in 2003 EML claimed that it could not afford to supply treated drinking water without government funding (Macdonald 2004). However, according to a representative from the Ministry of Health, the ministry tried on several occasions to put in a publicly treated water supply, but the company would not permit them to do so on their privately owned land (Timothy Young, personal communication, August 9, 2007). Following a formal request from the Fiji Mine Workers Union (FMWU) and the Citizens Constitutional Forum (CCF) in May 2003, the Oxfam Australian Community Aid Abroad Mining Ombudsman conducted an investigation into the mining activities at the Vatukoula Gold Mine the following November (Macdonald 2004). The case report, published in July 2004, recommended that "an independent audit of the occupational health and safety practices at the Vatukoula mine site be undertaken" (Macdonald 2004). In addition, the report recommended that independent environmental and social impact assessments be undertaken and be released publicly, "in a transparent and accountable manner" (Macdonald 2004). EML did not respond to the requests for comment on the 2004 report or to the recommendations the report set forth (Oxfam Australia 2006). The Mining Ombudsman returned to the site in 2005 to conduct a follow-up investigation and Gender Impact Assessment (GIA). Mine workers reported that newer mine management had taken some steps to improve safety, specifically by installing a new ventilation shaft. However, workers maintained that underground conditions were "very poor, with an intensely hot and wet environment, lack of proper respiratory equipment and consequent health concerns" (Oxfam Australia 2006).

Our study of the environmental risks of mining at Vatukoula also revealed that women are disproportionately affected by the environmental risks associated with the mining industry. Powerful forces of occupational discrimination and segregation by gender persist throughout many industries in Fiji (Asian Development Bank 2006). Despite the fact that there is no difference in the education levels achieved by men and women in Fiji, women do not have equal access to the benefits of employment at Vatukoula, while assuming much of the environmental burden. Women reported having less knowledge about the environmental and health risks of mining than men did, and reported feeling less able to avoid the environmental and health risks of mining compared to men. Finally, women also have less access to direct information about mining risks than men do; the study revealed that women tend to receive information about such risks from secondary sources. These findings highlight how foreign investment without appropriate consideration of local social norms can serve to further entrench existing social and cultural inequalities at the local level.

Bottled Water

The attractive labels on bottles of FIJI Water—another of Fiji's biggest industries, and a brand of bottled water known throughout the world—inform consumers that the plant is located "a continent away from the nearest industrialized civilization." Many of these consumers would be surprised to learn that Fiji itself is industrialized to some extent and that the firm's headquarters are located just a few miles from the Vatukoula mine, which has been minimally regulated in terms of environmental impact for over seventy years. FIJI Water's original owner, David Gilmour, also had a strong connection with the mining industry in Canada and used geologists from Barrick Gold Corporation to assist in the company's search for artisanal springs. Apart from these technical connections, this case also exemplifies how globalization without proper development planning can empower a relatively limited and powerful elite rather than spreading benefits more widely. While Fiji's economy may appear to be diversified in terms of sectors, the ownership patterns are still concentrated among foreign elite. For example, Gilmour also owns the Wakaya Club—Fiji's most prized tourist resort.

A few years ago, FIJI Water launched a major campaign to position itself as a green and sustainable business, outlining plans to go carbon negative (Fiji Water Company LLC 2008a). However, the benefits of FIJI Water's green efforts seem less clear to the residents of Vatukoula, and the impact of such efforts at an international level are not always felt by the domestic labor constituents of multinational companies. In fact, just months after our initial study, we learned that the Vatukoula community experienced a serious diarrheal outbreak due to contaminated drinking water, which hospitalized close to forty people and killed four children (B. Deskin, personal communication, March 31, 2008). How could this be happening so close to a place where pristine artisanal water is being bottled and shipped to the far reaches of the globe?

FIJI Water's website states that they "have taken direct responsibility for providing water access to the villages that surround their source in the Yaqara Valley" (Fiji Water Company LLC 2008b). Unfortunately, this promise has not yet extended to the several thousand residents of Vatukoula, many of whom have family members who are directly employed by FIJI Water, and who have been struggling with the mining company and government for years to get a treated drinking water supply in place in their community.

During our 2007 study, we found that another major environmental concern of Vatukoula residents is inadequate solid waste management, specifically the unsanitary conditions at the open dump site located in the community. A visit to the dump revealed yet another connection to nearby FIJI Water. Reels of discarded FIJI Water labels were in use by farmers as makeshift fencing along the dirt road approaching the dump site. Piles of packaging materials and discarded industrial plastic pellets, the same pellets used by FIJI Water to create their plastic bottles, were observed at the dump site. FIJI Water bottles were also everywhere, too many to be consumer waste. The mayor of neighboring Tavua Town later explained that indeed FIJI Water was dumping their industrial waste in Vatukoula and was paying the former mining company $1,100 FJD/month to do so. Romeo Kivi, a resident of Vatukoula, also noted that it was common knowledge that FIJI Water dumps their waste at Vatukoula; unmarked trucks can be seen passing his village daily carrying the discarded materials.

A representative of FIJI Water attempted to clarify this situation: "FIJI Water does not pay the gold mine to use the dump; the mine requests payment from any contactor who wishes to use the dump and in our case Tavua Plant Hire is contracted to dispose of our general waste from the plant. Tavua Plant Hire pays Vatukoula Gold Mine $1,500/month to use the dump, which is the closest officially sanctioned landfill to our plant" (R. Six, personal communication, August 5, 2008). The company also made it clear that since June 2007, they have dramatically reduced their use of the dump, and are in the process of phasing out the use of Tavua Plant Hire as their waste contractor. They made the following promise: "We will be contracting [with] an accredited waste disposal company to remove waste other than recyclables. In the past all waste went there but now bottles, labels, and label backings are all sent for recycling. We are continually working with our recyclers to further reduce the land fill with the intention to dispose of only food and bio-degradable items in the dump" (R. Six, personal communication, August 5, 2008).

FIJI Water now claims to be improving their environmental performance and giving back to the local community, but the many residents of Fiji who have been hearing such promises from both government and industry for generations are understandably skeptical. In 2007, the company founded the FIJI Water Foundation, which invested $150,000 in 2008 as a partner in the Rotary Pacific Water for Life Trust, to build sustainable water projects all over Fiji in communities determined by an external survey to have the highest levels of need (R. Six, personal communication, August 5, 2008). In addition to making the Rotary contribution, the foundation also provided water tanks, bores, piping, and necessary expertise directly to several other schools and communities that have applied for aid. Through this partnership with the Rotary Club, the company plans to bring water access to hundreds of communities (R. Six, personal communication, August 5, 2008).

Both FIJI Water and the owners of the Vatukoula Mine are foreign companies. Vatukoula's parent company has been a publicly traded corporation, while FIJI Water is a privately held corporation. However, their conduct vis-à-vis environmental compliance and social responsibility has been comparable.

The Role of Domestic Regulation

The Mining Act of 1978 is still the primary piece of legislation governing mining and subterranean activities in Fiji. While the act prohibits the pollution of waterways, and also requires the filling of any hole, shaft, pit, or other excavation site created by mining (The Mining Act of 1978), the fines imposed for violations of the act are extremely small, especially when levied against a large foreign corporation such as the Australian mine owners, EML. For example, the act calls for a fine not to exceed $100 FJD for anyone who "causes or permits the deposit or discharge of any rubbish, dirt, filth or debris or any waste water from any sink, sewer or drain or other dirty water or any chemical or other substance deleterious to animal or vegetable life, or any other noxious matter or thing, into any watercourse" (The Mining Act of 1978). The act allows the director to issue permits for discharge of wastes and mine tailings as deemed fit and also gives the director the power to require the discharging party to supply an alternative water supply to residents if their water supply is believed to have been compromised. The maximum fine imposed for any violation of the act is $200 FJD (The Mining Act of 1978). Under the Mining Act, the Mineral Resources Department (MRD) is responsible for inspections and environmental monitoring at Vatukoula. However, according to the Director of Environment, Epeli Nasome, these monitoring requirements are weak, and EML, on occasion, has blocked MRD inspectors from completing inspections (Epeli Nasome, personal communication, August 9, 2007).

The tourism and mineral water industries have enjoyed similarly weak environmental regulation and even weaker enforcement. The Fiji Director of Environment outlined the weaknesses of the existing Environmental Impact Assessment (EIA) process during our 2007 study: "The Department of Environment undertakes the whole process of approving EIA Reports through the powers of the Director of Town and Country Planning or through the own initiative of developers who recognize the environmental impacts on their developments and the need for the process to be done" (Epeli Nasome, personal communication, August 9, 2007).

In 2005 a new Environment Management Act was passed, which calls for EIAs for all new development projects, requires environmental bonds for mitigation purposes, and imposes strict fines (up to $1 million FJD) for violations (Environment Management Act of 2005). However, the specific regulations required to actually enforce the act were not promulgated until 2008 (Timothy Young, personal communication, September 16, 2008; Epeli Nasome, personal communication, August 9, 2007). The new regulations provide a mandate for the Department of Environment to undertake the EIA process through direct legislative requirements.

Domestic regulatory frameworks in developing countries may still take considerable time to develop to prevent a "race to the bottom," whereby multinational companies seek to take advantage of lax enforcement to obtain higher profits. While both the mining and bottled-water sectors that were studied in this investigation are determined to some extent by predetermined geological characteristics rather than factors such as tax incentives, there is still some room for discretionary preference. For example, mining companies are often willing to invest further in exploration of deposits in countries that have low labor costs while having a reasonable measure of political stability. The challenge for environmental justice advocates is to exert pressure on companies to improve compliance while not demonizing the companies to the extent that they pull out altogether from operating in such desperately poor locations. Indeed, mining companies are still more likely to tolerate risk than other sectors such as manufacturing and finance. Therefore, to move toward a common goal of development, a strategy is needed to foster improved environmental and social performance while not marginalizing the agents of multinational investment.

Conclusion: Corporate Social Responsibility and Environmental Justice

Critiques of globalization have often identified multilateral corporation as agents of environmental injustice because of their ravenous appetite for expedient profits that may preclude social and environmental concerns. Companies appear to follow paths of least resistance in terms of regulation because any compliance costs are believed to erode profitability. However, this view of corporate behavior is increasingly questionable because of a growing trend by which companies are identifying asymmetries in regulations as a threat rather than an opportunity. Given the range of corporate actors in the global arena, a race to the bottom may be workable for some corporations that do not have shareholder accountability or threats of litigation. For a growing cadre of companies, globalization has also created a network of accountability that they are unable to easily escape. Hence they feel that regulations may actually level the playing field and allow for more equitable competition.

However, in many parts of the developing world such competitive motivation is lacking across various sectors. This results in development disparities within countries that might be economically diversified but still show some of the symptoms of environmental injustice across each sector. Although extractive industries have often been singled out as being the most monopolistic and exploitative, other sectors may also take advantage of an absence of regulatory enforcement in the same way (Ali and O'Faircheallaigh 2007). As observed in the case of Fiji, multinational companies in mining and bottled water can exhibit similar symptoms of environmental injustice. Globalization may be held responsible for allowing foreign companies easier access to such developing markets but the story does not stop there. The same forces that allow for such foreign investment to potentially lead to exploitative and asymmetric development, may also empower institutions and agents that can provide regulatory oversight.

One paradigm that has received considerable attention in recent years as a global phenomenon is "corporate social responsibility" (CSR). While there has been considerable concern about the potential for using environmental dimensions of CSR as a means of co-opting opposition without substantive change, the growth of international institutions to monitor CSR has improved the likelihood that "greenwashing" can be minimized. Transnational global policy networks as manifest in organizations such as the Global Compact may be developed further to provide such a safety net against exploitation of CSR principles (Khagram and Ali 2008).

CSR reflects a pragmatic acceptance of the reality that corporations must achieve and retain the support of the communities affected by their operations. The driving force in this regard is often not a commitment to human rights or environmental sustainability per se, though aspects of company behavior may certainly be consistent with such a commitment. Neither is it simply an economic calculus based on the desire to enhance efficiency. Rather what is involved is a pragmatic calculation of what is needed to win the degree of community support required to avoid delay or disruption to company operations (Hamann 2003; Humphreys 2000). CSR may also be thought of as a "modern" or "enlightened" approach to maximizing efficiency, based on a recognition that in today's world, minimizing input costs and maximizing returns relative to risk requires corporations to utilize a calculus different from that employed in previous decades. Inputs would be minimized not only to reduce production costs, but also to minimize an extraction project's environmental footprint at each stage of the production change. For example, reducing the usage of energy fuels in a mining operation would reduce greenhouse gas emissions and other environmental impacts of producing those fuels in the first place, of transporting them to the mine site, of burning them, and of disposing of waste products.

In some cases this will involve actions that are "economically inefficient" in the short term. There is also an important environmental justice dimension of this matter that has been studied by Gouldson (2006) in his comparison of CSR performance in the European Union and the United States. The social license may ostensibly be easier to obtain from vulnerable impoverished communities and lead to subservience rather than true "buy-in." The tacit acceptance of a project may be misunderstood by companies as the "license" being granted, whereas resentment may build over time and lead to widespread resistance once communities have the social capital to protest and take direct action.

This dimension of CSR is directly relevant to the environmental effects of mining, because a failure to deal with these effects is often central to a failure to secure, or to the loss of, a social license to operate. For instance, the closure and ultimate abandonment of Rio Tinto's Bougainville copper mine in Papua New Guinea resulted in part from the widespread environmental damage associated with the project. Numerous proposed projects in every region of the globe have been delayed and many ultimately abandoned because of concerns regarding their potential environmental impacts, and it is evident that local communities and populations affected by multiple projects distinguish clearly between them on the basis of their expected environment impact (Ali and Grewal 2006).

However, the case of Fiji's mining and bottled-water sectors shows that CSR is still coming of age in the context of many developing countries. Dependence of an isolated economy on foreign investment per se is not a problem, but the qualitative aspects of that dependence in terms of accountability to international institutions must be ensured. Even with diversification of the economy, development may still not meet the standards of environmental and social justice without some larger transnational institutional pressures (Frynas 2006). The emergence of global norms such as corporate social responsibility shows some promise in this regard, but their efficacy is subject to the establishment of structures of global environmental governance. Such governance structures will inevitably be hybrids of public and private enterprise. Citizen pressure, either through ownership of shares or through deliberative democracy within a public context, is needed to diminish the growing cynicism about foreign investment in developing countries and the perceived injustices of globalization.

Notes

1. Calculated at constant 1995 prices, at factor cost (Fiji Islands Bureau of Statistics 2007).

References

Akcil, Ata. 2006. Managing cyanide: Health, safety and risk management practices at Turkey's Ovacik gold-silver mine. *Journal of Cleaner Production* 14(8): 727–735.

Ali, Saleem H., and Andrew Grewal. 2006. The ecology and economy of indigenous resistance: Divergent perspectives on mining in New Caledonia. *Contemporary Pacific* 18(2):361–392.

Ali, Saleem H., and Ciaran O'Faircheallaigh. 2007. Extractive industries, environmental performance and corporate social responsibility. Special issue of *Greener Management International* 52–53 (October–December).

Asian Development Bank. 2006. *Republic of the Fiji Islands, Country Gender Assessment.* Philippines: Asian Develoment Bank.

Dashwood, Hevina. 2007. Canadian mining companies and corporate social responsibility: Weighing the impact of global norms. *Canadian Journal of Political Science / Revue canadienne de science politique* 40(1):129–156.

Emperor Mines Ltd. 2006. *Emperor Mines Limited Annual Report 2006.* http://www.emperor.com.au/ar2006. Environment Management Act. 2005. Government of Fiji.

Evans, Peter. 1979 *Dependent Development.* Princeton: Princeton University Press.

Fiji Geochemical Laboratory. 2005. Certificate of Analysis Report, 2nd Quarter 2005. Suva: Mineral Resources Department, Government of Fiji.

Fiji Geochemical Laboratory. 2006. Certificate of Analysis Report 1st Quarter 2006. Suva: Mineral Resources Department, Government of Fiji.

Fiji Islands Bureau of Statistics. 2007. *Fiji Facts and Figures.* http://www.statsfiji .gov.fj/Fiji%20Facts%20%20Figures%20As%20At%20Jul%2007.pdf.

Fiji Islands Bureau of Statistics. 2008. *Fiji National Census of Population 2007.* http://www.statsfiji.gov.fj/.

Fiji Water Company LLC. 2008a. Our promise: Carbon negative. http://fijigreen .com/CarbonNegative.html.

Fiji Water Company LLC. 2008b. Water for Fiji. http://www.fijiwater.com/Water .aspx.

Frynas, Jedrzej George. 2006. The false developmental promise of corporate social responsibility: Evidence from multinational oil companies. *International Affairs* 81(3):581.

Gouldson, Andy. 2006. Do firms adopt lower standards in poor areas: Corporate social responsibility and environmental justice in the EU and the US. *Area* 38(4):402–412.

Grewal, David. 2008. *Network Power: The Social Dynamics of Globalization.* New Haven, CT: Yale University Press.

Hamann, Ralph. 2003. Mining companies' role in sustainable development. *Development Southern Africa* 20(2):237–254.

Hilson, Gavin, and James Haselip. 2004. The environmental and socioeconomic performance of multinational mining companies. *Minerals and Energy* 3:25–47.

Humphreys, David. 2000. A business perspective on community relations in mining. *Resources Policy* 26:127–131.

Khagram, Sanjeev, and Saleem H. Ali. 2008. Transnational transformations: From government-centric inter-state regimes to multi-actor, multi-level global governance? In Jacob Park, Ken Conca, Mathias Finger, et al., eds., *The Crisis of Global Environmental Governance.* London: Routledge.

Macdonald, I. 2004. *Mining Ombudsman Case Report: Vatukoula Gold Mine.* Carleton, Victoria, AU: Oxfam Community Aid Abroad.

Mining Act, Chapter 146. 1978. Government of Fiji.

Mitchell, Paul. 2006. *Giving Practical Meaning to CSR in the Mining Industry.* Paper presented at the Globe 2006 conference, Vancouver, Canada.

Oxfam Australia. 2006. Mining Ombudsman Case Updates 2005. Victoria: Oxfam Australia .Retrieved from: http://www.oxfam.org.au/resources/filestore/originals/OAus-MiningOmbudsmanUpdates-0806.pdf

Rajaram, Vasudevan, Subijoy Dutta, and Krishna Parameswaran. 2005. *Sustainable Mining Practices: A Global Perspective.* London: Taylor and Francis.

Reinecke, Wolfgang, and Francis M. Deng. 2000. *Critical Choices: The United Nations, Networks, and the Future of Global Governance.* Toronto: IDRC.

Stenson, Josephine. 2006. Disaster management as a tool for sustainable development: A case study of cyanide leaching in the gold mining industry. *Journal of Cleaner Production* 14(3–4):230–233.

Witte, Jan Martin, Wolfgang H. Reinecke, and Thorsten Benner. 2000. Beyond multilateralism: Global policy networks. *International Politics and Society* 2.

II

The Amplification of Inequality through International Donors and Institutions

5

Global Civil Society and the Distribution of Environmental Goods: Funding for Environmental NGOs in Ecuador

Tammy L. Lewis

How are environmental "goods" distributed across borders? In this chapter, I take a different slant on environmental injustice by examining the allocation of environmental goods, rather than environmental bads. Traditionally, the literature on environmental justice has largely focused on who gets the environmental "bads" of society—toxic waste, hazardous facilities, and poor air quality, to name a few. As movements shift from pointing out environmental injustices to seeking environmental justice and what Agyeman (2005) calls "just sustainability," we need to ask, who gets the environmental amenities? Parks? Water cleanup? Access to affordable public transportation? Resources for environmental improvements? Which communities get the "goods" to improve their quality of life?

By looking to goods as well as bads, I shift the conversation to a broader understanding of environmental inequality, one that looks to the full spectrum of distribution. An analogy can be made to income inequality. We cannot understand income inequality only by studying poor people.[1] Likewise, we cannot understand environmental inequality only by studying contaminated communities. We can devise environmental measures similar to those used to assess income inequality by including the entire range of distribution, though that is not the task of this chapter. We might ask, at what levels of environmental equality do we recognize just sustainability?

If we could quantify environmental "goods" and environmental "bads," a distribution score, like the GINI coefficient (a measure of inequality of income distribution) could provide indicators for whether the distribution of environmental goods and bads was getting more or less equal. This inequality has real consequences for responses to environmental change. As Gould (2006) argues, greater inequality in the distribution of environmental goods removes those at the top of the distribution from negative environmental feedback loops. Thus, those with the most political, social, and economic power are also those least likely to recognize environmental problems or have incentives to address them.

Historically, environmentally poor groups lead movements for environmental justice based on threats to their communities, and environmentally rich groups seek further environmental amenities, such as bike paths, brownfield cleanups, farmers' markets, and waterfront improvements. If environmental distributions proceed along "environmental class" lines much like income, we would expect the environmentally rich to get richer, and the environmentally poor to get poorer. Agyeman (2005) argues that groups for environmental justice and for environmental sustainability have the potential to blend frames to work for "just sustainability." However, this may be increasingly difficult if those at the top are seeking environmental goods and those at the bottom are trying to avoid environmental bads. The two ends do not see the same "environment."[2]

In this chapter, I focus on a specific environmental good: transnational environmental aid. How is environmental aid distributed? What efforts are supported by environmental aid and which are left out? I use Ecuador to illustrate how and why the distribution of environmental aid matters for environmental justice.

North-South Environmental Politics and Environmental Aid

In a globalized world, environmental problems are framed as "global" problems with global solutions. In this context, actors cross borders to ask for and offer environmental assistance. At both the United Nations Conference on Environment and Development (UNCED) in Rio de Janeiro in 1992 and the United Nations' World Summit on Sustainable Development in Johannesburg in 2002, poorer nations asked richer nations to help protect their environments.

The global North has increasingly offered "environmental aid" to the global South. Environmental aid comes from many types of donors for many types of projects. Donors include governments, multilateral agencies, and private organizations, such as foundations and nongovernmental organizations (NGOs). Projects range from environmental education to mapping conservation to technical assistance with policy writing.

How is the aid, an environmental good, distributed? As in many transnational assistance programs, the donors and the recipients do not always agree on priorities. Southern environmentalists complain that

Northern environmentalists focus on "green" issues such as biodiversity and land conservation, at the expense of "brown" issues such as water pollution and land degradation (Guha and Martinez-Alier 1997; Taylor et al. 1993). The brown issues are akin to environmental justice concerns, because they are focused on protecting local residents' health and livelihoods. Guha (1999) argues that "while Northern greens have been deeply attentive to the rights of victimized or endangered animal and plant species, Southern greens have generally been more alert to the rights of the less fortunate members of their own species."

Anthropologists and environmental sociologists have shown how different conceptions of "environment" have generated these conflicts between groups in the global North and the global South.[3] Some have suggested that environmentalists (conservationists in particular) from the global North are "ecoimperialists," who have ignored the needs of indigenous people in favor of protecting the environment (Guha and Martinez-Alier 1997). Power relations play out in the construction of what is and is not an environmental problem and consequently whether or not it is addressed. For instance, are "global" problems such as ozone depletion more pressing than "local" problems such as water contamination? Donors have the capacity to impose their interpretations and interests through the distribution of aid.[4]

At Rio in 1992, the buzz was around the concept of "sustainable development"—integrating environmental concerns with social and economic justice. Despite the conceptual attention given to social and economic concerns, at UNCED, agreements focused on protecting forests and biodiversity in the global South with little attention to justice. Leaders from the global South considered that focus hypocritical since the nations of the global North had already depleted those environmental resources in the name of their own economic development. At the UN's 2002 World Summit on Sustainable Development, new topics emerged: clean water and sanitation, sustainable energy, sustainable agriculture, health, and still, biodiversity. In ten years, it appeared that the South's agenda had made it to the UN. Headlines from the conference reported on calls for increased environmental aid for the environment. The conventional wisdom was and is that transnational cooperation and aid are critical to improving the environment. Case studies bear this out (Keck and Sikkink 1998; Lewis 2000; Rothman and Oliver 1999; Wapner 1996). However, which aspects of the environment are prioritized?

Funding for environmental projects, an environmental "good," has been unevenly distributed beyond borders. It is distributed unevenly among nations in transnational interactions, and it is distributed unevenly in terms of types of organizations (Lewis 2003, 2005). In previous research, I analyzed which nations were the targets of environmental aid. I found that U.S. donors (foundations and United States Agency for International Development) were more likely to fund nations with environmental richness (biodiversity) than those with environmental poverty (polluted water), even when controlling for political, economic, and security interests (Lewis 2003). In a study focused on which types of organizations received environmental aid to work in Ecuador, I found that the majority of grants and grant dollars went to U.S.-based organizations working in Ecuador rather than Ecuadorian organizations. Environmental goods went to U.S. organizations more often than Ecuadorian ones (Lewis 2005).

These North-South debates and the literatures in social movements, environmental sociology, and development frame the Ecuadorian case.[5] In Ecuador, the distribution of environmental goods—funding for projects—has shaped the choices of Ecuadorian environmental NGOs and has largely ignored environmental justice advocates. By way of funding, the global North has played a strong hand in directing the environmental agenda of this small nation. What this has meant is that projects have tended to focus on issues of importance to a "global" community, such as biodiversity protection. Environmental justice concerns have not been the focus. This makes sense since the effects of environmental injustice are most acutely felt locally. This social process is written on the land of Ecuador.

Environmental Problems in Ecuador

Ecuador is a useful country to study in relation to social-environmental issues because it is representative of other Latin American countries and thus provides a glimpse into the region in general. Socioeconomically, it is a "typical" Latin American nation: it is 25 percent Amerindian; in 2006, its GDP was $4,500; 41 percent of its citizens live below poverty; it has a large external debt; and it is resource dependent, with 40 percent of the country's revenue coming from petroleum extraction (World Bank 2006).

Ecuador also suffers from many of the same environmental problems that are pervasive in Latin American and the Caribbean: deforestation, soil erosion, and industrial pollution, to name a few. As in the rest of Latin America, Ecuador's major cities (Guayaquil, Quito, and Cuenca) struggle with issues associated with environmental poverty: problems with water quality, sewage management, air pollution, industrial pollution, and municipal solid waste (Southgate et al. 1995). Sixty-two percent of Ecuador's 13 million people are urban dwellers (World Bank 2006).

Ecuador is also useful to study because of its environmental richness. Ecuador represents a "biodiversity hotspot." Despite being a small nation, about the size of Colorado or Nevada (283,560 square kilometers), it has four distinct bioregions: the Galápagos Islands, the coast, the sierra, and the Amazon. Scientists count it among the top ten megadiverse countries in the world on the basis of its high number of plant and animal species, and its high number of endemic species. It contains over 20,000 plants, a fifth of which are endemic. The small nation contains 10 percent of the world's plant species and 17 percent of the world's bird species (Manosalvas et al. 2002).

Ecuador's rate of deforestation is 1.4 percent, higher than the average rate in Latin America of 0.4 percent (World Bank 2006). In the period from 1990 to 2000, Ecuador's forested area decreased from 43 to 38 percent (World Bank 2004). This is especially troubling to international conservationists given Ecuador's high degree of biodiversity. They have worked with nongovernmental organizations and the state to help preserve lands. The percentage of land protected nationally is very high: 18 percent (compared to 11 percent in Latin America, and conservationists' goal of 10 percent worldwide). However, the government has permitted oil extraction and other environmentally damaging activities within protected areas. This damages the ecosystem (soil and water contamination) and risks the health of indigenous people living in the Amazon region.

In addition to the socioenvironmental problems related to oil extraction in the Amazon basin, some of Ecuador's other problems include destruction of mangroves due to shrimp farming, difficulties stemming from tourist development of the ecologically sensitive Galápagos Islands, and environmental health problems caused by pesticides used in the production of cut flowers and by fumigation along the Colombia border, which is part of the U.S. "Plan Colombia," designed to eradicate coca.

While all of these problems affect both nature and humans, on a spectrum some have a more direct and immediate impact on nature and some a more direct and immediate impact on humans. For example, deforestation has a more direct and immediate impact on animal ecosystems and other areas of the natural world, while industrial pollution in cities has a more direct and immediate impact on human health.

Deforestation tends to take place in rural areas with lower human population densities, and industrial pollution in urban areas with higher human population densities. Clearly, though, these are interrelated issues. Returning to Guha's quote, which species get the attention of environmental aid: plant and animal or human?

Environmental Organizations in Ecuador—the Broad View

Ecuador has had a long history of interacting with the international community on environmental issues. Its environmental groups have received sponsorship from international agents for over thirty years. In 1978, the United States Agency for International Development provided support for Fundación Natura, Ecuador's first environmental NGO. Support from abroad has been a consistent aspect of the Ecuadorian environmental sector. To understand how the transnational funding has affected organizations over time, I conducted interviews with directors of environmental organizations, aid agencies, and foundations in Quito during 2006 and 2007. I also conducted an organizational survey.[6]

Being in the capital of Quito, you get a skewed sense of what the main environmental issues are in Ecuador. This is because the majority of groups with offices in the capital are relatively resource-rich organizations with a primary focus on conservation. These organizations are in the capital because that is where donors meet with their beneficiaries. Smaller and less resourced groups are in the field, doing their work, largely unseen and unnoticed in Quito. For this reason, the organizational survey is particularly useful in a broad understanding of environmental organizations—it makes visible the goals and work of organizations that are not in Quito. There are approximately 200 organizations in Ecuador with "environment" being their primary focus.

Over half of the groups responding to the survey are national-level NGOs. Their interests are in issues that encompass all of Ecuador—for example, national environmental policies. Local NGOs and international NGOs are almost equal in proportion (17.5 and 15 percent respectively). The majority (57 percent) of the environmental groups are located in the capital (Quito), while the two other major cities (Guayaquil on the coast and Cuenca in the sierra) contain over 11 percent of groups; the rest of the groups are distributed throughout the country, including two groups in the Galápagos and groups in the Amazon.

Of particular importance to the theme of this chapter is the organizations' receipt of international funding. Over three-quarters of the responding groups received funding through donors. The most common sources of funding are foreign sources (foundations, INGOs, and foreign governments). Fifty percent of groups received at least half of their funding from foreign sources, nineteen organizations (24 percent) received some foreign funding, nine organizations (11 percent) received no foreign funding, and twelve groups did not report. In terms of organizations' budgets, at the top, more than 10 percent of organizations have budgets over US$1 million and just under 10 percent of the groups have no budgets. Ninety percent of the organizations working on environmental issues in Ecuador believe that international funding is "somewhat" to "very important" in resolving the environmental problems that they are working on.

Organizations cover a broad spectrum of issue areas, but three issues dominate: environmental education, biodiversity conservation, and sustainable development. Other issues less frequently mentioned included labor rights, public health, and environmental justice. Half of the organizations' main issue areas had changed since the organization was founded. The groups report that the reasons for changes were largely due to availability of funding (70 percent). Other reasons topping the list included "needing to secure available resources" and "donor priorities." The survey indicated that resource issues (i.e., availability of environmental goods) rather than changes in the organization's mission or leadership drove changes in issue area. This theme was reinforced in interviews.

Ecoimperialists, Ecodependents, Ecoresisters, and Ecoindependents

As the overview of the organizational survey suggests, the environmental sector in Ecuador is diverse: it contains international, national, and local groups, some rich and some poor groups, it covers all geographic areas of the country, and though the main issues areas are biodiversity conservation and sustainable development, many themes are addressed, including environmental education, water pollution, and deforestation. I outline composites of four types of environmental groups. They are not equal in size, scope, or influence. They represent "ideal types." I define the types according to key dimensions: degree of receipt of environmental aid from abroad, primary issue area, type of projects executed, how it contributes to themes related to environmental justice, and Ecuadorian views of each type of group.

Type 1: Ecoimperialist Organizations

These are transnational environmental groups (also called international nongovernmental organizations or INGOs) that bring environmental goods (i.e., foreign funds) with them to Ecuador to focus primarily on biodiversity protection, often with additional goals of supporting sustainable economic development. They are viewed as ecoimperialist because they set up shop in Ecuador with their own funds to do what they want to do. Many view them as foreign intruders imposing their will on the people, land, and policies of Ecuador. A national environmental leader remarked, "They don't listen to nationals; they are top down." Of the groups working in Ecuador's environmental sector, these have the largest budgets, often over $1 million.

An example of an INGO project is the Nature Conservancy's (TNC's) project to create a tortoise conservation area in the Galápagos Islands. Through this work, TNC is attempting to restore natural pools for giant tortoises. The pools had been degraded due to invasive species and cattle ranching. TNC works with a local organization, Fundar Galápagos, to execute the program. A director of a similar organization remarked, "We work at the species level and the site level. Protected areas are the cornerstone of conservation. . . . Human well-being is important, but it is not our expertise." This project and others like it do not have environmental justice as a goal. However, increasingly, economic (though not social) concerns are included in biodiversity protection. Often these organizations couple land conservation with ecotourism development. The guiding principle behind adding economic aspects is to make conservation pay for itself.[7]

Though "ecoimperialist" is a strong term to use in describing these groups, it reflects the sentiment of some national and local organizations in the environmental community, especially as recent INGO practices have changed. Previously, these organizations have acted as intermediaries—channeling funds from (often) U.S. offices to Ecuadorian NGOs, which would implement project priorities of the foreign-based INGO. A recent trend among INGOs, however, is to execute their projects themselves rather than by distributing funds to national and local groups. For instance, the Wildlife Conservation Society implements projects directly, with their own staff, without engaging Ecuadorian NGOs. This practice, which essentially bypasses Ecuadorian institutions, has led to complaints among Ecuadorian NGOs, despite the fact that the employees of WCS are Ecuadorian. Not all of the groups have done this. For example, in The Nature Conservancy example cited above, TNC works with an Ecuadorian organization to carry out the project.

A second criticism in the ecoimperialist vein comes from the indigenous groups that believe that foreign organizations are attempting to buy land to control the water resources and to privatize reserves—literally an imperialist objective. The Nature Conservancy is the main target of this claim, though the land-purchase strategy of biodiversity protection is one that TNC uses in North America, not in Ecuador. The national coordinating body of Ecuadorian environmental groups does not allow INGOs into its group.

Type 2: Ecodependent Organizations

These are Ecuadorian groups that are dependent on environmental goods from abroad to carry out projects focused on biodiversity protection and sustainable development. More than 50 percent of their budget comes from other countries. These national-level groups have offices in the capital and their focus is not on a narrow geographic area. Though their budgets are well above average (of all environmental organizations in the country) and they are able to maintain full-time staff, their budgets vary over time, based on whether they have foreign contracts. An example of an ecodependent organization is Fundación Jatun Sacha (FJS). FJS works in cooperation with Conservation International to reforest biodiversity hotspots, one of Jatun Sacha's internal goals. Over the years, a number of NGOs of this type have come and gone in boom-and-bust fashion, as foreign development organizations initiated and then ended large conservation programs. Many of these national groups started as purely conservation organizations but have felt the need to add people into the mix because that is what the foreign donors have added to their portfolio of projects. In this way, they mirror the ecoimperialists: they do not have environmental justice as a goal. At this point in time, a relatively small number of groups dominate the national scene.

Organizations whose priorities are not conservation or sustainable development complain that they have not been able to master "donor speak" in such a way that they can complete for contracts with these groups. The ecodependent organizations have well-established relationships with their donor-partners and the donor-partners reinforce the strength of these groups by funding them over time, which in turn, builds reputations and begets more funds. For the most part, donors have not been risky in their giving, but have relied on their traditional "best-bet" strategies, reinforcing the relationships. Informants complain of nepotism, cronyism, and corruption.

While in many cases, the national-level dependent organization cooperates with the INGO on shared goals, and there are numerous "win-win" possibilities, ecodependence comes at a cost. The most obvious problem is that these groups lack autonomy in goal setting. When there is funding for conservation, groups work on conservation. When the funding shifts to sustainable development, groups work on sustainable development. If there is no funding for air pollution, groups do not work on air pollution. One disgruntled NGO leader explained, "They [INGOs] have plenty of money for their own project ideas, but not for ours." Another noted, "We are dancing to the rhythm of the donors." In this way, the national agenda is written abroad. In Ecuador, like most of Latin America, there is no tradition of philanthropy, and large NGOs cannot rely on membership for their funding base.[8]

A second major problem is that the international funding process breeds competition rather than cooperation among national groups. The INGOs distribute a request for proposals for projects they would like to see completed. Then, the national groups compete to secure limited project funding, often withholding scientific information from each other. This splits the organizations, which could potentially be working together for a common agenda. These groups become more like consultants exchanging services for fees rather than groups organized for a common end. In this type of project funding, it is difficult for them to form alliances with other like-minded groups because they are going from proposal to project to proposal, and so on, working for a paycheck and to fund their programs rather than working for a common agenda with other national groups. These groups are self-aware and seek funding independence or "sustainability," though none have achieved this.[9] They also say that the biggest failure of Ecuadorian environmentalism is the failure of organizations to work together on a common agenda. Other Ecuadorian groups that fit this profile include Aves y Conservación and EcoCiencia.

Type 3: Ecoresistance Organizations
This type of group receives little to no environmental goods from abroad and they focus on issues that groups in the global North would frame as "environmental justice" (however, they are not framed that way in Ecuador). Their websites are not translated into English for the ease of

donors to read. Their primary goal is to resist the forces of "development," particularly resource extraction, due to its negative impacts on the environment and communities. Rather than focus on projects, they focus on "processes." For example, through workshops, they teach communities how to monitor their environment, grab media attention, and pressure the government. In this way, ecoresistant organizations facilitate the process of local, popular movements standing up to fight in defense of their territories and rights.

An example of an ecoresistant organization is Acción Ecológica (AE). AE did not disclose its funding sources to me, but explained their funding philosophy: "It depends whether we accept foreign funds. We are very cautious. It is unacceptable to accept funds that come with an agenda or from a bank. Our funds come from social organizations. [Funding sources] must match our priorities and our agenda. Those are the conditions" (translated from Spanish).[10] AE was founded in the 1980s and over the years, their campaigns have focused on a range of issues, including resisting oil extraction in the Amazon, helping coastal communities prevent the expansion of shrimp farming into mangroves, demanding changes in the structures of international financial institutions (IFIs) to favor Latin America, and recently, working with a local organization, Quito para Todos/Colectivo Cuidadana (Quito for All/Citizens' Collective), to improve the quality of life in Quito. Other organizations of this type include Defensa y Conservación Ecológica de Intag (DECOIN), whose main fight is against foreign mining, and FUNDECOL, which works on the coast to prevent further development of large-scale shrimp operations. AE is allied with South-South networks, such as the Latin American network against genetically modified organisms.

AE's acts of resistance to oil extraction, deforestation, and mining are reactive, a quality of many environmental justice movements. However, it is also forward looking in its calls for the restructuring of IFIs and its work to build sustainable local communities. The "environmental justice" frame is not used in Ecuador. The label "radical" is partially a proxy for it, though not a perfect fit. Other organizations call AE radical, meaning extreme and impractical. To AE, it means being concerned with workers and social and economic justice. AE's critique of sustainable development helps to distinguish it from the ecodependent organizations. To paraphrase (and translate) from their website, they essentially argue that the concept of sustainable development is used to justify almost any proposal that favors economic growth and exploitation of natural resources. Its inherent logic is that economic growth solves the problems of inequity. However, the AE website argues that economic growth is the cause of environmental problems, not the solution to them, and furthermore, it does not address inequity or inequality. AE argues for sustainable campaigns to meet needs through proper management of natural resources through food sovereignty, energy sovereignty, and so on. This perspective represents a clear break with the organizations that work for sustainable development (over 77 percent of organizations responding to the survey). This type of organization and the projects that it promotes are most like environmental justice groups and actions in the global North.

The ecodependent groups call these organizations "radical" and note, "They don't get much done, all they do is talk, talk, talk." However, leaders in those mainstream groups also call the ecoresisters "essential" because they voice a critique of development and extraction that would otherwise be absent. These groups are underrepresented in the sample data presented above for a few reasons. First, since they receive less funding, they are less likely to have a web presence and staffing to respond to survey requests. Second, the frames of groups working in this area are not necessarily "environmental"; rather, many consider themselves social justice groups with a focus on the environment. These groups were not identified in the sampling frame.

Type 4: Ecoindependent Sustainability Organizations

These groups receive no environmental goods from abroad and are characterized by their pragmatic and innovative approaches to gaining resources. They focus on local issues relevant to communities' quality of life, such as access to clean water and green spaces as well as human health, and they are typically urban. They are eco*independent* because their issues are local, they set their own agendas, and they raise the funds locally to accomplish their goals. They are *sustainability* organizations because they are also seeking environmental amenities. As noted above, the environmental justice frame is not a prevalent frame in Ecuador. Though these organizations share some aspects of EJ—for example, a focus on human health—their frame is broader; in the United States, these groups might be called "sustainable community organizations."

A group that exemplifies this type is Vida para Quito (Life for Quito). Vida para Quito is a nonprofit organization created by the municipality of Quito and the city water company to do "works that improve environmental health and the quality of life of the city and its inhabitants" (Vida para Quito website, translated). Vida para Quito is funded through a voluntary local tax contribution of up to 25 percent of total tax. When Quito residents fill out their tax forms, they can check a box that indicates they would like a portion of their taxes to go to Vida para Quito. This is an especially creative way of generating a budget in a culture in which philanthropy is not common.

The organization leads a number of programs, including urban park development, urban reforestation, recycling, environmental education, river recuperation, and other programs. It uses local resources to attain environmental goods. Its projects are geographically focused and the amenities it promotes have the potential to help a wide swath of Quiteños, not just tourists visiting the ecoreserves. For example, the Ciclo-Q bikeway project provides a way for people to use their bikes as a safe means of transportation in an automobile-centric city. This reduces air pollution, increases public safety, and provides an inexpensive means of transportation. The projects of the ecoindependent sustainability organizations attempt to limit environmental bads and increase environmental goods for a broad segment of the urban population.

Vida para Quito is fairly well known among Quiteños because of its funding structure, and residents have more positive views of the organization than they have of environmental organizations in general. This may be due to the fact that NGO leaders are considered to be among a higher class, and average Ecuadorians do not know how or where the NGOs spend the money. Vida para Quito, by contrast, must report data publically, since it is subject to the "transparency law." Its budget and the salaries of its staff can be found online. In 2007, half of a percent of its funding was spent on staff costs and over 98 percent of its budget was spent on investment in construction and services.[11] An environmental professional remarked that groups funded independently like Vida para Quito "will be around for fifty years." This is a long life in a sector where groups come and go, year to year.

Environmental Goods: Who Gets Them and Who Decides?

Who decides if Ecuador should prioritize saving the rainforest, creating ecotourism, resisting foreign development of natural resources, or creating bikeways along the streets of Quito? The social and ecological landscape of Ecuador is being created in the image of donors, not in the image of Ecuadorians. Ecuadorian NGOs' dependence on foreign funding (foreign distribution of environmental "goods") shapes the agenda of Ecuadorian environmentalism and has limited the growth of organizations focused on environmental justice. In this way, dependence on foreign funding further entrenches environmental inequities.

For the most part, Ecuadorian organizations that have the greatest capacity are chasing foreign funding rather than setting their own agenda. Funding from the global North is channeled through Ecuadorian environmental NGOs and as a result of donor choices, most Ecuadorian environmental organizations are focused on biodiversity projects rather than the environmental issues of concern to locals. While biodiversity protection is important, the unintended consequence of supporting it through environmental aid is that other issues, such as environmental justice, are not addressed.

The prominence of ecoimperialist and ecodependent organizations lets them overshadow organizations with justice concerns. Social and economic justice are not conceptualized as part of the environmental agenda. Nevertheless, ecoresisters, though few in number, push their broader conception of environmentalism into public discourse, most notably through television and newspapers. They have less capacity to implement "projects," and instead focus on empowering and mobilizing local actors whose concerns are primarily economic and social justice in issues related to the environment, in that order. Ecoindependent sustainability organizations have not embraced "environmental justice" as a frame and it is unlikely that they will; nonetheless, the actions they have taken have served a diverse segment of urban populations, at least on issues of quality of life and public health, but not on jobs and democracy. The types of groups least likely to receive "environmental goods" from the global North are those that work most for environmental justice.

What is occurring in Ecuador is not unlike what has occurred with the U.S. movement. Aid (from within the United States) for U.S. organizations has not been distributed equally across different types of projects and organizations. In a recent analysis, Brulle (2009) found that environmental health, environmental justice, and the green/antiglobalization organizations receive just 2 percent of the income of the U.S. environmental movement. By contrast, preservation groups receive over 50 percent. In many ways, transnational civil society relationships mirror dependency relationships within nations and between international aid organizations and governments from the global South. Organizations in the South are dependent on Northern donor priorities. The distribution of environmental goods promotes the interests of the "global" (Northern) community. Despite this, the existence of alternative organizations, such as Acción Ecológica(ecoresisters) and Vida para Quito (ecoindependents), suggests that greater local autonomy is possible.

Notes

Thanks to JoAnn Carmin, Russ Dalton, Bob Edwards, and Patrick Gilham for sharing their organizational surveys with me. Special thanks to JoAnn Carmin and Ken Gould for their ongoing dialog. This research was supported by the Fulbright Commission and by Muhlenberg College's Class of '32 Research Professorship.

1. There have been some studies that address aspects of environmental amenities. For instance, this line of thinking can be found in Robert Bullard's (1990) classic book, *Dumping in Dixie*. Though Bullard focuses primarily on the distribution of "bads," he also writes that getting an area declared a Superfund site is positive. Though ironic, being able to get this designation for a site ensures some commitment to cleanup. Bullard shows that Superfund sites have disproportionately been sited in white communities. Similarly, the Environmental Protection Agency has charged higher fines for polluters in white neighborhoods.

2. See Gould, Lewis, and Roberts 2004 on the difficulty of forming coalitions among various progressive organizations.

3. See, for example, Escobar 1995.

4. Power relations are inherent in the distribution of resources. In the social movement literature, researchers debate whether patronage for social movement organizations is beneficial or whether it co-opts organizations. For works on this topic, see Brulle 2000; Jenkins and Eckert 1986; Jenkins and Halci 1999; McAdam 1982; McCarthy, Britt, and Wolfson 1991; McCarthy and Zald 1977; and Walker 1991.

5. My analysis also fits into a tradition in development studies of understanding the consequences of Northern interventions in issues of the South. This is analogous to the issue raised by social movement theorists—understanding the consequences of elite intervention for indigenous activities. Both question whether powerful groups are able to co-opt weaker groups to promote the powerful groups' interests. In the development literature, there is a range of findings. On one end of the spectrum, some argue that international interactions create the growth of a "world culture"; on the other end of the spectrum are those who highlight diversity and resistance in the global South to the global North's neoliberal agenda. See Frank, Hironaka, and Schofer 2000 for the world culture argument, and Taylor et al. 1993 for the resistance argument. This work contributes to the growing body of literature on transnational social movements: Bandy and Smith 2005; Carmin and Hicks 2002; Della Porta and Tarrow 2005; Keck and Sikkink 1998; Martin 2003; Pellow 2007; Rodrigues 2003; Smith and Johnston 2002; and Tarrow 2005.

6. The survey population consists of organizations with offices in Ecuador working on environmental issues with valid e-mail addresses. Of the population of 176 organizations, 45 percent responded to the survey (*n* = 80). The survey

was conducted in Spanish. All of the translations into English for this chapter are by the author. I supplemented the survey with thirty-five interviews of key actors in the environmental movement sector. For more information on the data collection procedures, contact the author.

7. These projects are not always entirely devoid of environmental justice themes; rather, the themes that might be framed as environmental justice, such as human health, are often tertiary. Reforestation projects are framed as a means by which locals can protect watersheds and thus provide clean water. Clean water for local communities is not the central goal of the program; however, it is included as another potential benefit. This aim has been added in the thirty years since international agents have engaged in environmental issues in Ecuador. Initially, it was enough to focus on conservation; over time, human aspects have been added, as has been true throughout the world with the rise of the concept of sustainable development. Additionally, ecoresistance to ecoimperialism has forced INGOs to include local benefits in projects because "pure conservation" has not succeeded on the ground.

8. Relationships among national NGOs, the state, and INGOs is different in countries that have membership organizations, such as those in the Czech Republic (see Carmin and Jehlička 2005).

9. For example, Jatun Sacha charges a fee for volunteers to work at their reserves; Fundación Maquipucuna uses its reserve to attract ecotourists where it sells its own organically grown, bird- and butterfly-friendly coffee. Most national groups have numerous strategies such as these.

10. A director of a mainstream organization noted that AE receives a small amount of funding from a California-based organization. In the 1990s, AE received small grants from a number of European countries, including Spain, Italy, and Germany.

11. See www.vidaparaquito.com.

References

Agyeman, Julian. 2005. *Sustainable Communities and the Challenge of Environmental Justice.* New York: New York University Press.

Bandy, Joe, and Jackie Smith, eds. 2005. *Coalitions across Borders: Transnational Protest and the Neoliberal Order.* Lanham, MD: Rowman & Littlefield.

Brulle, Robert J. 2000. *Agency, Democracy and Nature: The U.S. Environmental Movement from a Critical Theory Perspective.* Cambridge, MA: The MIT Press.

Brulle, Robert J. 2009. The U.S. Environmental Movement. In Kenneth A. Gould and Tammy L. Lewis, eds., *Twenty Lessons in Environmental Sociology,* 211–227. New York: Oxford University Press.

Bullard, Robert. 1990. *Dumping in Dixie.* Boulder, CO: Westview Press.

Carmin, JoAnn, and Barbara Hicks. 2002. International triggering events, transnational networks, and the development of the Czech and Polish environmental movements. *Mobilization* 7(3):305–324.

Carmin, JoAnn, and Petr Jehlička. 2005. By the masses or for the masses?: The transformation of voluntary action in the Czech Union for Nature Protection. *Voluntas* 16(4):401–421.

Della Porta, Donatella, and Sidney Tarrow. 2005. *Transnational Protest & Global Activism*. Lanham, MD: Rowman & Littlefield.

Escobar, Arturo. 1995. *Encountering Development: The Making and the Unmaking of the Third World*. Princeton, NJ: Princeton University Press.

Frank, David John, Ann Hironaka, and Evan Schofer. 2000. The nation-state and the natural environment over the twentieth century. *American Sociological Review* 65:96–116.

Gould, Kenneth. 2006. Promoting sustainability. In Judith Blau and Keri Iyall Smith, eds., *Public Sociologies Reader*, 213–229. Lanham, MD: Rowman & Littlefield.

Gould, Kenneth, Tammy L. Lewis, and J. Timmons Roberts. 2004. Blue-green coalitions: Constraints and possibilities in the post 9–11 political environment. *Journal of World Systems Research*. Special issue: Global social movements before and after 9–11. Winter 10(1):90–116.

Guha, Ramachandra. 1999. *Environmentalism: A Global History*. New York: Longman.

Guha, Ramachandra, and Juan Martinez-Alier. 1997. *Varieties of Environmentalism: Essays North and South*. London: Earthscan.

Jenkins, J. Craig, and Craig M. Eckert. 1986. Channeling black insurgency: Elite patronage and professional social movement organizations in the development of the black movement. *American Sociological Review* 42:249–268.

Jenkins, J. Craig, and Abigail Halci. 1999. Grassrooting the system? The development and impact of social movement philanthropy 1953–1990. In Ellen Condliffe Lagemann, ed., *Philanthropic Foundations: New Scholarship, New Possibilities*, 229–256. Indianapolis: Indiana University Press.

Keck, Margaret E., and Kathryn Sikkink. 1998. *Activists beyond Borders: Advocacy Networks in International Politics*. Ithaca, NY: Cornell University Press.

Lewis, Tammy L. 2000. Transnational conservation movement organizations: Shaping the protected area systems of less developed nations. *Mobilization* 5(1):105–123.

Lewis, Tammy L. 2003. Environmental aid: Driven by recipient need or donor interests? *Social Science Quarterly* 84(1):144–161.

Lewis, Tammy L. 2005. Foundation funding for the global environment: Green altruism or green imperialism? Paper presented at the conference of the American Sociological Association, Philadelphia.

Manosalvas, Rossana, Jorge Mariaca, and Jaime Estrella. 2002. Guia metodologica para el acceso de recursos genericos. In Carmen Josse, ed. *La biodiversidad del Ecuador: Informe 2002*, 60–78. Quito: Ministerio del Medio Ambiente, UICN.

Martin, Pamela. 2003. *The Globalization of Contentious Politics: The Amazonian Indigenous Rights Movement*. New York: Routledge.

McAdam, Doug. 1982. *Political Process and the Development of Black Insurgency 1930–1970*. Chicago: University of Chicago Press.

McCarthy, John D., David W. Britt, and Mark Wolfson. 1991. The institutional channeling of social movements by the state in the United States. *Research in Social Movements, Conflicts and Change* 13:45–76.

McCarthy, John D., and Mayer N. Zald. 1977. Resource mobilization and social movements: A partial theory. *American Journal of Sociology* 82(6):1212–1241.

Pellow, David. 2007. *Resisting Global Toxics: Transnational Movements for Environmental Justice*. Cambridge, MA: MIT Press.

Rodrigues, Maria Guadalupe Moog. 2003. *Global Environmentalism and Local Politics: Transnational Advocacy Networks in Brazil, Ecuador, and India*. Albany: State University of New York Press.

Rothman, Franklin Daniel, and Pamela E. Oliver. 1999. From local to global: The anti-dam movement in southern Brazil 1979–1992. *Mobilization* 4(1):41–57.

Smith, Jackie, and Hank Johnston, eds. 2002. *Globalization and Resistance: Transnational Dimensions of Social Movements*. Lanham, MD: Rowman & Littlefield.

Southgate, Douglas, Kenneth Frederick, John Strasma, Allen White, Lori Lach, John Kellenberg, and Patricia Kelly. 1995. *An Assessment of Urban Environmental Problems in Ecuador*. Under contract for the United States Agency for International Development. Madison: University of Wisconsin–Madison.

Tarrow, Sidney. 2005. *The New Transnational Activism: Movements, States, and International Institutions*. New York: Cambridge University Press.

Taylor, Bron, Heidi Hadsell, Lois Lorentzen, and Rik Scarce. 1993. Grass-roots resistance: The emergence of popular movements in less affluent countries. In Sheldon Kamieniecki, ed., *Environmental Politics in the International Arena*, 69–89. Albany: State University of New York Press.

Walker, Jack L. 1991. *Mobilizing Interest Groups in America: Patrons, Professions, and Social Movements*. Ann Arbor: University of Michigan Press.

Wapner, Paul. 1996. *Environmental Activism and World Civic Politics*. Albany: State University of New York Press.

World Bank. 2004. Environment at a glance 2004 Ecuador. http://siteresources.worldbank.org/INTEEI/Data/20806987/Ecuador.pdf.

World Bank. 2006. Ecuador. *Little Green Data Book*. http://siteresources.worldbank.org/INTEEI/936214-1146251511077/20916989/LGDB2006.pdf.

6

Environmental Justice, Values, and Biological Diversity: The San and the Hoodia Benefit-Sharing Agreement

Saskia Vermeylen and Gordon Walker

Recent commentaries have identified a number of ways the field of environmental justice scholarship is evolving (Walker and Bulkeley 2006; Sze and London 2008; Holifield, Porter, and Walker 2009). First, as demonstrated in this book, this scholarship is giving attention to the application of the environmental justice frame in new places and contexts around the world (Walker 2009). Second, it is extending its scope to include increasingly diverse forms of socioenvironmental concern, moving far beyond the racial distribution of pollution, toxicity, and technological risk with which the early phases of environmental justice activism were primarily concerned. Third, it has developed a more pluralistic view of the multiple interconnected concepts of justice that are part of an environmental justice framing and the practices of claim making that this involves (Schlosberg 2004, 2007). In this chapter we explore these spatial, material, and theoretical currents and their interrelation through the case of the San in southern Africa and their claims for benefit sharing in the exploitation of biological diversity for commercial gain. Through exploring the various forms of value and notions of justice revealed in the San's pursuit of a benefit-sharing agreement, we demonstrate the challenges involved in contextualizing environmental justice within what constitutes a particular and distinctive cultural and political setting in the developing world.

The San are former hunter-gatherers and the oldest surviving inhabitants of Southern Africa. The arrival of pastoralists and agriculturalists of the Bantu-language group (in the last 500 to 2,500 years) and white settlers (in the last 300 years) has resulted in the assimilation, subordination, or even persecution, of the San peoples. About 100,000 San survive today in the Kalahari basin, but while their physical survival may no longer be at risk, their cultural survival is highly precarious. While local and regional variation exists, the vast majority of the San have lost their land rights and with that, the opportunity and skills to hunt and gather food. They are almost invariably poor by local standards, and few can survive on subsistence farming because this requires access to land, suitable soil and climate, and some capital in the form of livestock or fences to protect their crops. Many depend for their livelihood on seasonal farmwork (often paid in kind) and the collection of bush food. In countries like Namibia and Botswana food aid from the government is important. Seen as an archetypical hunting and gathering society, the San are subject to numerous ethnographic studies, documentaries, films, postcards, and so on (Suzman 2001).

The very specific environmental resource we focus on in this chapter is *Hoodia gordonii*, a traditional (medicinal) plant of the San that was patented without their prior consent by a state institution, the South Africa Council for Scientific and Industrial Research (CSIR), which then licensed its development and commercial use to multinational companies. Belatedly a benefit-sharing agreement has been negotiated between the San and the CSIR, as required under the Convention on Biological Diversity (CBD), which demands "equitable" benefit sharing from the use of biodiversity between companies and indigenous local communities. By examining both how this benefit-sharing agreement and search for an equitable outcome have been structured and pursued and how this process has been viewed by local people, we reveal how different notions of what constitutes justice and different forms of value are at the core of a process that continues to be in dispute.

Through the Hoodia case study, we are embedding the concept of justice in the well-developed discourse regarding indigenous peoples' rights and their struggle to determine their own destiny.[1] The attitude of the international institutional community toward indigenous peoples has changed from being "assimilationist" in the ILO Convention 107 toward the recognition of indigenous peoples' self determination rights in the UN Declaration on the Rights of Indigenous Peoples. Within the context of the Hoodia case study, concepts such as traditional knowledge, commodification, property, indigeneity, customary law, sui generis protection, and self-determination rights are all focal points in the debate about indigenous peoples' property rights and self-determination rights. However, based on our own observations in the field we feel there is not only a need to better define these concepts because a lot of the literature and policy frameworks are out of tune with some of the daily realities lived by indigenous peoples, but it is important from an ethical point of view to gain a better understanding of what these concepts mean in different contexts and cultural settings. As some of the most prolific anthropologists have argued (e.g., Strathern, 2004; Kirsch 2004), the meaning of "traditional knowledge," "commodities," and "property" are tainted by a discourse of an international community that has a track record of stereotyping traditional communities as the binary opposite of Western communities, with little regard to the realities of their socioeconomic and political life.

It is against this background of frameworks that capture and are consistent with different values and practices, without essentializing and reducing the cultural differences to binary opposites, that we explore the notion of environmental justice. By embracing pluralistic approaches toward justice we are skeptical about the imposition or expectation of universal norms and values. Instead, we are endorsing the recognition of a diversity of values, experiences, and cultures. Inspired by the work of the legal philosopher Felix Cohen,[2] who has devoted his scholarship to honoring the values of diverse groups, including protecting the constitutional rights of Indian natives, we aspire to incorporate a multiplicity of value systems in the environmental justice debate. Cohen's celebration of diversity as an alternative to the classicists' attempt to force uniformity on law through abstract concepts reflects Douzinas and Warrington's (1994) idea that injustice begins at the point when the language of one is imposed on the other, or when similarity is imposed on difference. In keeping with this view, in this chapter, we draw on the case of Hoodia to examine how and why justice as a concept means that acceptance of the "other" is recognition and appreciation of what is irreplaceably unique.

The Justice in Environmental Justice

The discourse of environmental justice as it first emerged in the distinctive political context of the United States, emphasized particular notions of justice and how this might be understood. Many observers have characterized environmental justice as primarily, if not entirely, a discourse of distributive justice, concerned with outcomes and who gets what in terms of environmental benefits and burdens. Wenz (1988, 4), for example, argues that distribution is the "chief topic" of environmental justice concerns and is the "substantive justice" that matters in a material sense in terms of the burdens and benefits received (Bell 2004). A number of other authors, however, have persuasively argued that to only understand environmental justice as a matter of distribution is limited and incomplete. For example, Low and Gleeson (1998, 24) argue that "attention must be paid not only to the substance of justice, justice of outcomes and consequences, but also to the justice of procedure." Schrader-Frechette (2002) puts forward the Principle of Prima Facie Political Equality as the objective for correcting problems of environmental justice, combining distributive with participative justice. Drawing on Young (1990), she argues that a combined conceptualization is needed because "purely distributive paradigms tend to ignore the institutional contexts that influence or determine the distributions" (Schrader-Frechette 2002, 27). Both Torres (1994) and Schlosberg (2007) make a similar point in arguing that broad, inclusive, and democratic decision-making procedures are a tool, or indeed a precondition, for achieving distributional justice.

While it has become relatively commonplace to acknowledge that environmental justice claim making is "bivalent," incorporating both distribution and procedure, Schlosberg (2004) goes further to add a third concept of recognition. At the core of misrecognition are cultural and institutional processes of disrespect and denigration that devalue some people in comparison to others, meaning that there are unequal patterns of recognition across social groups. This, he argues, makes environmental justice "trivalent" (Schlosberg 2004) with issues of recognition distinct from, but closely connected to, those of distribution and procedure. In constructing this argument he draws from justice theorists such as Young (1990), Fraser (1997, 1999), and Honneth (1995), who each argue, although in different ways, that misrecognition in the form of insults, degradation, and devaluation is fundamental to the damage and constraint inflicted on individuals and communities and to the production of distributional inequalities. As with procedural justice, an integrated argument is made that sees recognition as both a subject and a condition of justice. It is a distinct, separate form and experience of injustice and terrain of struggle, but deeply tied to distributional inequalities. Schlosberg (2007, 26) in this way nicely conveys the interconnections at work between recognition, participation, and distribution: "If you are not recognized you do not participate; if you do not participate you are not recognized. In this respect justice must focus on the political process as a way to address both the inequitable distribution of social goods and the conditions undermining social recognition."

While in part a pluralistic understanding of environmental justice rests on acknowledging that it can take these multiple interconnected forms, a full account also needs to recognize the diversity of value systems and cultural contexts in which each form of justice is made sense of. This has become all the more necessary as the use of the environmental justice frame has moved around the globe, applied in diverse contexts and to different forms of environmental concern. In terms first of distributive justice, a pluralistic view of justice finds necessary diversity in the criteria of distribution to be applied because "there are many different social goods (and evils) whose distribution is a matter of justice, with each kind of good having its own particular criterion of distribution" (Miller 1995, 2). More fundamentally, Walzer (1983) contends that naming and giving meaning to any particular good or bad (including environmental ones) is a social process, particular and produced rather than universal. Schroeder et al. (2008, 550) similarly argue, specifically in the context of environmental justice cases in the developing world, that the concepts of benefits and burdens "are always relative, both in absolute terms and with respect to any particular group of potential resource users."

Much the same applies to the cultural basis of understandings of procedural justice and what this constitutes. How voice is "given" and to whom (defined culturally and/or spatially), how representation legitimately achieved, how meaningful involvement is enabled, and the degree to which differentials in power can in any way be equalized within decision-making forums, are each culturally shaped and situated components of determining what constitutes justice in procedure.

What constitutes justice in procedure becomes a particularly important issue when this question is posed against the background of indigenous land-right claims. Indigenous peoples have highlighted that rights to land, traditional institutions, cultural practices, and intellectual property rights are inseparable and interrelated. Not only are indigenous peoples struggling to get their legal rights over land and resources recognized, they also want to have the freedom to make their own decisions about how to use and manage natural and cultural resources. However, as Borrows (2002) argues, the current sociolegal and political platform through which indigenous peoples can claim restitution of land forces indigenous peoples to engage with a discourse that does not necessarily reflect the social context experienced by indigenous peoples. The criteria for indigenous status in native title claims enforce an engagement with primordialist and essentialist concepts of culture. Indigeneity is fixed in time and place and is not socioeconomically and historically contextualized. This strategy can lead to the exclusion of indigenous peoples who have lost the connections with their ancestral land. For example, Canadian and American courts have rendered some indigenous land-right claims invalid because the plaintiffs did not appear native enough. While in the past normative arguments such as the concept of *terra nullius* have not only justified colonial acquisition of territory, they were also a reflection of the bias against the political and social organization of indigenous peoples. These biases, according to Tully (1994), continue to influence the current debate about native title claims and are forming the basis against which native title claims are judged. It will be difficult to respond appropriately to compensatory and procedural demands for justice with regard to indigenous land-right claims as long as Western-based legal norms and values are used to judge them (Dodds 1998; Tully 1994). Borrows (2002) has explored alternative approaches and his attempt to incorporate indigenous norms and values in common law presents a new potential political and legal order for indigenous peoples.

There are other dimensions to how procedural justice is structured for indigenous peoples, relating closely also to the ways in which their cultures are or are not given recognition. The ability to participate depends on language skills, and the capacity to participate in decision-making processes (Whiteman and Mamen 2002). Hierarchical approaches to decision making (e.g., by government, corporation, or NGO without community consent) may ignore established indigenous processes of decision making in which power is more flatly and widely distributed. In terms of providing feedback to the wider community, procedures for explanation and justification may also need to be culturally framed (Whiteman and Mamen 2002). If perceptions of procedural justice are within the tenets of traditional law, appropriate feedback may have to include social, environmental, and spiritual reasoning.

Such recognition of both the multiple concepts of environmental justice that can be at work, and the plurality of value and cultural systems through which these are understood and mediated, calls for a relative and scaled understanding of what constitutes environmental justice rather than one based on notions of universality and conformity (Debbane and Keil 2004). That is not to say that the meaning of justice is born anew in each place and each time that claims are made and disputes materialize. There will be common reference points but the ways these are interpreted, combined, and operationalized are open to variety and diversity. As we will now see, this becomes particularly clear when the traditions for adjudicating justice in a historically embedded yet evolving indigenous cultural and physical space, are intersected by an international process for establishing the sharing of commercial benefits from biological diversity.

The CBD and Benefit-Sharing Agreements

The recognition that biological diversity is a distinctive resource for which claims of ownership and benefit from exploitation can be made is enshrined within the Convention on Biological Diversity. This states that national governments have sovereign rights over their biological resources and requires that access to these resources occur under the prior informed consent of source-country governments and on mutually agreed terms (Articles 15.4 and 15.1 respectively). Among its objectives, the CBD mentions the "fair" and "equitable" sharing of benefits resulting from commercial and other uses of genetic resources (Article 15.7), and as such it constitutes one of number of examples of pieces of international environmental legislation that incorporate justice or equity principles (Okereke 2006). Article 8(j) of the CBD stipulates that in cases wherein the knowledge of indigenous and local people has contributed to the commercial or other uses of biological resources, the benefits must also be shared with the indigenous and local people (Mulligan 1999). While the CBD creates the obligation to respect, preserve and maintain traditional knowledge, innovations, and practices, and promote their wider use with the approval of indigenous and local communities, it does not describe how this is to be achieved (Tobin 2001). "Fair" and "equitable" remain undefined in the CBD and widely divergent opinions have existed over the interpretation and implementation of these terms (Henne 1997; Mugabe et al. 1997; Mulligan 1999; Artuso 2002).

While fundamentally the CBD is concerned with questions of distribution—who should benefit from the exploitation of an environmental resource—it has also been recognized that to achieve what might be seen as a just agreement, a fair and inclusive process of negotiation and settlement is required. In 2002, Article 15 of the CBD was elaborated with the Bonn Guidelines, which recognized the need for participation of stakeholders other than governments in the implementation of the convention and for introducing a new ethic to the CBD. For example, prior informed consent (PIC) is set as a precondition to access while bottom-up approaches are advocated to promote the direct participation of indigenous communities (Herkenrath 2002; Tully 2003). To a significant degree, the debate about benefit sharing in the case of the San and the Hoodia plant has been framed by the requirements and evolving practice of implementing the CBD. What is unclear, however, is how far this acknowledgment of the need to widen involvement and to recognize the distinctive claims of indigenous groups extends in practice. For the San people in particular, to what extent has the process and outcome of negotiation that puts substance onto the bones of what is required by the CBD been able to satisfy their expectations of what justice should constitute? And what does this reveal about the values and understanding that different actors bring to the debate?

The San Views of the Benefit-Sharing Agreement

The story of Hoodia is probably one of the most famous bioprospecting case studies. It first caught worldwide attention when a British newspaper reporting on Hoodia as a new appetite suppressant mentioned the extinction of the San. Very quickly the case attracted a fair amount of negative publicity, which eventually sparked, in 2001, the start of benefit-sharing negotiations between the San and South Africa's Council for Scientific and Industrial Research (CSIR)—which had registered a patent in 1996 without any attempt at obtaining prior informed consent from the San. Originally hunter-gatherers, the San have lost out (often violently) to successive groups of pastoralists and agriculturalists. Scattered around the Kalahari basin, surviving communities are now among the most marginalized and stigmatized in their respective countries. The benefit-sharing agreement made by the San with CSIR regarding the commercialization of the Hoodia plant, is detailed in table 6.1.[3]

Wynberg (2004a, 241) laments the absence of prior informed consent from the holders of traditional knowledge (the San), and she poses fundamental questions such as

Who qualifies as the rightful community or group from whom consent should be obtained? Can knowledge be attributed to a single group or individual? Is the privatisation of traditional knowledge through intellectual property rights not contrary to the belief of many communities that such knowledge is collectively held, for the benefit of the broader community? Can bioprospecting in fact deliver development benefits and social justice?

To address these concerns, fieldwork was carried out in three San communities in Namibia (Omatako, Vergenoeg, and Blouberg) and one San community in South Africa (Andriesvale) in the period July-October 2004. The communities were selected to capture some of the diversity of circumstances in which the San may find themselves, including culture, geography, the situation with regard to land rights, and general socioeconomic conditions. The San's perceptions of the Hoodia benefit-sharing agreement were collected through the use of participant observation, life stories, and over 100 informal and semistructured interviews.

Table 6.1
Timeline and terms of Hoodia benefit-sharing agreement

Timeline of agreement
1963: Knowing about its use by San, CSIR (a state-owned South African research institute) starts researching Hoodia and "discovers" its appetite-suppressant quality
1996: CSIR begins with filing patent applications for P57 around the world
1997: CSIR signs contract with Phytopharm, which allows the latter to further develop P57
1998: UK patent and world patent are secured for P57.
1998: Phytopharm signs sublicensing agreement with Pfizer to develop and commercialize P57
2001: Survival International informs San (WIMSA) about the P57 patent.
2001: Negotiations start between San and CSIR about the P57 project and CSIR apologizes for not consulting with the San.
2003: Benefit-sharing agreement
2004: Pfizer pulls out; new agreement with Unilever
2007: Signing of new benefit-sharing agreement with Hoodia growers
2008: Unilever pulls out of the project.

Terms of agreement
CSIR will pay the San 8% of all the milestone payments it receives from Phytopharm.CSIR will pay the San 6% of all the royalties CSIR receives.
The San have proposed the following in terms of distribution of the profits from the Hoodia:
75% equally divided between the San of Namibia, Botswana, Angola, and South Africa
   - 30% of each country's proceeds should cover the administration of the country's San Council
   - 70% should go to development projects
10% as working capital to the Hoodia Benefit Sharing Trust
0% to be kept by WIMSA as an emergency reserve
5% to WIMSA for administrative purposes

Justice as Procedure and Recognition

With regard to procedural justice, first, doubts must be expressed to what extent the process can be characterized as participatory. For example, in Namibia only a handful of all the interviewees knew about the Hoodia benefit-sharing agreement; the vast majority of the people interviewed had never heard about it, let alone had their opinion been sought prior to signing the agreement. The interviewees in Namibia who have heard about the agreement could be described as the "elite" San—that is, the individuals who have been elected as representatives of the community in organizations like the San Council and the Working Group of Indigenous Minorities in Southern Africa (WIMSA). The situation in South Africa was slightly better. The community members who were interviewed knew about the agreement, but the majority complained that their opinion was not sought prior to signing it. They lamented the lack of communication between the "elite" San and the majority of the community. None of the community members interviewed was able to relate any details of the contents of the agreement. For example, they did not know that the royalties are to be shared equally between the San in South Africa, Namibia, Botswana, and Angola; they did not know for what purposes the Hoodia was going to be used; they were not aware that Pfizer had pulled out of the deal; nor were they involved in the new negotiations between CSIR and Unilever.

Apart from being nonparticipatory, the process can also be criticized for its failure to create an environment that could have assisted the San in their negotiations. As confirmed by Wynberg's (2004a, 2004b) observations, communities dealing with bioprospecting and benefit-sharing agreements require legal and strategic assistance in dealing with these issues. This has been clearly absent in the case of the Hoodia agreement. Only a few people were selected to represent the interests of their communities and they lacked the appropriate knowledge and skills for effective negotiation of intellectual property rights and benefit-sharing agreements. During the fieldwork, people who are part of the Hoodia Trust Fund complained that they were not adequately trained by the CSIR to manage the project and the potentially high amounts of money that could be accrued once the Hoodia product is commercialized. Stories were told that it took them two years to open a bank account and none of the Hoodia Trust Fund members had any knowledge of accounting. They further complained that their requests for training and assistance were denied by the CSIR. Complaints were also voiced about their (non-San) representatives, that they have no clear understanding what benefit-sharing agreements entail. After attending a workshop about the pros and cons of benefit-sharing agreements (which was organized by academics), people involved in the Hoodia Trust Fund argued that they have made crucial mistakes and that neither the San nor their representatives knew about alternative nonmonetary benefits. High-profile leaders in the community complained that the agreement was closed under conditions set out by non-San peoples and that the San's opinion was neither respected nor even sought. Procedural deficiencies were in this way accompanied by more fundamental processes of misrecognition.

Doubts must be raised as to whether either the outcome of, or the process behind, the benefit-sharing agreement has respected one of the prevailing ethical norms in the San society, namely, egalitarianism. The San's society has been described by anthropologists as one that functions free of hierarchy and power structures and without formal political institutions (Lee 2003; Guenther 1999; Woodburn 1982). Decisions are made through a process of intensive talking and lively discussions or, in other words, through consensus. The idea is that all members of the community should have the chance to contribute to the debate before a decision is made. This guarantees that all people have had access to information and each and everyone can contribute to the formation of this information (Guenther 1999).

Looking at the situation in the field, both in Namibia and South Africa, a schism can be identified between "ordinary" community members and "elite" community members. In their struggle for the recognition of their basic human rights, the San were pressured by NGOs, donors, and governments to organize themselves and appoint leaders. Increasingly, it is expected that the San speak with one voice. During the fieldtrips in Namibia numerous San have complained about their leaders. Their behavior in community meetings provided visible evidence of their higher status. Meetings were partially conducted in Afrikaans, while outside the meetings people communicated in their native language. It has been reported that using Afrikaans, the language of the whites and the outside world, signifies a certain status.

Similar observations can be made for the Hoodia benefit-sharing agreement. One of the CSIR's prerequisites for starting the negotiations about the benefit-sharing agreement was that the San had to organize themselves in such a way that it was easier for the CSIR to deal with them (e.g., by setting up a Board of Trustees). They expected that the San would speak with one voice and a few people should represent the entire community. The San's identity is highly diversified and consequently opinions about intellectual property rights and benefit sharing tend to differ widely across communities (see Vermeylen 2008). It may be practically impossible to negotiate with a group of more than 100,000 people, but enforcing a managerial style that sits uncomfortably with their traditional values has led to tensions among the San. A society that was previously characterized by egalitarianism and avoidance of prestige is now faced with a new sort of San "elite" who are visibly better off (houses, cattle) and consider themselves superior to other community members. Furthermore, the difference between the "elite" San and the "ordinary" San has been aggravated through the lack of communication between the two groups. Concerns must be voiced that this process of acculturation will be further fed by the Hoodia benefit-sharing agreement. People who were interviewed also expressed their worries that once the money from the Hoodia benefit sharing is distributed to the communities through the trust funds, tension will erupt in the community. In short, the way the Hoodia benefit-sharing agreement came into being shows that it mainly regulates an economic relationship; the main concern was redistribution of money and no attention was given to the social impacts of the agreement.

In hunter-gatherer societies such as the San, a high priority is accorded to the avoidance of conflicts, and dispute resolution is believed to be far superior to that used in Western societies (Ury 1990, 1995). Resolution of disputes was essential for small seminomadic groups that needed each other's cooperation in order to survive in nature.

Silberbauer (1982) and Lee (2003) note several characteristics that can be distilled in the San's decision-making process. Decisions that affect the band as a whole always come into being as the result of a process in which everyone in the community participates. Discussions seldom take place in a single event, but rather emerge over days during ordinary conversations among friends, relatives, and neighbors. If more serious decisions have to be made and factions emerge, the San will involve a wider audience and include those members of the community who are not taking part in the initial discussion. In this way the different factions can test how the wider community responds to the issues they are discussing and, possibly, may influence members' opinions. Direct confrontation with the opposition is avoided and their inclusion is frowned on. However, the opposition party can use the same technique.

Decisions in band societies[4] such as the San are made by consensus. This does not mean unanimity of decision or opinion, just as egalitarian does not mean equality. As Silberbauer (1982) argues, it is important to understand that consensus is not a synonym for democracy. Democracy, he continues, "is about equality of opportunity of access to positions of legitimate authority and the limitations this imposes on the exercise of power" (p. 31). As such it is an organizational framework "ruled" by the majority (in a representative democracy) that makes and executes decisions. Band societies, on the other hand, make decisions on the basis of a series of judgments that can be formed because everyone had access to a common pool of information. According to Silberbauer, consensus arrives when "people consent to judgment and decision" (p. 31). Consensus is reached when there is no longer a significant opposition to the decision, which is different from accepting by unanimity.

It was also noted that the Hoodia benefit-sharing agreement has raised high and somewhat unrealistic expectations. Some of the San believe that they are sitting on a potential gold mine and that they will become multimillionaires overnight. The recent signing of a new bioprospecting agreement between the San of Southern Africa and the CSIR has reinforced this feeling. The new agreement regulates a partnership between the South African San Council and the CSIR with regard to researching the indigenous knowledge of the San people on the usage of indigenous plants, to the benefits of both parties (as claimed in the joint press release). The leader of the South African San Council argues that the agreement is beneficial in the sense that it records and conserves the San's indigenous knowledge and provides proof of ownership and possible use of the San knowledge in future development projects. Two weeks prior to the signing of the agreement, when community members in Andriesvale were questioned about this new agreement, they were not aware of it. Furthermore, they seemed reluctant to sign such an agreement for two reasons. First, some argued that the Hoodia benefit-sharing agreement has so far shown no concrete results and question why they should sign a new agreement. Second, some people felt very uncomfortable with the idea of generating together with a third party a database of their traditional knowledge. They felt as if they would lose control over their resources and knowledge and had fundamental problems with this concept of joint partnership unless the terms and conditions were clear from the start. Anthropologists have also identified the importance of trust among members of ethnic groups and trust in the system as important concepts in San societies (Hitchcock 2002). In other words, the new agreement shows the same flaws as the Hoodia benefit sharing, namely not being participatory. Consistent with what Greene (2004) suggests, it could be argued here that raising the expectations that large sums of money are going to be transferred to the San may have been an effective strategy (although there is no proof of a deliberate strategy) to persuade local communities to accept the Hoodia benefit-sharing agreement and the new bioprospecting project.

As time went on, it seems increasingly unlikely that the high expectations that have been raised when signing the benefit-sharing agreement will ever be fulfilled. As mentioned above, the first major setback occurred when Pfizer announced in July 2003 that it was going to withdraw from the P57 agreement and returned the licensing rights to Phytopharm. However, in June 2004, Phytopharm announced that it had sublicensed the P57 commercialization rights to Unilever, with the intention of developing and marketing an appetite-suppressing energy bar (Chennells 2007). Then, in December 2008 after spending €10 million on research, Unilever decided to withdraw from the licensing agreement relating to the development of products based on the CSIR patent. More than ten years after the patent was registered by the CSIR and more than five years after the San have signed the benefit-sharing agreement, there are currently no signs that a Hoodia product will soon be on the market.

Distributive Justice

Looking at distributed pattern of actual and potential outcomes from the exploitation of Hoodia, a number of dimensions can be identified that complicate the realization of what might constitute distributive justice. The benefit sharing under the initial agreement was structured in monetary terms. The share the San would receive from the milestone payments and the royalties—8 and 6 percent of the payments made to CSIR respectively—may sound reasonable, but their actual value is not clear at this stage. The fact that the Hoodia was originally expected to be commercialized as a drug, but then the focus shifted to a food supplement, meant that its total market value and thus the absolute benefit share would be lower than the San had been expecting. Now that there is no sublicense agreement with a company to commercialize Hoodia as a slimming or dietary product, these expectations must be further lowered. However, as a result of all the publicity for the Hoodia as an appetite suppressant, the international demand for Hoodia as a natural product exploded, with literally hundreds of Hoodia dietary products being advertised on the Internet. Poaching and illegal harvesting of the product became a problem to such an extent that in October 2004, Hoodia was registered in Appendix II of CITES, but in many areas the protection came too late and the Hoodia became extinct, cutting off the San from their "life force." On the back of this development, the San were able, in March 2007, to negotiate a new benefit-sharing agreement specifically with the Hoodia farmers who were organized in the Southern African Hoodia Growers Association. While, initially, the agreement entitles the San to a modest £2 per dried kilogram of Hoodia exported, at the moment it seems that the Hoodia *growers'* benefit-sharing agreement might potentially be—in all its modesty—more "lucrative" than the initial benefit-sharing agreement, but with proceeds distributed just to the farmers rather than to the San as a wider community.

A second issue relates to the notions of value embodied in an agreement conceived in terms of a financial outcome. The San who were interviewed were less interested in monetary benefits than in receiving nonmonetary benefits like schools, hospitals, access to land, agricultural projects, and housing. They argued that distributing money was problematic for several reasons. First, they were worried that the money would not be used for the right purposes and would be mainly wasted on alcohol. Second, they were also worried that even when the money was managed through a trust fund, this could raise problems because the management of the trust fund was so far nontransparent. Third, there was a general consensus that the CSIR, or any other company or third party for that matter, could not be trusted. Especially the San in Andriesvale argued that in the past they were promised a better economic life by the South African government when some of their land was returned. They now complained that these were "empty" preelection promises; in reality, the economic situation was not further improved and they were still dependent on government aid and were not able to start their own "development projects." Furthermore, they argued that in the long term, nonmonetary benefits would be more beneficial than monetary benefits because the improvements with nonmonetary benefits would be more sustainable and less dependent on issues like trust and dependency. This shows that those interviewed have a different conceptualization of distributive justice than just monetary benefits alone. For example, questions were asked why they were not more closely involved in the scientific work of the CSIR. Some of the participants in the research showed a keen interest to learn from the Hoodia project and wanted to understand the scientific and chemical process behind the P57 compound. Ultimately, they wanted, in due time, to have San researchers working with their own traditional medicinal plants either with or without the support of the CSIR. So far they were disappointed in the level of cooperation between the CSIR and the San community members; they felt they had been left behind by the CSIR.

In addition to questions about the level and type of benefits, there are questions about the beneficiaries. Who are the "community" to whom justice needs to be done and how is this to be defined? Some anthropologists (e.g., Widlok 1999) claim that the current botanical knowledge of the San does not surpass that of neighboring agriculturalists. Furthermore, the Hoodia grows in Namibia only in areas currently not inhabited by the San and fieldwork observations confirmed that it is no longer known to or used by the San. The Nama and Damara in Namibia, on the other hand, are still using the Hoodia. While the San are clearly the oldest surviving indigenous group of Southern Africa, botanical knowledge that would have been exclusively theirs has since passed to other groups of more recent ancestry or arrival. Some of these groups have interacted with the various San groups to the extent that they are ethnically (Nama) or linguistically (Nama and Damara) linked. It should be clear that controlling the appropriation of knowledge through allocating exclusive property rights on the basis of ethnicity is neither practicable (ultimately requiring DNA tests) nor desirable because it can increase racial animosity and tension with the official, nonethnic policies of postapartheid states. As publicity around the Hoodia benefit-sharing agreement has gathered momentum, increasingly other groups such as the Nama (supported by the Namibian government) have raised their voice and in the most recent stakeholder meeting (January 2009), Nama community leaders were invited to explore a San-Nama agreement (personal communication, February 2009). While this symbolic reaching out to the Namas must be applauded, the fact is that the Damaras—whose use of *Hoodia currorii* was reported as early as 1907 by Vedder and Schultze (see Barnard 1992)—might further aggravate and expose the problems associated with embedding the concept of biodiversity conservation in a Western framework of exclusive property rights.

While it is beyond the scope of this chapter, one of the most controversial aspects of the access and benefit-sharing debate relates to the way traditional knowledge is used and commercialized. Vermeylen (2008) has reported that opinions differ widely within the communities studied as to whether to commodify traditional knowledge, but the way benefit-sharing agreements are conceptualized and presented suggests that there is an expectation that indigenous peoples will speak with one voice. Although during the fieldwork carried out over a period of three years, a diversity of opinions were recorded—a result that is not surprising when the local context is taken into account, as well as current socio-

economic and political circumstances at the local and community level—
an acceptance of commodification in principle seemed to be widespread
in some communities. However, as further explored in Vermeylen 2008,
the acceptance of commodification should not only be translated into an
economic compensation. As the following quote illustrates, regardless of
its commercial status, the symbolic and cultural value of Hoodia should
never be underestimated:

When you eat the Hoodia you can feel the supernatural powers coming from
above. When you smell the Hoodia and taste it on your tongue you will feel how
it stimulates you, how it controls your hunger, how it gives you power and
energy. . . . When you eat the Hoodia in the veld you can enjoy the powers of
the plant. When I notice some symptoms of cancer, I eat the plant, I talk to the
plant; the plant gives me new power and energy and in return I can give all the
bad energy back to the plant; the plant knows how to deal with these bad energies. . . . You can not experience these powers and energies of the Hoodia in
pills; we gave the power away for money. Everything we had here is gone because
we traded the supernatural powers for money, for simple things . . . but the
Hoodia was good for us.[5]

This indicates that the process of commodification is challenged by
some San as resulting in the Hoodia losing its "life force" and power to
"heal." The commodification of the Hoodia is seen as another example
in the historical process of marginalizing the San's culture and way of
life—a process that closely ties together the injustice of misrecognition
with the distributive outcomes that are then imagined and achieved. The
benefit-sharing agreements only compensate the economic value of a
commodity because this is the only value that is given recognition. One
of the biggest challenges faced with regard to distributive justice is therefore to find ways to both utilize and compensate for the cultural values
that indigenous peoples like the San attribute to what others view only
in commercial and monetary terms.

Conclusion

The case of the San and the Hoodia has clearly demonstrated both the
situated process needed to make sense of what environmental justice
constitutes, and the multiple notions of justice that need to be brought
to bear. While we can find clear evidence for Schlosberg's argument that
environmental justice is multivalent, that it incorporates interrelated
notions of justice as distribution, procedure, and recognition, we also
have to closely interrogate assumptions as to what constitutes value,
community, fair process, and fair outcome in applying each of these forms

of justice in this distinctive context. Expectations that the fair distribution of value can be understood only in monetary terms, that a hierarchical structure of representation can be assumed in negotiations, that property rights can be conceived in exclusive, individualistic terms, and that the "worthy" community of justice can be simply defined, are all confounded by an approach to sharing benefit that risks fundamentally misrecognizing the cultural foundations of the San as an indigenous group. Williams and Mawdsley (2006: 669) make a similar point in arguing that

regardless of the theoretical lens through which concepts of injustice are viewed . . . a close examination of differences in the context in which struggles for environmental justice are located is required. There has to be critical engagement with these differences—including those of history, culture, state structure, and public discourse—if environmental justice is not to fall in to the trap of staying within a world that is "thinly known."

The parameters and hazards of this "trap" are all the more readily exposed when, as in the case we have examined, an attempt is made to embody justice within an essentially neoliberal international legislative regime. When the presumptions and assumptions of this regime crash against the situated particularities of its implementation and negotiation it is hardly surprising that discontinuities in value and process are to be found, although their intensity might vary from context to context. We can therefore finish our discussion by considering what alternative legal models for doing justice might be possible that are better able to embody such diversity in context.

As we have established, the concept of environmental justice seeks to ensure equity based on the participation of those affected in order to produce outcomes that treat all affected groups fairly. According to Shelton (2007), equity not only comports with notions of justice, equity also relates to law in the sense of providing contextualized justice. In this perspective, the relationship between justice and law should be explored against the background of an understanding of the limits of positive law, or indeed as a critique of the universal norms and values as embodied in the spirit of the Enlightenment. Instead of embedding justice in a dominant and abstract positivist legal discourse that ignores the politics of power (Minda 1995), justice should be interpreted in terms of what Lyotard (1984) calls complex narratives or local discourses of different cultural and theoretical perspectives. Parallel to the arguments used by scholars like Felix Cohen with respect to justice, postmodernist legal scholars refute the concept of law as an autonomous, self-generating activity because there can be no fixed foundation on which to ground legal justification once and for all (Minda 1995). Instead, law should be defined as something that offers an insight into the community that law is to serve (Donovan and Anderson 2003). This links to the idea developed by De Sousa Santos (2002) that law and justice, so far, have only recognized one time-space dimension but, as De Sousa Santos argues, society is regulated by a plurality of legal orders. Therefore law and justice need to be understood not so much within the context of norms and rules, but rather as narratives or rhetorics. As Gewirtz (1996) argues, law is not just a mechanism that draws up policies that shape culture; on the contrary, law becomes almost like an "artifact" that reveals a specific culture. The central inquiry is about the story of law and not the rule of law. The attention should subsequently be focused on those who are the subject or object of law and specifically on those who, as Wright (2001) argues, have been kept subordinated by formal law.

The point we are making is that the concept of environmental justice can only work when comparable weight is given to each stakeholder's perspective and value system. This equity is the prerequisite to achieving true conciliation between different cultures of praxis. Although it poses a great challenge, we find great inspiration in the work of Leon Sheleff (2000), who argues that custom is an important source of law for all legal systems. For Sheleff, custom exists in the present; it consists of the standards, norms, and criteria that a community finds acceptable when seeking justice. As such, custom exists in any legal system, whether a judge needs to make a decision in the high court or an elder needs to make a decision in the xhotla (traditional courthouse in Botswana). At the end of the day judges and elders alike must consider the sentiments of the people when justice is being sought.

Notes

1. For concise overviews see, for example, Lenzerini 2008; Anaya 2003; Blaser, Feit, and McRae 2004; Ivison, Patton, and Sanders 2000; Keal 2003; Venne 1998; and Battiste and Henderson 2000.

2. For an overview of Cohen's work, see Mitchell 2007.

3. For more information see Stephenson 2003; Wynberg 2004a, 2004b; and Wynberg, Schroeder, and Chennells, 2009.

4. Band societies consist of a small kin group, which is usually not larger than an extended family. Two main characteristics of band societies are egalitarianism and consensus-based decision making.

5. Interview with Andriesvale informant, June 21, 2007, translated from Afrikaans to English.

References

Anaya, J. 2003. *International Law and Indigenous Peoples*. Dartmouth: Hants.

Artuso, A. 2002. Bioprospecting, benefit sharing, and biotechnological capacity building. *World Development* 30:1355–1368.

Barnard, A. 1992. *Hunters and Herders of Southern Africa: A Comparative Ethnography of the Khoisan Peoples*. Cambridge: Cambridge University Press.

Battiste, M., and Henderson, J. Y. 2000. *Protecting Indigenous Knowledge and Heritage: A Global Challenge*. Saskatoon: Purich.

Bell, D. 2004. Environmental Justice and Rawls' Difference Principle. *Environmental Ethics* 26:287–306.

Blaser, M., H. A. Feit, and G. McRae. 2004. *In the Way of Development: Indigenous Peoples, Life Projects and Globalisation*. London: Zed Books.

Borrows, J. 2002. *Recovering Canada: The Resurgence of Indigenous Law*. Toronto: Toronto University Press.

Chennells, R. 2007. *San Hoodia Case: A Report for GenBenefit*. New Delhi: Research and Information System for Developing Countries.

Debbane, A. M., and R. Keil. 2004. Multiple disconnections: Environmental justice and urban water in Canada and South Africa. *Space and Polity* 8(2): 209–225.

De Sousa Santos, B. 2002. *Toward a New Legal Common Sense: Law, Globalisation, and Emancipation*. London: Butterworths.

Dodds, S. 1998. Justice and indigenous land rights. *Inquiry* 41:187–205.

Donovan, J. M., and E. H. Anderson. 2003. *Anthropology & Law*. New York: Berghahn Books.

Douzinas, C., and R. Warrington. 1994. *Justice Miscarried: Ethics, Aesthetics and the Law*. Hemel Hempstead: Harvester Wheatsheaf.

Fraser, N. 1997. *Justice Interruptus: Critical Reflections on the "Postsocialist" Condition*. New York: Routledge.

Fraser, N. 1999. Social justice in an age of identity politics: Redistribution, recognition and participation. In L. Ray and A. Sayer, eds., *Culture and Economy After the Cultural Turn*, 25–52. London: Sage.

Gewirtz, P. 1996. Narrative and rhetoric in the law. In P. Brooks and P. Gewirtz, eds., *Law's Stories: Narrative and Rhetoric in the Law*, 2–13. New Haven, CT: Yale University Press.

Greene, S. 2004. Indigenous people incorporated? Culture as politics, culture as property in pharmaceutical bioprospecting. *Current Anthropology* 45: 211–238.

Guenther, M. 1999. *Tricksters & Dancers: Bushman Religion and Society*. Bloomington: Indiana University Press.

Henne, G. 1997. Mutually agreed terms in the CBD: Requirements under public international law. In J. Mugabe, C. Barber, G. Henne, L. Glowka, and

A. La Viña, eds., *Access to Genetic Resources: Strategies for Sharing Benefits*, 71–91. Nairobi: ACTS Press.

Herkenrath, P. 2002. The implementation of the Convention on Biological Diversity—A non-government perspective ten years on. *Review of European Community & International Environmental Law* 11:29–37.

Hitchcock, R. K. 2002. "We are the First People": Land, natural resources and identity in the central Kalahari, Botswana. *Journal of Southern African Studies* 28:797–824.

Holifield, R., M. Porter, and G. Walker. 2009. Spaces of environmental justice: Frameworks for critical engagement. *Antipode* 41:591–612.

Honneth, A. 1995. *The Struggle for Recognition: The Moral Grammar of Social Conflicts*. Cambridge, MA: MIT Press.

Ivison, D., P. Patton, and W. Sanders. 2000. *Political Theory and the Rights of Indigenous Peoples*. Cambridge: Cambridge University Press.

Keal, P. 2003. *European Conquest and the Rights of Indigenous Peoples: The Moral Backwardness of International Society*. Cambridge: Cambridge University Press.

Kirsch, S. 2004. Property limits: Debates on the body, nature and culture. In E. Hirsch and M. Strathern, eds., *Transactions and Creations: Property Debates and the Stimulus of Melanasia*, 21–39. New York: Berghahn Books.

Lee, R. 2003. *The Dobe Ju/'hoansi*. Toronto: Wadsworth.

Lenzerini, F. 2008. *Reparations for Indigenous Peoples: International and Comparative Perspectives*. Oxford: Oxford University Press.

Low, N., and B. Gleeson. 1998. *Justice, Society and Nature: An Exploration of Political Ecology*. London: Routledge.

Lyotard, J.-F. 1984. *The Postmodern Condition: A Report on Knowledge*. Trans. G. Bannington and B. Massumi. Minneapolis: University of Minnesota Press.

Miller, D. 1995. Equality in post-modern times. In D. Miller and M. Walzer, eds., *Pluralism, Justice and Equality*. New York: Oxford University Press.

Minda, G. 1995. *Postmodern Legal Movements: Law and Jurisprudence at Century's End*. New York: New York University Press.

Mitchell, D. 2007. *Architect of Justice: Felix S. Cohen and the Founding of American Legal Pluralism*. Ithaca, NY: Cornell University Press.

Mugabe, J., C. Barber, G. Henne, L. Glowka, and A. La Viña. 1997. *Access to Genetic Resources: Strategies for Sharing Benefits*. Nairobi: ACTS Press.

Mulligan, S. P. 1999. For whose benefits? Limits to sharing in the bioprospecting "regime." *Environmental Politics* 8:35–65.

Okereke, C. 2006. Global environmental sustainability: Intragenerational equity and conceptions of justice in multilateral environmental regimes. *Geoforum* 37:725–736.

Schlosberg, D. 2004. Reconceiving environmental justice: Global movements and political theories. *Environmental Politics* 13:517–540.

Schlosberg, D. 2007. *Defining Environmental Justice: Theories, Movements and Nature*. Oxford: Oxford University Press.

Schrader-Frechette, K. 2002. *Environmental Justice: Creating Equality, Reclaiming Democracy*. New York: Oxford University Press.

Schroeder, R., K. S. Martin, B. Wilson, and D. Sen. 2008. Third World environmental justice. *Society & Natural Resources* 21:547–555.

Sheleff, L. 2000. *The Future of Tradition: Customary Law, Common Law and Legal Pluralism*. London: Frank Cass.

Shelton, D. 2007. Equity. In D. Bodansky, J. Brunnee, and E. Hey, eds., *Oxford handbook of international environmental law*, 639–662. Oxford: Oxford University Press.

Silberbauer, G. 1982. Political process in G/wi bands. In E. Leacock and R. Lee, eds., *Politics and History in Band Societies*, 23–35. Cambridge: Cambridge University Press.

Stephenson, D. 2003. *The Patenting of P57 and Intellectual Property Rights of the San Peoples of Southern Africa*. In cooperation with and with the special assistance of the South African San Council, as representatives of the Working Group of Indigenous Minorities in Southern Africa, and First Peoples Worldwide. Available at http://www.firstpeoples.org.

Strathern, M. 2004. Introduction: Rationales of ownership. In L. Kalinoe and J. Leach, eds., *Rationales of Ownership: Transactions and Claims to Ownership in Contemporary Papua New Guinea*, 1–12. Wantage: Sean Kingston.

Suzman, J. 2001. *An Introduction to the Regional Assessment of the Status of the San in Southern Africa*. Windhoek: Legal Assistance Centre.

Sze, J., and J. London. 2008. Environmental justice at the crossroads. *Social Compass* 2(4):1331–1354.

Tobin, B. 2001. Redefining perspectives in the search for protection of traditional knowledge: A case study from Peru. *Review of European Community & International Environmental Law* 10:47–64.

Torres, G. 1994. Environmental burdens and democratic justice. *Fordham Urban Law Journal* 21:431–460.

Tully, J. 1994. Aboriginal property and Western theory: Recovering a middle ground. *Social Philosophy & Policy* 11:153–180.

Tully, S. 2003. The Bonn Guidelines on access to genetic resources and benefit sharing. *Review of European Community and International Environmental Law* 14:84–98.

Ury, W. 1990. Dispute resolution notes from the Kalahari. *Negotiation Journal* 6:229–238.

Ury, W. 1995. Conflict resolution among the Bushmen: Lessons in dispute system design. *Negotiation Journal*, October, 379–389.

Venne, S. H. 1998. *Our Elders Understand Our Rights: Evolving International Law Regarding Indigenous Peoples*. Penticton: Theytus Books.

Vermeylen, S. 2008. From life force to slimming aid: Exploring views on the commodification of traditional knowledge. *Applied Geography* 28:224–235.

Walker, G. 2009. Globalising environmental justice: The geography and politics of frame contextualisation and evolution. *Global Social Policy* 9:355–382.

Walker, G., and H. Bulkeley. 2006. Geographies of environmental justice. *Geoforum* 37(5):655–659.

Walzer, M. 1983. *Spheres of Justice.* New York: Basic Books.

Wenz, P. S. 1988. *Environmental Justice.* Albany, NY: SUNY Press.

Whiteman, G., and K. Mamen. 2002. Examining justice and conflict between mining companies and indigenous peoples: Cerro Colorado and the Ngäbe-Buglé in Panama. *Journal of Business and Management* 8:293–329.

Widlok, T. 1999. *Living on Mangetti: "Bushman" Autonomy and Namibian Independence.* Oxford: Oxford University Press.

Williams, G., and E. Mawdsley. 2006. Postcolonial environmental justice: Government and governance in India. *Geoforum* 37(5):660–670.

Woodburn, J. 1982. Egalitarian societies. *Man* 17:431–451.

Wright, S. 2001. *International Human Rights, Decolonisation and Globalisation.* London: Routledge.

Wynberg, R. 2004a. Bioprospecting delivers limited benefits in South Africa. *European Intellectual Property Review* 26:239–243.

Wynberg, R. 2004b. Rhetoric, realism and benefit sharing: Use of traditional knowledge of Hoodia species in the development of an appetite suppressant. *Journal of World Intellectual Property* 7:851–876.

Wynberg, R., D. Schroeder, and R. Chennells. 2009.*Community Consent and Benefit-Sharing: Lessons Learned from the San Hoodia Case.* Dordrecht: Springer.

Young, I. 1990. *Justice and the Politics of Difference.* Princeton, NJ: Princeton University Press.

7
Global Environmental Governance and Pathways for the Achievement of Environmental Justice

Beth Schaefer Caniglia

The UNFCCC COP15 meeting erupted after its first week in Copenhagen, bringing to a head the clash between the climate justice movement, a range of formally accredited nongovernmental organizations (NGOs), and a United Nations agency charged with the facilitation of a binding agreement among sovereign nation-states to curtail climate change. Banners, pamphlets, t-shirts, and buttons were displayed by thousands of participants from around the world. Slogans such as "System Change, Not Climate Change," "There Is No Planet B," "Politicians Talk; Leaders ACT," and "HOPENHAGEN: Earth's Body Guard" were some of the most prominent messages communicated. Activists were everywhere—inside the official negotiating halls, at the People's Summit called the Klimaforum, at numerous side events and celebrations, and in the streets and the jails of Copenhagen. Scientists, ministry personnel, moderate NGOs, and business representatives became increasingly radicalized as they waited in line, day after day, to commence the work they hoped to accomplish inside the Bella Center. They, too, chanted, played musical instruments, danced to keep warm, and eventually some even walked out of the official meetings to join protestors in the streets. So many left Copenhagen disappointed, not only in the weak agreement governments finally reached but in the ability of the UN to organize an efficient, effective conference.

COP15 illustrates a conundrum in global governance that is growing more difficult to solve: international institutions, like the United Nations, are often forced to mediate between the grievances of civil society and the sovereignty of nation-states. As civil society grows more aware of and engaged in international institutions, it becomes more important to understand the limits those institutions grapple with and the circumstances under which such institutions incorporate the voices of nonstate actors. Each sector of the United Nations is populated by particular agencies that are charged with addressing particular problems or enacting particular programs under their purview. At the international level, the achievement of environmental justice is facilitated and constrained by institutions of environmental governance. Formal international environmental governance is managed by the United Nations, particularly through the United Nations Environment Program (UNEP), the United Nations Commission on Sustainable Development (UNCSD), the United Nations Development Program (UNDP), and a myriad of specific treaty secretariats, which oversee such issue areas as oceans, climate change, ozone, and whaling (Ivanova and Roy 2007). Advocates for environmental justice clearly recognize that global environmental governance institutions provide important channels through which to effect change, both at home and abroad (Keck and Sikkink 1998; Porter, Brown, and Chasek 2000; Caniglia 2001; Bernstein 2001). Many are uncertain, however, which institutions provide the most efficient avenues for change and whether engagement in intergovernmental institutions like the United Nations will ever result in significant reform (Ivanova and Roy 2007; Pellow 2007).

Two UN agencies stand out as central targets in the struggle for environmental justice: The UN Commission on Sustainable Development (UNCSD) and the UN Framework Convention on Climate Change (UNFCCC). The UNCSD is the only institution specifically charged with articulating, implementing, and monitoring policies that harmonize the three pillars of sustainable development: environment, economy, and equity. In recent years, however, NGO attendance at UNCSD meetings has waned and some highly respected NGOs have become frustrated with the organization's efficacy. In contrast, attendance at the UNFCCC talks has increased (Smith 2004; Roberts and Parks 2007). Why is it that nonstate actors are abandoning the UNCSD in favor of this platform and how might this affect our chances to expand environmental justice policies at the global level?

Drawing on theories of institutional change and social movements, I examine the UNFCCC and UNCSD to assess their likelihood of incorporating the voices of nonstate actors and creating more just international environmental law. Based on this analysis, I find that specific characteristics of the UNCSD lead it to be better poised to facilitate global frameworks that support environmental justice. Treaty organizations like the UNFCCC also have an important role to play; however, NGOs and other nonstate actors are more limited in such hard-law environments. As a result, I argue that advocates for environmental justice should chart an integrated strategy that includes targeting the UNCSD and the specific treaty organizations that are relevant to their interests.

International Institutions and Social Movements

International policy frameworks provide models of appropriate nation-state behavior that can be leveraged by social movement organizations and other NGOs to pressure their governments to change (Boli and Thomas 1997; Meyer et al. 1997; Finnemore and Sikkink 1998; Frank, Hironaka, and Schofer 2000). Although social movement scholars have long emphasized the "outsider" status that social movements and other nonstate actors hold vis-à-vis institutional centers of policymaking (Tarrow 1998), recent scholarship has shown that movement groups and nonstate actors often work on the inside of such structures (Zald 2000; Caniglia 2001; Pellow 2007; Roberts and Parks 2007). International institutions, in particular, are often described as being in a symbiotic relationship with NGOs, governments, and intergovernmental organization (IGO) personnel (Gordenker and Weiss 1995; Risse-Kappen 1995; Willetts 1996, 2006). And nonstate actors, especially NGOs, are often given credit for pushing nation-states toward universal standards by the work they do inside IGOs in articulating progressive visions for the future (Boli and Thomas 1997; Finnemore and Sikkink 1998; Caniglia and Sarabia 2003).

There are skeptics and critics who argue that NGOs and social movement groups should avoid joining forces with international institutions, because their goals may be moderated or co-opted by policymaking authorities (Riker 1995; Fisher 1997; Third World Network 2004; Gordenker and Weiss 1995). Others highlight the powerful influence "outsider" strategies can yield by bringing media attention to grievances and mobilizing conscience constituents on behalf of movement goals (Skolnick 1969; Meyers 2006; McCarthy and Zald 1977, 1987). As David Meyers (2006) points out, however, insider and outsider strategies can work together to move decision makers in more progressive directions than either strategy can achieve in isolation. The *radical flank effect*, where protests and demonstrations outside policymaking institutions serve to move decision makers toward more moderate advocates inside policymaking institutions (McAdam 1982 Haines 1984; Jenkins and Ekert 1986; Minkoff 1994; Meyers 2006), is equally important to international policymaking as it has been shown to be for American social movements.

Theories of institutional change and political opportunity structures also directly apply. The relative ability of international policy institutions to exclude (or discourage) participation by their critics tends to reinforce the status quo in international law (Clemens and Cook 1999; Chiang 1981; Willetts 2006). The United Nations and its corresponding agencies walk a fine line as they attempt to bring together nation-states to solve international problems. On the one hand, the UN's primary purpose is to facilitate the collective interests of nation-states. In the process of bringing states to consensus, however, they often rely on pressure provided by NGOs, industry, scientists, and other nonstate actors to help move states toward the policies the UN has identified as either desirable or feasible. This balancing act places the UN in a difficult situation as a mediator between nation-states and civil society—a situation that is increasingly coming to a head at international conferences. The United Nations and its corresponding agencies grant consultative and observer status to NGOs and have waxed and waned historically regarding their tendencies toward openness to nonstate actor participation (Weiss and Gordenker 1996; Willetts 1996, 2006; Chiang 1981; Third World Network 2004; Tarrow 1988, 2005). Engagement by a diversity of nonstate actors—both inside the institutions and from the outside—creates the conditions cited by institutional change scholars that facilitate change. Therefore, the openness of international environmental policy institutions is an important variable in the equation to bring about environmental justice.

According to Clemens and Cook (1999, 451), "Institutional change is most likely when (a) models of action are understood to be discretionary, (b) social heterogeneity is high, and (c) social networks are fragmented and cross important social cleavages." This perspective is rooted in the idea that increased heterogeneity will decrease the "common ground" of shared understanding, which plays a critical role in the maintenance of social systems. Since hybrid forms of governance that incorporate nonstate actors are increasingly common, we should expect to find nonstate actors exerting more influence on the articulation of international policy—especially in environmental governance (Karkkainen 2004; Hemmati 2002). However, hybrid forms of governance are less common and more symbolic within "hard-law" treaty institutions than they are within "soft-law" agencies of the United Nations, which requires us to consider a variety of pathways through which NGOs, social movement groups, and other nonstate actors can effectively influence each of these types of international law (Tarrow 2005; Willetts 1996).

To explore these factors and chart a pathway toward increased justice in the articulation and implementation of international environmental law, the UNCSD and UNFCCC will be reviewed. These organizations represent different forms of institutions of global environmental governance. The UNCSD is a "soft-law" institution, which means the policy statements it produces represent consensus-based recommendations. While soft-law recommendations can be strengthened over time and become enforceable, they start out as guiding principles and states face no serious sanctions if they do not implement them. The UNFCCC, on the other hand, is dedicated to the articulation, adoption, implementation, and monitoring of an international treaty. Countries that sign and ratify such treaties make commitments to abide by the rules and deadlines specified in the treaty and stand to be sanctioned if they do not conform to treaty obligations. Hard-law institutions are less open to nonstate actor participation, and their politics are more likely to reflect international relations well beyond the scope of their immediate concern, since countries use international treaties to gain favor and to leverage a variety of gains and losses. But soft-law institutions tend to fly below the radar, stick closer to the issues at hand, and have more room for the consideration of new ideas.

Theoretically, close examination of the UNFCCC and UNCSD encourages us to apply institutional-change and political-opportunities scholarship in the contexts of soft and hard law as frameworks through which to formulate a systematic set of strategies to push international environmental governance toward the achievement of environmental justice. I will start with a review of the UNFCCC, since it has received so much recent media attention. For reasons that will unfold, however, I argue that any strategy for the achievement of environmental justice at the international level should include the UNCSD. A relatively brief review of each organization will ensue, followed by a series of recommendations for ways they can be strengthened as avenues for nonstate actor input.

The UNFCCC and the Kyoto Protocol Treaty

Like the UNCSD, the UNFCCC was initiated at the Rio Earth Summit in 1992. The goal was to create a binding treaty for the reduction of greenhouse gas emissions in the face of mounting evidence that these emissions were responsible for increasingly erratic weather patterns, including global warming. At the summit, the UNFCCC succeeded in articulating a shared set of principles that included acknowledgment that climate change required immediate cooperative action. Relevant to our concern with environmental justice, the UNFCCC asked nations to "protect the climate system . . . on the basis of equity and in accordance with their *common but differentiated responsibilities and respective capabilities*" (quoted in Roberts and Parks 2007, 3). However, North–South politics, along with a poor political environment in the United States, signaled that an effective treaty would be difficult to achieve (Roberts and Parks 2007; Fisher 2004; Pulver 2005).

Despite these difficulties, the Kyoto Protocol was negotiated only five years following Rio. Based on the principle of *common but differentiated responsibilities*, the parties agreed that industrialized nations (Annex I countries) would be required to reduce their collective greenhouse gas emissions by just over 5 percent of 1990 levels by 2012, while developing nations (non–Annex I countries) would be allowed to increase their emissions over the same time period. Agreement was also reached that the treaty would not enter force until fifty-five countries ratified the treaty and the total emissions represented by Annex I Signatories reached 55 percent of total 1990 carbon dioxide emissions (UNFCCC 2008). The contested nature of the protocol is illustrated by the fact that this participation goal was not reaching until 2005—ten years after the first Conference of the Parties (COP) met in Berlin—when Russia ratified the treaty.

The general ethos surrounding the Kyoto Protocol was mixed from the beginning. Everyone knew the targets established were insufficient to mitigate climate change (Fisher 2004; Newell 2008). Industrialized nations were bifurcated in their enthusiasm: EU countries, New Zealand, and Japan most vocally argued that the protocol represented an important symbolic step forward that would provide a learn-by-experience opportunity on the road to transforming the Earth's carbon footprint. The United States and Australia strongly opposed the principle of *common but differentiated responsibility* on the grounds that it provided an unfair advantage to their competitors, especially China, India, and Brazil. Developing countries retorted to this complaint that it was industrialized nations who were responsible for over half of all greenhouse gas emissions and, thus, it should be their responsibility to make the largest contribution to their reduction. In other words, the development potential of Southern nations should not be compromised to solve a problem that was overwhelmingly caused by the industrialized nations of the North (Roberts and Parks 2007).

Because the protocol was ratified so late in its first term, many nations and NGOs alike have treated it like a trial to create the institutional and economic mechanisms needed to implement a more rigorous treaty after 2012. The two COP meetings prior to COP15 in Copenhagen were particularly forward-looking and began sketching out potential modifications of the Kyoto Protocol that would lead to a more effective and truly transformative treaty. A surge of optimism accompanied the election of Barack Obama to the U.S. presidency in 2008, because Obama promised to rejoin the UNFCCC process and develop a carbon cap and trading system in the United States. Australia experienced a change in leadership and became a Signatory, indicating that momentum *was* gaining.

Unfortunately, this momentum seems to have stalled if not reversed at the most recent Copenhagen meeting, which failed to produce the binding treaty it promised and, according to many, lost ground compared to previous COP meetings (Athanasiou 2010; "Summary of the Copenhagen Climate Change Conference" 2009; Gomez 2010). The UN process, which is typically marked by evolving consensus over agreement language, devolved during the Copenhagen meeting. Just when it seemed that the meeting would fail to produce any agreement, Obama crashed a backroom meeting between top negotiators from Brazil, China, India, and South Africa and brokered what resulted in the Copenhagen Accord ("President Obama's Dramatic Climate Meet" 2009). The long-term emission reductions that were included in earlier versions of the agreement were omitted in the end, although an agreement in principle to cap temperature increases at 2 degrees Celsius was reached. A bloc of developing nations vehemently objected to both the content of the accord and the processes by which it was negotiated, but in the end the majority of nations endorsed the document.

Moderates and long-time observers of the process argue that the Copenhagen Accord paved the way for incremental progress toward more profound commitments. Timmons Roberts wrote illustratively in his blog on Copenhagen (2009): "In the end, we got an inadequate deal, but it was a realist's deal that may lead to some forward progress."

The UNFCCC and Environmental Justice

Drawing on Clemens and Cook's (1999) criteria, I would score the UNFCCC as moderate in all three categories. Diversity of attendees is restricted by typical hard-law privilege of government officials. As a result, the social cleavages that are emphasized are those between North and South governments, rather than encompassing the range of Major Groups included at the UNCSD. While models of action are somewhat contentious, because solving the immense challenges of climate change places us in unprecedented territory, the methods used to adjudicate options are found across institutions of international treaties and restrict the input of nonstate actors (Dodds 2004).

The UNFCCC provides revealing insights into typical UN treaty organization structures. Treaties are binding agreements between and among nation-states and distinctly privilege government officials in their negotiations. Systematic barriers restrict the extent and avenues of NGO and other nonstate actors' participation, and while these barriers disadvantage all nonstate actors, they often particularly disadvantage groups from the developing world (Willetts 1996). The UNFCCC has been cited as being more favorable to NGO participation than some other treaty secretariats (Pulver 2005), but barriers to NGO participation are present. These barriers limit NGO effectiveness and structure the repertoires of strategies available for nonstate actor influence.

Accreditation to attend UNFCCC meetings is more difficult to acquire than attendance at the UNCSD. In part, this is because the UNFCCC is a focused area, while the UNCSD encompasses the entire scope of sustainable development. In addition, the UNFCCC is less likely to accredit smaller, local organizations, because the secretariat emphasizes the international character of those who apply. Just under 70 NGOs attended the 1995 negotiations, but in 1997 more than 230 NGOs were represented by over 3,500 people (Pulver 2005) and in Copenhagen the number surged to approximately 40,000 accredited representatives of nongovernmental organizations. Early on, NGO access to the negotiating floor was restricted by the secretariat because of the heavy influence of business and industry NGOs (BINGOs);[1] the secretariat wanted to restrict the influence of BINGOs and chose to banish all nonstate actors from the negotiating floor to achieve this result.[2]

Nonstate actors are given *one* formal intervention opportunity at each negotiating meeting of the UNFCCC. At the plenary session, each sector of nonstate actors is able to present opening comments to governments. Otherwise, interventions by NGOs must follow the available informal channels, and the NGO community—at the UNFCCC and at other hard-law forums—has found creative ways to exercise limited influence through these channels (see Dodds 2004). These circumstances require NGOs to build informal ties of trust with secretariat officials and members of government delegations that can be mobilized at critical

Table 7.1
Interview responses regarding the benefits of consultative status and informal ties with IGOs

Benefits of consultative status	Benefits of informal relationships
• Receipt of UN documents	• Interpretation of UN documents
• Distribution of position papers	• Feedback on position papers
• Access to UN meetings	• Insight into country delegation positions and political context
• Guidelines for agency accreditation and Meeting participation	• Insight into other UN agencies and personnel
	• Consideration when opportunities arise
	• Information and introduction re: other organizations with similar interests
	• Co-sponsorship of events and projects
	• Funding opportunities
	• Inside, "privileged" information

moments to increase NGO responsiveness and influence (Caniglia 2001; Dodds 2004 Hemmati 2002). Table 7.1 highlights the distinct benefits that NGOs receive from formal consultative status and informal ties with intergovernmental personnel.

To strengthen their position at the UNFCCC, NGOs formed a loose self-organizing committee, which meets daily and has been coordinated by Climate Action Network (CAN). CAN is a massive network of NGOs from around the world and carries a great deal of scientific and moral authority as a representative of civil society interests at the climate change talks; they also publish *ECO*, a daily NGO newsletter that reviews and comments on the negotiations expected to take place that day. Members of government delegations have been known to approach CAN to have statements published in *ECO*, which is one indicator of how successful this publication has been at elevating NGO viewpoints inside the UNFCCC (Pulver 2005). Throughout the negotiating sessions, the NGOs arrange meetings with government delegations and lobby those delegates in hallways, bathrooms, just about anywhere they can find them. One NGO delegate is reported to have taken up smoking as an excuse to congregate with government delegates as they smoked outside the negotiating hall![3]

In general, NGO influence is restricted to these informal avenues of access. As Newell (2008) points out, NGOs at the UNFCCC are restricted to traditional lobbying, shame-and-blame strategies, and watchdog roles. This does not suggest that nonstate actors cannot influence the process;

clear evidence exists that they have and will continue to press governments toward more equitable and creative solutions to climate change
(Pulver 2005; Roberts and Parks 2007). Nonetheless, because governments are accountable to the obligations made under treaties like the
Kyoto Protocol, those governments tend to restrict the extent to which
nonstate actor voices are included at the table.

While the UNFCCC has worked to keep access relatively open to
nonstate actor participation, including industry, youth, indigenous
peoples, scientists, and NGOs, in Copenhagen access to the Bella Center
became a central point of contention, particularly during the second
week of meetings. The conference facilities dictated that only around
one-third of the accredited NGOs could be in the building at one time.
As a result, lines of people running several football fields in length barely
moved in the cold and sometimes snowy Copenhagen winter. I personally
stood in line six hours on the second Monday before being told that no
further accreditation would take place that day. On Tuesday, I was in
line for seven hours outside in the snow and two hours inside the building before getting my coveted pass. By Wednesday, NGO admissions
were halted before noon, and by Friday, only ninety representatives from
a range of NGOs were allowed in the building. An alternative site several
miles from the conference center was opened for accredited participants
on Thursday, but the attendance there was very low. During my six days
in Copenhagen, I spent fewer than five hours inside Bella Center, nearly
twenty hours in line, and over $3,000.

The costs to representatives of developing-country NGOs and indigenous peoples were notable. Trust and transparency came into question,
contributing considerably to the overall sense of desperation and failure
in Copenhagen. A group of over fifty NGOs, including Climate Action
Network Europe, Friends of the Earth International, and Third World
Network, submitted a letter to Connie Hedegaard (president of COP15)
and Yvo de Boer (executive secretary of UNFCCC) denouncing the participation limits. Part of the letter reads: "The negotiations under the
UNFCCC and the Kyoto Protocol have a huge and increasing impact on
the lives of ordinary people all over the world. Their participation in the
climate negotiations as members of civil society and peoples' movements
is absolutely crucial for ensuring that the Copenhagen outcomes are just,
effective and legitimate" ("NGOs Slam 'Undemocratic' UN Talks"
2010). Several videos on YouTube feature the sea of people waiting in
line, day after day, and several others highlight that even those on the
inside were met with closed-door meetings and severe participation

restrictions. One video pictures Ben Powless of the Indigenous Environmental Network (IEN) and other members of the indigenous peoples' caucus being completely ignored during a meeting where they were invited to discuss their views on the UNFCCC's forest initiative REDD (*REDD* 2009).

Despite the problems, several interesting dynamics make Copenhagen a fascinating puzzle for international governance. To begin with, the lines between "outsiders" and "insiders" were blurred more than at any other conference I have attended over the past fifteen years. Accredited groups staged approved demonstrations inside Bella Center. This practice is not unprecedented, but the number and range of those in Copenhagen took the practice to a new level. Avaaz and Climate Action Network International staged elaborate presentations of the Fossil of the Day Awards, the indigenous peoples' caucus played drums and chanted prayers, and on Wednesday, December 16, at least 100 accredited participants, including some government delegates, staged a walkout and joined protestors on the outside to demand system change and climate justice. Yvo de Boer was visibly angry with "inside" NGO representatives who confronted him about access restrictions (EUXTV 2009). "Is that how you want to do it?" he asked. "I have been reasonable throughout my three years in this job . . . are you willing to talk to me or do you wish to fight me?" Access problems were not unique to NGOs. One of China's top delegates was refused entrance three times, even though he had all the necessary accreditation paperwork (The Copenhagen Post 2009). Industry representatives, ministry employees, scientists, and journalists alike faced the long, cold lines and access restrictions in Copenhagen. The three ministry employees who were in line with me chanted, "What do we want? Access! When do we want it? Now," along with everyone else in line, illustrating the diffusion of movement tactics across sectors.

"Insider" and "outsider" dynamics were further complicated by interactions among governments. Some delegations were present and actively involved in crafting agreement language during the entire two weeks of conference meetings. Others, like the United States and China, swept in during the final days of the conference and usurped the UN negotiation process in backdoor meetings. After Obama spoke at the Friday plenary, Morales of Bolivia and Chavez of Venezuela chastised these backdoor tactics and joined a coalition of several governments that refused to accept the Copenhagen Accord because of its flagrant disrespect of the negotiation process. Though most delegations came on board to support the accord, some were concerned that these dynamics could threaten the legitimacy of UN negotiations for the near future and could require a reconsideration of the entire UN conference model of evolving consensus through face-to-face negotiations (Hultman 2009).

The UNFCCC meeting in Copenhagen suggests a clash between the standard operating procedures of hard-law venues and rising global scrutiny of international affairs. For the moment, however, business as usual restricts access to government delegations and their accredited representatives. The UN and its constituent hard-law agencies will have to go further than saying they are participatory to satisfy the increasing demands of nonstate actor groups. Of course, broadening participation in a true sense is extremely difficult, given an international system based on the sovereignty of nation-states, rather than on the self-determination of individual citizens. With that in mind, I now turn to a soft-law institution that is much more amenable to nonstate actor participation.

The UNCSD

Formulated during the 1992 United Nations Conference on Environment and Development (the UNCED "Earth Summit"), the UNCSD was established to facilitate and monitor the implementation of UNCED conference agreements, most notably Agenda 21, which is the broad-sweeping sustainable development agenda for the twenty-first century drafted during the Earth Summit. The commission's focus has subsequently expanded to include oversight of the Barbados Program of Action for Small Island Developing States[4] and the Johannesburg Plan of Implementation.[5] The commission is a high-level forum, meaning it involves minister-level government officials as well as senior-level United Nations staff members (and often heads of state), and meets in New York City annually in a two-year cycle of review and policy. The range of government ministers engaged at the CSD varies widely and includes such areas as energy, natural resources, agriculture, oceans/fisheries, development, forestry, and occasionally foreign affairs. The United Nations Division for Sustainable Development serves as the secretariat for the UNCSD.[6]

The Division for Sustainable Development is charged with three primary goals: "Integration of the social, economic and environmental dimensions of sustainable development in policy-making at international, regional and national levels; Wide-spread adoption of an integrated, cross-sectoral and broadly participatory approach to sustainable development; and Measurable progress in the implementation of the goals and targets of the Johannesburg Plan of Implementation" (UN Department of Economic and Social Affairs 2010).

Like all UN agencies, the UNCSD is an intergovernmental forum first, designed to serve the needs of member governments. The creation of the CSD was welcomed by the majority of UN member nations and their constituents, but often for different reasons. Developing countries were pleased that the CSD elevated development within the "environmental" governance system (Doran and Van Alstine 2007). Industry, too, was pleased to see development more central to the discussion (Bernstein 2001). NGOs, citizen groups, and more environmentally progressive states were hopeful that the CSD would serve as a prominent rule-making and oversight organization and elevate environmental issues to compete with the international financial institutions, which they saw as frequent trump cards played against international and national environmental and labor laws. UNEP was rumored to object strongly to the need for a new environmental body and was especially indignant when the CSD was assigned to act as the coordinating body for the environmental efforts of the United Nations.

Despite the wishes of those who wanted the CSD to be a strong, rule-making body with enforcement capabilities, the commission's mandate is primarily normative. The CSD drafts principles related to the achievement of Agenda 21 and sustainable development in the language of "shoulds" rather than "shalls" and serves more as a consensus-building organization than an enforcement agency. On the positive side, this was intended to encourage open discussion and adoption of agreements on language that might go beyond what many countries would otherwise accept. In practice, especially in recent years, it has frequently led to lengthy discussions over subtle shades of language that often end up watered down to a lowest common denominator that does not hold the force of law.

Over its fifteen years, the CSD has undergone two reviews. The first took place in 1997 at the UN General Assembly, also known as the Rio +5 session. The news was generally disappointing, since most attendees concluded that little notable progress had been made in the first five years after adoption of Agenda 21. Criticisms were most scathing in two areas: that financial commitments fell short of Agenda 21 targets and that there was confusion over how to measure the achievement of sustainable development. Attendance at CSD meetings in 1997 indicated a healthy, vibrant organization, in which most Major Groups organizations and member nations invested with hope and vigor. This was also the first year for the multistakeholder dialogs, designed to facilitate collaborative and rigorous review of each year's focal topics (e.g., energy, agriculture, tourism, etc.), which will be described in more detail later.

The second review took place in the run-up to and during the Johannesburg World Summit on Sustainable Development, which took place in 2002. Although most agreed that progress toward the achievement of Agenda 21 goals was not significantly greater in 2002 than it was in 1997, the organization was deemed a success on other important levels. Attendance at the annual meetings in New York remained high, diverse, engaged, and motivated. In the area of multistakeholder participation, the CSD was recognized as a leader, providing a model for nonstate actor inclusion for the rest of the UN system (Hemmati 2002). In the field of sustainable development specifically, the Indicators Project received accolades for the progress its participants had made toward developing a useful and consensus-based set of measurements and criteria with which to document sustainable development activities at local, state, and international levels (Shah 2004). Furthermore, no one could debate the fact that sustainable development had become a household word in many nations around the world, although key Northern governments like the United States and Australia continued to resist (if not deny) serious commitments to balance the three pillars of sustainable development.

Many are hopeful that the CSD will be revitalized at the 2012 review in Mexico City. First suggested by a quasi-nongovernmental organization called Stakeholder Forum, discussions among key governments have resulted in a consensus that a high-level review of the CSD could catalyze renewed momentum for this commission and increase international awareness of the importance of an integrated sustainable development strategy when addressing pressing issues such as climate change:

Sustainable Development has suffered from a lack of public, political and media attention. As a result the profile of the sustainable development agenda has gradually declined since the Rio Earth Summit in 1992, momentum for change has been lost, and the efficacy of the Commission on Sustainable Development has subsequently been questioned. In this context, Climate Change and the Millennium Development Goals have subsumed the international agenda. To encourage governments around the world to deliver on the commitments made at Rio and Johannesburg, and to address the multi-faceted challenges for the future, an open, inclusive, high-profile global event is required to initiate and accelerate change and hold the international community to account (*The Denostia Declaration* 2008).

The UNCSD and Environmental Justice

Drawing from the theoretical framework previously articulated, the UNCSD provides an excellent intervention point for activists who hope to advance policy instruments that favor environmental justice. In particular, it meets all three criteria set forth by Clemmens and Cook (1999). Levels of social heterogeneity are among the highest in any UN body and are certainly the highest and most purposively created among the two organizations reviewed here (Hemmati 2002; Doran and Van Alstine 2007). Over 200 nonstate organization representatives attended the first UNCSD meeting in 1993, and by 2000, there were over 700 in attendance (Dodds 2002). All associated meetings are open to accredited nonstate actors, and the commission provides small grants to enable traditionally underrepresented groups to send delegates (CBI 2002). Responsibility for the achievement of sustainable development is clearly ascribed to nonstate actors in Agenda 21 under the rubric of the Major Groups, which include youth, farmers, women, indigenous peoples, scientists, NGOs, industry, trade unions, and local authorities. Organizations in each of these Groups is authorized to send representation to the UNCSD meetings, provided they seek and gain consultative or observer status. The commission also has a broader interpretation of the types of groups that can gain observer status than most UN agencies, allowing local and regional organizations to apply as long as their work falls within the purview of the UNCSD.[7] Coordination of Major Groups input is handled within the secretariat by an NGO liaison. The extent to which these nonstate organizations are able to passively observe official meetings, organize their own meetings (in the form of caucuses and side events), present their projects, intervene or speak at official sessions, and negotiate/lobby directly with government officials is unprecedented (Hemmati 2002; Dodds 2004).

Partnerships Fairs have been a part of CSD annual meetings since 2004 and include training sessions and highlight successful partnerships across stakeholder groups that are recognized by the UNCSD secretariat for their work toward the implementation of Agenda 21. Most partnerships are between or among governments, industry, scientists, and NGOs, while only a small number incorporate the least represented groups, such as indigenous peoples, women, and youth (UN Division for Sustainable Development 2007). To encourage wider participation in such partnerships, the CSD organizes an annual Partnerships Fair, hosts an interactive partnerships website, and publishes *Partnerships Wire*, a newsletter featuring partnership initiatives and insights. According to the Secretary

General's report, 207 partnerships had participated in Partnerships Fairs since their inception.

Given the diversity of attendees, it should not be surprising that "social networks are fragmented and cross important social cleavages" (Clemens and Cook 1999, 451). The commission is notorious as a site where the contentious dimensions of international environmental politics collide: North versus South, rich versus poor, and the classic balancing act required between people, prosperity, and planet. Despite such conflicts, the commission and its participants are flexible and resilient, often reinventing themselves,[8] which is but one indicator that the commission's "models of action are understood to be discretionary" (Clemens and Cook 1999, 451). This discretionary nature comes in part from the nature of soft-law governance, since "the obligatory component is discretionary" (Emadi-Coffin 2002). However, the sweeping scope of the sustainable development project, coupled with the hybrid-governance character of the UNCSD, builds in discretion at multiple levels.

Therefore, while the UNCSD is a soft-law body with a broad and sometimes amorphous mandate, these very characteristics increase the likelihood that nonstate actor interventions can influence policies in their favor. In the area of environmental justice in particular, the institution is an ideal target. The explicit acknowledgment of the central role of women, farmers, indigenous peoples, NGOs, and youth in the achievement of UNCSD goals opens doors that are closed in most venues of global environmental governance; the explicit acknowledgment that equity is central to the achievement of sustainable development provides leverage that does not exist elsewhere (Roberts and Parks 2007). To facilitate the pursuit of these goals, the UNCSD has developed multiple mechanisms for the inclusion of nonstate actors, which provide unprecedented opportunities for social movements to work directly with governments to craft policies focused on environmental justice.

Points of Improvement for the UNCSD

The policy potential of the UNCSD stems predominately from its openness to vastly broader participation of the Major Groups than is afforded by other institutions of global environmental governance. Two specific innovations already cited—the Multi-stakeholder Dialogues and the Partnerships Fairs—are examples of the creative governance that have prospered at the UNCSD. More recently, however, the innovations have slowed, and attendance of NGOs and other nonstate actors has declined. I believe this decline is largely due to a subtle disenfranchisement of nonstate actor participation, which can be best seen in changes made in the multistakeholder dialogues.

While the overall integration of major groups at the UNCSD has vastly increased since Johannesburg, the interactive dialogs with Major Groups have lost much of their effectiveness. The UNCSD Multi-stakeholder Dialogues, first launched at CSD6 in 1997, have served as a model for hybrid governance across and beyond the UN system (Hemmati 2002; CBI 2002). Their earlier effectiveness stemmed largely from their facilitative structure, which enabled ample time for focused, interactive exchange. Post-Johannesburg, the length of the dialogs has been vastly shortened, leaving insufficient time for collaborative and synthetic exchange.

Pre-Johannesburg, the dialogs consisted of twelve hours of focused discussion, broken into four 3-hour sessions. These were typically held over the course of two days, and efforts were made to ensure they were scheduled at times that did not compete with other sessions. Each session began with 8-minute opening statements by each major group and one 8-minute statement each from a Northern and Southern government representative. After these statements, the floor was opened for 2-minute reaction statements from authorized participants who wished to clarify, extend, or build on the ideas that had been entered for consideration. Most years, the chair of the dialog meeting, who was usually also the chair of the UNCSD and a high-level government official, choreographed the conversation to encourage collaborative problem solving and the resolution of long-standing sectoral disagreements. The results were impressive to observe, especially in those years when multisectoral initiatives, such as the Sustainable Agriculture and Rural Development initiative (SARD) and the Multi-stakeholder Review of Voluntary Initiatives, were born from the dialogs and endured well beyond the UNCSD meetings.

Ten years later, during CSD16, the dialogs were allotted approximately one-third of the time, broken into 1.5-hour slots, spread across the two weeks of meetings, and they competed with other sessions. The challenges presented by this structure were highlighted by the first dialog at CSD16. Each major group was asked to present a three-minute statement representing their sectors' views on agriculture and rural development. The difficulty of this task was illustrated by the fact that only one of the groups presented a statement in three minutes or less. While some interaction took place between the Major Groups and governments, there was certainly insufficient time to address any dimension of agriculture or rural development in a way that recognized its complexity. In essence, this dialog bit off far more than it could chew and retired substantive rigor in favor of symbolism.

The purpose of the dialogs is to facilitate collaboration between governments and the Major Groups. The pre-Johannesburg dialogs were characterized by mutual exchange of best practices, the establishment of new models for the achievement of sustainable development, and synergistic outcomes that continued Major Group–government interaction beyond the dialog sessions and well after the UNCSD meeting. The strides gained were in large part facilitated by a structure that encouraged conversations that were focused on very specific dimensions of the year's theme.

For example, CSD6, which focused on the role of industry in achieving sustainable development, featured four sessions at its dialog: responsible entrepreneurship, voluntary initiatives, technology cooperation and assessment, and industry and freshwater. Each of these specific topics was addressed in a three-hour conversation, enabling extensive and thorough discussions that confronted and often overcame strong sectoral disagreements. These 1997–2001 dialogs frequently addressed questions of program implementation, monitoring, reporting, and multistakeholder review; they allowed time for the Major Groups to highlight their perspectives on existing programs and make suggestions for their improvement on the ground. Such detailed and complex analyses were only possible given (1) a focused topic and (2) ample time.

Recently, a new director of the Division on Sustainable Development was appointed. At the intersessional meeting in February 2009, the new director asked an NGO representative how "new energy" could be infused into the UNCSD. Given the analysis here, one clear recommendation would be to return to previous models of Major Group participation that allowed ample time for debate and discussion with governments regarding specific policy dimensions of the achievement of sustainable development. Likewise, this goal would be a valuable target of NGO/social movement activities at the UNCSD.

General Evaluation of the Case Studies

This case analysis has been based on Clemens and Cook's (1999) model of institutional characteristics that facilitate change. This choice is based on the realization that institutions tend to reproduce dominant social arrangements and resist intervention from less powerful actors. Institutional-change scholars and students of the role of culture in institutions have shown, however, that NGOs, norm entrepreneurs, and other underrepresented groups have—in both historical and contemporary times—exerted influence in such resistant institutions (Clemens and Cook 1999; Finnemore and Sikkink 1998; Meyer et al. 1997; Boli and Thomas 1997; Wuthnow 1989). However, certain characteristics of institutions make them more amenable to change than others. Specifically, Clemens and Cook (1999) argue that (a) diversity of participants, (b) representation that crosses significant social cleavages, and (c) contested models of action are all facilitative of social change. My argument, then, is that social movements should be aware of how institutions of global governance compare along these lines.

The UNFCCC meeting in Copenhagen was relatively open to a diversity of participants during the first week of meetings, but as heads of state arrived, most NGOs and other nonstate actors were systematically banished from the building. Excluding such a wide range of nonstate actors limits the diversity of views, and the prominent social cleavages become those that exist between nation-states, rather than those that exist across other important sectors of society. This is precisely what happened to the discourse in Copenhagen: countries increasingly focused on which nations were responsible for the majority of greenhouse gas emissions, what they had gained during the era of dirty development, and how reductions in greenhouse gas emissions would lead to unequal disadvantage among nation-states. The target emission reductions found in early versions of the negotiating text disappeared, and only the least-common-denominator acknowledgment of the need to keep temperature rises to below 2 degrees Celsius remained. Despite the cacophony of banners, signs, buttons, and t-shirts on display, calling for an aggressive, binding agreement, governments closed out the crowd like players at the free-throw line and focused on scoring political points. And, given a geopolitical climate marked by the tensions of economic crisis and war (among others), Clemens and Cook's framework would predict similar outcomes in most hard law institutions.

Soft-law institutions like the UNCSD do not typically garner the same level of attention as treaty institutions like the UNFCCC. Their work tends to stay below the radar, since the language being debated and honed does not imply immediate change. Likewise, the sense of urgency that drove thousands of activists to Copenhagen does not surround institutions of soft law. However, this is precisely why such venues hold the most promise for incorporating the views of nonstate actors. The CSD in particular is arguably the most open institution in the United

Nations system. They have accredited the widest range of nonstate actors, including local and regional organizations; they have structured dialogs, which are designed to bring this diversity of participants into conversation with each other; and they have partnership fairs that encourage and feature cross-sectoral cooperation. The breadth of sustainable development has produced an impressive array of working models, such as beach and hotel certification programs, multistakeholder reviews of voluntary industry initiatives, indigenous people's tribunals, and agricultural subsidy reviews, to name just a few. In recent years, I have witnessed a narrowing of public participation at the CSD; however, I suspect this narrowing is equally the result of NGOs and other nonstate actors divesting from this institution, rather than from government attempts to limit access. One outcome of understanding how institutions compare in these regards would be for NGOs and social movement groups to invest their scarce resources in the venue most amenable to change. Given that many NGOs in the global South in particular lack sufficient resources to participate in numerous international meetings, this strategy might increase the effectiveness of a group's interventions. On the other hand, this comparison suggests that an effective movement-wide strategy might be loosely designed to target each institution in ways that emphasize the specific opportunities it affords. This approach is already pursued by some NGOs active at the UNCSD, as illustrated by the following comment made to me during a recent interview: "We look at the CSD as the workshop where we create consensus on the language of sustainable development. Once we have the language, then we can lobby for the implementation of that language in other venues of the United Nations, but without the language we cannot make progress on environmental rights or environmental justice."

This comment also highlights a possible division of labor that exists not only between these specific institutions but between the broad categories of international institutions they represent. Generally speaking, soft-law institutions like the UNCSD serve as centers for the negotiation of global norms of appropriate nation-state behavior (Boli and Thomas 1997; Finnemore and Sikkink 1998; Emadi-Coffin 2002); such norms then find specificity and forcefulness in treaty organizations like the UNFCCC. In fact, my interview participants confirm that these two organizations in particular are seen by some NGOs to work in tandem in the climate policy arena: "Just now, groups are returning to CSD—some who left after Jo'burg [Johannesburg]—because they are concerned about climate change. They said, okay, let's give this another try and see if the CSD can influence the climate change talks. They, too, see the CSD as a testing ground for language." That said, however, I argue that if a group has only enough resources to engage in one of these institutions, the UNCSD is likely to provide the most satisfying results in terms of policy changes that support environmental justice.

As I indicated in my discussion of the strategies pursued by NGOs at the UNFCCC, nonstate actors—especially those who have engaged for many years in international negotiations—have developed a standard set of intervention strategies that facilitate their influence at hard-law forums (see Dodds 2004). Soft-law forums like the UNCSD offer a wider range of strategies, which sometimes serves to diffuse NGO efforts in these forums. In previous studies, I have elaborated in detail on scholarship that suggests NGO and movement efforts in such arenas are most effective in the area of norm articulation (Caniglia 2001, Caniglia and Sarabia 2003). Karkkainen (2004) describes forums like the UNCSD as hybrid governance structures, where broad stakeholder participation in the articulation of standards and models of action predominate. I have also argued that it is just this type of arena where NGOs and other nonstate actors can have the most impact on the evolution of environmental policies, because this state of policy winnowing and concept debate allows "norm entrepreneurs" (Caniglia 2008; Finnemore and Sikkink 1998) to engage governments, industry, and other power brokers in a more creative and open forum of discussion than institutions of hard law afford (Caniglia and Sarabia 2003). Therefore, given that the UNCSD illustrates the most amenable characteristics for NGO/social movement effectiveness, I have elaborated above some specific recommendations for changes to the multistakeholder dialogs that I feel will pave an even more effective path for the articulation of policies at the UNCSD that facilitate environmental justice.

Discussion and Conclusions

Issues of justice are central to the achievement of sustainable development (Roberts and Parks 2007; O'Connor 2008; Lewis, Gould, and Roberts 2003). Despite this agreement, the achievement of environmental justice via international institutions has been hampered by numerous crosscutting debates, national interests, and a decentralized international environmental governance structure. This chapter has tried to clarify some of the confusion surrounding the global environmental governance system by examining two types of institutions. The UNCSD is a soft-law agency of the United Nations system and is charged to bring together diverse stake-holders to build sets of consensus principles regarding the achievement of sustainable development. And the UNFCCC is the secretariat for the Kyoto Protocol—a hard-law treaty that holds government signatories accountable to their commitments to reduce greenhouse gases.

Drawing from theories of institutional change and social movement strategies, I put forth a framework by which to evaluate each of these institutions as potential sites for advancing environmental justice policies. Due to their organizational designs, neither of these institutions can stand alone in this task. Rather, I recommend that environmental justice advocates develop a multilayered strategy to target each of these organizations in the ways they are best suited to support the movement. The UNFCCC provides access points for NGOs and environmental justice advocates to engage, but those intervention points are limited due to the hard-law nature of treaty negotiations. Collaborative exchange between governments and nonstate actors is limited to strictly consultative forums, including side events and panels. NGOs face similar limitations across the UN system (Emadi-Coffin 2002; Dodds 2004) and have honed a toolkit of strategies to effectively nudge governments in the direction of their interests. Most of these strategies require multiple years of participation in UN meetings to leverage them effectively, because they require informal relationships of trust with intergovernmental and governmental representatives to operate most effectively (Dodds 2004. Nonetheless, numerous UN-savvy environmental NGOs have joined forces to target UNFCCC talks. Pulver's (2005) examination of how NGO positions gained favor over those of opposing industry BINGOs illustrates that environmental justice advocates can indeed impact negotiations in this and other hard-law venues.

In the end, however, any strategy for the articulation of more justice-oriented policies should target the UNCSD. Charged with oversight of the implementation of Agenda 21, the organization is the only United Nations agency specifically responsible for advancing all three pillars of sustainable development—the environment, economy, and equity. From the organization's inception following the Rio Earth Summit in 1992, the UNCSD has brought together NGOs, women's groups, farmers, scientists, youth, industry, local authorities, and governments North and South in an effort to achieve a just and sustainable balance between development and the natural environment. Numerous factors have caused NGOs and the media to deemphasize the UNCSD in recent years, including an increased focus on climate change. Recent tendencies within the UNCSD to minimize dialog with NGOs and other major groups have perpetuated the trend of important stakeholders abandoning the institution. However, the UNCSD still occupies a unique position in the architecture of global environmental governance as the most open and inclusive site for the articulation of principles for the achievement of sustainable development—a unique role that can be harnessed for the advancement of environmental justice.

Notes

1. There are currently nine NGO constituencies: BINGO (business and industry NGOs), ENGO (environmental NGOs), TUNGO (trade union NGOs), IPO (indigenous peoples' organizations), LGMA (local government and municipal authorities), RINGO (research-oriented and independent organizations), YUNGO (youth NGOs), Faith (faith-based NGOs), and Gender (gender-based NGOs).

2. To learn more about conflict between BINGOs and NGOs at the UNFCCC, see Pulver 2005.

3. Personal interview.

4. The Barbados Programme of Action (BPoA) was adopted at the first Global Conference on Sustainable Development of SIDS in Barbados in 1994.

5. The Johannesburg Plan of Implementation was drafted at the World Summit for Sustainable Development, which was held in Johannesburg, South Africa, in 2002.

6. To manage this jurisdictional overlap in a way that reduced redundancy and increased cooperation, the UN charged the UNCSD with coordinating the activities of several environmentally focused IGOs. Originally, the UNCSD accomplished this coordination under the umbrella of the Inter-Agency Cooperation Committee. In 1993, the IACC was replaced by the Division for Sustainable Development (DSD), which currently serves as the official secretariat for the Commission on Sustainable Development.

7. Most UN agencies restrict observer and consultative status to international organizations, which must show memberships that span multiple nations.

8. After the UNCSD NGO Steering Committee was affectively abandoned in 2001, the NGOs reinvented their self-governance structure as SDIN, which currently serves as the informal coordinator of NGO participation at the commission. Similarly, the commission itself has consistently morphed to encompass emerging trends. One recent example is the inclusion of "Partnership Fairs" to facilitate successful multisectoral partnerships engaged in the implementation of commission goals.

References

Athanasiou, Tom. 2010. After Copenhagen: On being sadder but wiser, China, and justice as the way forward. http://www.ecoequity.org/2010/01/after-copenhagen/.

Bernstein, Steven. 2001. *The Compromise of Liberal Environmentalism.* New York: Columbia University Press.

Boli, John, and George M. Thomas. 1997. World culture in the world polity: A century of international non-governmental organization. *American Sociological Review* 62:171–190.

Caniglia, Beth Schaefer, and Daniel Sarabia. 2003. Articulating sustainable development: Multi-stakeholder dialogues & the creation of global environmental discourse. Paper presented at the Annual Meeting of the American Sociological Association, Atlanta, August.

Caniglia, Beth Schaefer. 2001. Informal alliances vs. institutional ties: The effects of elite alliances on environmental TSMO network positions. *Mobilization* 6(1):37–54.

Caniglia, Beth Schaefer. 2008. CSD then and now: How the CSD dialogue has changed and what was lost along the way. *Outreach Issues*, May 15, 8–9.

Chiang, Pie-Heng. 1981. *Non-Governmental Organizations at the United Nations: Identity, Role and Function.* New York: Praeger.

Clemens, Elizabeth, and James Cook. 1999. Politics and Institutionalism: Explaining Durability and Change. *Annual Review of Sociology* 25:441–466.

Consensus Building Institute (CBI). 2002. Multi-stakeholder dialogues: Learning from the UNCSD experience. DESA/DSD/PC3/BP4. Boston: Consensus Building Institute.

Copenhagen Post. 2009. http://www.cphpost.dk/climate/91-climate/47721-top-delegate-refused-cop15-access.html.

The Denostia Declaration. 2008. Stakeholder Forum. http://www.earthsummit2012 .org/fileadmin/files/Earth_Summit_2012/Earth_Summit_2012_Donostia_Declaration __2_.pdf.

Dodds, Felix. 2002. The context: Multi-stakeholder processes and global governance. In Hemmati, Minu, ed., *Multi-Stakeholder Processes for Governance and Sustainability,* 26–39. London: Earthscan.

Dodds, Felix, and Michael Strauss. 2004. *How to Lobby at Intergovernmental Meetings or Mine is a Café Latte.* London: Earthscan.

Doran, Peter, and James Van Alstine. 2007. The Fourteenth Session of the UN Commission on Sustainable Development: The Energy Session. *Environmental Politics* 16(1):130–141.

Emadi-Coffin, Barbara. 2002. *Rethinking International Organization: Deregulation & Global Governance.* New York: Routledge.

EUXTV. 2009. Yvo de Boer tells NGOs to leave COP15 talks in Copenhagen. December 16. http://www.youtube.com/watch?v=-nU9-gWtyHw.

Finnemore, Martha, and Kathryn Sikkink. 1998. International norm dynamics and political change. *International Organization* 52:887–917.

Fisher, Dana R. 2004. *National Governance and the Global Climate Change Regime.* Lanham, MD: Rowman & Littlefield.

Fisher, William F. 1997. Doing good? The politics and antipolitics of NGO practices. *Annual Review of Anthropology* 26:439–464.

Frank, David John, Ann Hironaka, and Evan Schofer. 2000. The nation-state and the natural environment over the twentieth century. *American Sociological Review* 65(1):96–116.

Gomez, Jim. 2010. End to bickering urged to achieve new climate pact: Environmental officials say bickering and mistrust must end for sake of new UN climate pact. Associated Press, February 26. http://abcnews.go.com/Business/wireStory?id=9953398.

Gordenker, Leon, and Thomas G. Weiss. 1995. NGO participation in the international policy process. *Third World Quarterly* 16:543–555.

Haines, Herbert H. 1984. Black radicalization and the funding of civil rights: 1957–1970. *Social Problems* 32:31–43.

Hemmati, Minu. 2002. *Multi-stakeholder Processes for Governance and Sustainability: Beyond Deadlock and Conflict*. London: Earthscan.

Hultman, Nathan. 2009. The Copenhagen governance gap. December 16. http://www.brookings.edu/opinions/2009/1216_copenhagen_hultman.aspx.

Ivanova, Maria, and Jennifer Roy. 2007. The architecture of global environmental governance: Pros and cons of multiplicity. In Lydia Swart and Estelle Perry, eds., *Global Environmental Governance: Perspectives on the Current Debate*, 48–66. New York: Center for UN Reform Education.

Jenkins, J. Craig, and Craig M. Ekert. 1986. Channeling black insurgency. *American Sociological Review* 51:812–829.

Karkkainen, Bradley C. 2004. Post-sovereign environmental governance. *Global Environmental Politics* 4(1):72–96.

Keck, Margaret E., and Kathryn Sikkink. 1998. *Activists Beyond Borders: Advocacy Networks in International Politics*. Ithaca, NY: Cornell University Press.

Lewis, Tammy, Kenneth Gould, and J. Timmons Roberts. 2003. From blue-green coalitions to blue-green partnerships? Creating enduring institutions through just transition, climate justice and the World Social Forum. Paper presented at the 2003 American Sociological Association Annual Meeting, San Francisco.

McAdam, Doug. 1982. *Political Process and the Development of Black Insurgency, 1930–1970*. Chicago: University of Chicago Press.

McCarthy, John, and Mayer Zald. 1977. Resource mobilization and social movements: A partial theory. *American Journal of Sociology* 82(6):1212–1241.

McCarthy, John, and Mayer Zald. 1987. Appendix: The trend of social movements in America: Professionalization and resource mobilization. In Mayer Zald and John McCarthy, eds., *Social Movements in an Organizational Society*, 337–392. New Brunswick, NJ: Transaction Books.

Meyer, John, John Boli, George M. Thomas, and Francisco O. Ramirez. 1997. World society and the nation-state. *American Journal of Sociology* 103:144–181.

Meyers, David S. 2006. *The Politics of Protest: Social Movements in America.* Oxford: Oxford University Press.

Minkoff, Debra C. 1994. From service provision to institutional advocacy: The shifting legitimacy of organizational forms. *Social Forces* 72:943–969.

Newell, Peter. 2008. Civil society, corporate accountability and the politics of climate change. *Global Environmental Politics* 8(3):122–153.

NGOs slam "undemocratic" UN talks. 2010. Oneworld.net, March 7. http://uk.oneworld.net/article/view/164207/1/.

O'Connor, David. 2008. Governing the global commons: Linking carbon storage and biodiversity conservation in tropical forests. *Global Environmental Change* 18(3):368–374.

Pellow, David Naguib. 2007. *Resisting Global Toxics: Transnational Movements for Environmental Justice.* Cambridge, MA: MIT Press.

Porter, Gareth, Janet Welsh Brown, and Pamela S. Chasek. 2000. *Global Environmental Politics.* 2nd ed. Boulder, CO: Westview Press.

President Obama's dramatic climate meet. 2009. Politico, December 18. http://www.politico.com/news/stories/1209/30801.html.

Pulver, Simone. 2005. A public sphere in international environmental politics: The case of the Kyoto Protocol negotiations. Paper presented at the 2005 Berlin Conference on the Human Dimensions of Global Environmental Change: International Organizations and Global Environmental Governance, December 2–3, 2005.

REDD: *Indigenous Peoples Not Allowed to Speak at UNFCCC.* 2009. SommerFilms, December 10. http://www.youtube.com/watch?v=brsqUgbBHu0&feature=related.

Riker, James V. 1995. From cooptation to cooperation in government-NGO relations: Toward an enabling policy environment for people-centered development in Asia. In Neoleen Heyzer, James V. Riker, and Antonio B. Quizon, eds., *Government-NGO Relations in Asia: Prospects and Challenges for People-Centered Development,* 91–130. New York: St. Martin's Press.

Risse-Kappen, Thomas. 1995. *Bringing transnational relations back: Non-State Actors, Domestic Structures and International Institutions.* Cambridge: Cambridge University Press.

Roberts, J. Timmons. 2009. In the end, a realist's deal. *Copenhagen Journal,* December 21. http://today.brown.edu/articles/2009/12/cop15-final.

Roberts, J. Timmons, and Bradley C. Parks. 2007. *A Climate of Injustice: Global Inequality, North-South Politics, and Climate Policy.* Cambridge, MA: MIT Press.

Shah, Reena. 2004. CSD indicators of sustainable development—recent developments and activities. Paper presented at the Assessment of Sustainability Indicators Workshop, Prague, Czech Republic.

Skolnick, Jerome. 1969. *Politics of Protest: The Skolnick Report.* Hendersonville, TN: Ballentine Press.

Smith, Jackie. 2004. The World Social Forum and the challenges of global democracy. *Global Networks* 4:413–421.

Summary of the Copenhagen Climate Change Conference, 7–19 December 2009. 2009. *Earth Negotiations Bulletin.* http://www.iisd.ca/vol12/enb12459e.html.

Tarrow, Sidney. 1988. National politics and collective action: Recent theory and research in Western Europe and the United States. *American Review of Sociology* 14:421–440.

Tarrow, Sidney. 1998. *Power in Movement: Social Movements and Contentious Politics*, 2nd edition. Cambridge: Cambridge University Press.

Tarrow, Sidney. 2005. *The New Transnational Activism.* Cambridge Studies in Contentious Politics. Cambridge: Cambridge University Press.

Third World Network. 2004. *The Cardoso Report on UN-Civil Society Relations: A Third World Network Analysis.* www.twnside.org.

UN Department of Economic and Social Affairs. 2010. http://www.un.org/esa/dsd/dsd/dsd_index.shtml.

UN Division for Sustainable Development. 2007. Secretary General's Report on Partnerships. http://www.un.org/esa/dsd/dsd_aofw_par/par_csdfair17_docu.shtml.

UN Framework Convention on Climate Change. 2008. Kyoto Protocol: Status of ratification. http://unfccc.int/kyoto_protocol/status_of_ratification/items/2613.php.

Weiss, Thomas G., and Leon Gordenker, eds. 1996. *NGOs, The UN, & Global Governance.* Boulder, CO: Lynne Rienner.

Willetts, Peter. 1996. *The Conscience of the World: The Influence of NGOs at the United Nations.* Washington, DC: Brookings Institution

Willetts, Peter. 2006. The Cardoso Report on the UN and Civil Society: Functionalism, global corporatism or global democracy? *Global Governance* 12:305–324.

Wuthnow, Robert. 1989. *Communities of Discourse: Ideology and Social Structure in the Reformation, the Enlightenment, and European Socialism.* Cambridge, MA: Harvard University Press.

Zald, Mayer N. 2000. Ideologically structured action: An enlarged agenda for social movement research. *Mobilization* 5:1–16.

III
Networked Responses to Global Inequality

8

Governing and Contesting China's Oil Operations in the Global South

Patricia Widener

Research indicates that each step of the oil supply chain has the potential to threaten the health of communities and ecosystems,[1] while oil extraction and the related elements of the supply chain often fail to promote local employment, technology transfers, and local economic linkages (Arakan Oil Watch 2008; Caldwell 1986; Karl 1997; Renner 2002). Unless coupled with a state and industry commitment to the environment and to participatory spaces for affected communities, oil extraction has proven to be detrimental to neighboring communities and ecosystems. To be sure, oil-related injustices are twofold. On the one hand, they have been perpetuated nationally by unresponsive state leaders who have failed to provide the most basic necessities for the most oil-impacted communities. On the other hand, they have also been perpetuated by Northern corporations, policies, and consumption patterns, which seek fossil fuels worldwide. Combined, these national and global inequities have generated nearly three decades worth of local, national, and transnational oil disputes.

It is within this milieu of conflict and inequity that Chinese oil operators have expanded overseas. Chinese firms began entering Africa's oil fields in the early 1990s and courting and being courted by South American leaders a decade later.[2] China's state-owned enterprises (SOEs), which have expanded into new terrain or replaced Northern firms and financiers when they have abandoned politically risky ventures or low-yield fields,[3] may even aggravate human rights abuses, labor injustices, and ecological destruction if they weather political instability, short-term profit demands, community protest, and social unrest better than Northern firms.

In defense of China's overseas operations, there is no "enforceable code" with regard to human rights for China's SOEs to follow (Meintjes 2000, 94), while global standards on labor issues, affected communities, and the environment remain inadequate and unjust in places where oil is found. Nevertheless, and in contrast to egregious charges against China, its engineers and technocrats are equipped with the technology and skills to meet Northern standards, or even improve on them, if those standards are demanded.

Adding to these diverging assessments, which call attention to extreme injustices on the one hand and adherence to international standards on the other, this chapter explores how China's needs and technological competence materialize unequally in the global South. For Chinese oil operators, international social and environmental standards (though weak and with few enforcement mechanisms) and community and labor dialogs (though not consensus-seeking and perhaps street-side) are realized in Latin America in order to demonstrate international goodwill. On the other hand, lesser standards and greater abuses are realized in parts of Africa and Asia to secure much-needed hydrocarbons, regardless of global stigmatization.

This chapter suggests that these two paths are not determined by China's state leaders or technocrats, as some accounts would lead us to believe. Latin America's active civil society, with a history of contesting injustices, and its democratically elected leadership, along with the copresence of transnational advocates, labor unions, and Northern multinational corporations (MNCs), govern China's operations. Indeed, environmental, labor, and community groups in Latin America are better able to monitor and curb the more appalling aspects of the industry than their fragmented and vulnerable counterparts in parts of Africa and Asia, where civil society has been weakened by authoritarian regimes. On this point, Northern advocates have been critical initially in raising international social and environmental standards among public and private financiers and the oil industry, while supporting affected communities in the global South in challenging Northern corporations.

Finally, this chapter argues that an advocacy vacuum currently exists in China. That is, there are Chinese oil operators without the copresence of independent Chinese activists, scholars, journalists, and nongovernmental organizations (NGOs) to inform, monitor, and question the former's practices. An alternative assessment of North-South advocacy campaigns points to the potential role of Pan-Pacific networks between China and South America, led by the more experienced South American organizations. However, if Pan-Pacific networks materialize, it is unclear whether they will adopt conservation-only policies influenced by Northern organizations, enact the more exacting and encompassing environmental justice paradigm to eliminate the threat of petrochemical toxins, or launch an original Sino-Latino orientation to global justice, which may advance or dilute the existing Northern interpretation.

China's Pendulum: Domestic Rights and Abuses

Before speculating on how China's overseas operations are trailing, meeting, or exceeding Northern standards and on how Southern activists and NGOs are mobilizing in response to China's presence, this section introduces China's domestic policies with regard to labor and the environment in order to shed light on its global operations. In China, for example, the ongoing arrests of political activists, inadequate labor safeguards, inequitable distribution of resources between rural and urban populations, and a legacy of environmental negligence paint a dismal picture. If transported overseas, these practices could prove disastrous for ecosystems and communities near oil facilities.

Labor Struggles

In China, protest gatherings of more than 100 people have risen from nearly 9,000 in 1993 to approximately 74,000 in 2004, with the majority involving laid-off workers chanting communist slogans against oppression, farmers protesting land seizures and environmental contamination, and ethnic minorities resisting repression (Shirk 2007, 56–57).[4] Rural peasants and/or migrant laborers in urban factories describe thirty-hour shifts and physically abusive workplaces, while older workers identify a disinvestment in the workplace and a subordination of skill building, due to an increasingly capitalistic orientation to production (Lee 2007).

In contrast, workers in China also have the right to unionize, to file grievances, and to form representative committees (Lee 2007; Guthrie 2006), while multinationals, such as Wal-Mart and McDonald's—which have resisted union formation in the United States—have agreed to support the state-run union in China (Barboza 2008). In addition, Chinese citizens view human rights as including "guaranteed jobs and wages" as "part of the larger bundle of rights" (Guthrie 2006, 24), which are not realized in the United States. Yet in spite of these rights, incongruities exist. For instance, the sole union available to workers is the All China Federation of Trade Unions, while "underground unionists" have been arrested and imprisoned (Lee 2007, 192).

The balance between worker rights and national need is precarious in a less socialist and more capitalistic marketplace that includes joint ventures between foreign firms and local governments (Lee 2007). In the domestic workplace, China appears unable to merge worker-centric policies and protections with profit-oriented production, a divide that portends poorly for semiskilled workers overseas. Moreover, it remains doubtful whether the more benevolent aspects of socialism, which remain on the decline domestically, will be exported, including employment for life and worker representation for non-Chinese laborers in China's overseas operations.

Environmental Damage and Repair

With regard to the environment, China's domestic dereliction has created persistent pollution over Beijing, swaths of desertification and dust storms, polluted and toxic rivers, and greenhouse gas emissions (Economy 2004; Fishman 2005; Shirk 2007; Richerzhagen and Scholz 2008). A number of large-scale environmental justice (EJ) struggles have surfaced including a mobilization effort of more than 20,000 people to contest chemical plants polluting local water sources, an additional 15,000 who demonstrated against a pharmaceutical factory's water pollution, and a third protest against a battery factory (Shirk 2007). If accurate, these numbers far exceed community-based EJ campaigns in most other places. Communities near the Hongwei Petrochemical Park have also identified a higher cancer risk as well as a cerebral palsy cluster, which they have linked to the plants' operations ("Pollution in China" 2007; Ribet 2007). Regionally, China has ignored or discounted how its domestic projects, such as dam construction on the Upper Mekong River, impact nations downstream, and how its industrial practices and desertification have led to transnational smog (Guttal 2008; Economy 2004; Fishman 2005). Globally, China has failed to commit to international initiatives or policies to lower its greenhouse gas emissions (Richerzhagen and Scholz 2008; Gu, Humphrey, and Messner 2008), though neither has the United States.

In contrast to this growing list of environmental injustices, international pressure for a cleaner environment produced a more environmentally aware population and state leadership during China's bid to host the 2008 Summer Olympic Games. In particular, China's bid succeeded in part because of Beijing's agreement to reduce the area's air and water pollution and to properly dispose of solid wastes produced during the games ("UNEP and Beijing Sign Pact" 2005). China also invited proposals for green urban planning, including garden rooftops, for the selected city Liuzhou (Tyrnauer 2008), while Beijing banned the production and use of thin plastic bags ("Poking Holes in China's Plan to Ban Plastic

Bags" 2008; "China Bans Free Plastic Shopping Bags" 2008). The latter effort though may be mere posturing with limited enforcement. Yet, while China increases its protection over its local environment, it has demonstrated limited will to protect the global environment or to contribute to international environmental governance mechanisms (Chan, Lee, and Chan 2008). Indeed, China's limited understanding of environmental injustice and ecological burden may generate even more substandard practices if permitted by draconian political leaders elsewhere.

Deciphering China's Ethical Capital

Deciphering China's ethical capital is as murky as understanding its domestic practices with regard to labor and environmental issues. Enderle's (2000) work on China's Confucian and socialist ethics and international influences following China's "Open Door" policy in 1978 provides insight into the pressures between its technocrats, on the one hand, and its socialist leaders on the other. To Enderle (2000), Confucian values emphasize a government responsive to its citizens, wise use of natural resources, and the pursuit of knowledge, which could include Western technology and environmental values, while international influences could include the recognition of and respect for human dignity and human rights.

China's efforts to learn from Western, or Northern, technological advances are clear. Beijing invests in research and development, educates its scientists, engineers and managers overseas, opens its doors to international consultants, requires foreign investors to transfer research and technological knowledge in exchange for market access, and creates joint ventures with the world's largest oil companies, including BP, Royal Dutch/Shell, and Exxon Mobil, to produce internationally competitive petroleum companies (Altenburg, Schmitz, and Stamm 2008; Zhang 2004). The social and ecological disasters associated with each one— the BP explosion and spill in the Gulf of Mexico in 2010, Shell's operations in Nigeria, and the *Exxon Valdez* oil spill in Alaska in 1989— say much about the inherent risks in the supply chain and the inadequate safeguards of these operators. In addition, and in the absence of urgent profit pressures, China's technocrats could actually invest in and even develop advanced and least damaging technology, including the production of hybrid and fuel-efficient cars (Altenburg, Schmitz, and Stamm 2008). In truth, Chinese leadership appears attentive to demonstrating their globally competitive skills and capacities, in *some* places (Andrews-Speed and Vinogradov 2000).

While Enderle minimizes the socialist contributions to China's ethical practices, other than to note its state- and community-based orientations, socialist ideals practiced domestically are informative of China's overseas activities. First, the socialist emphasis on community is in relation to the motherland and the state; it is not necessarily directed toward a global civil society or to nonlocal, non-Chinese, and non-socialist communities, where China seeks petroleum. Second, Chinese socialism marginalizes environmental responsibilities and articulates a meager perception of civic and human rights, placing Chinese officials and SOEs in a situation when operating overseas, of which they have limited experience and understanding and into which affected people have been defining and contesting injustices for years.

Overseas Operations

These domestic inconsistencies command special attention when analyzing China's overseas operations. One would expect the domestic realization of greater rights and standards than those practiced overseas, which has been demonstrated during times of colonialism and neocolonialism. In this case, China's leadership perpetuates and enables human, labor, and environmental abuses both domestically and internationally. Yet as a newcomer to the oil industry, China expresses a desire to demonstrate its understanding of and ability to meet Northern standards. However, this demonstration appears to be one of a follower or a mimic, rather than a leader or inventor. Therefore, when operating alone in China or overseas or as the primary oil entity with minimal national controls, Chinese oil companies may fail to meet even the substandard Northern benchmarks.

Taken together, China is likely to adopt Northern standards for *some* of its international practices that are monitored by affected groups and responsive state leaders, while perpetuating inferior standards elsewhere, including in parts of Africa and Asia and even within China itself. Therefore concerns that China is operating its overseas facilities in a manner that is inferior to China's domestic operations are unfounded. Such fears underestimate the social and environmental commitments of state leaders that have been demanded by affected people especially in Latin America.

Access to Africa and Asia

In a withering assessment of China's operations overseas, one journalist warned that the international community "may miss the clarion call of

Chinese petro-imperialism and the ensuing screams of the next Darfur" (Clasper 2005, 42). Indeed, China's operations in Sudan and Burma are particularly alarming.[5] China is criticized for its neocolonial practices, including exploring for and extracting oil in Burma, which in a climate of political oppression has led to land seizures, local economic destabilization, and polluted rivers (Arakan Oil Watch 2008).[6] It has also been criticized for arming Sudan, heightening internal displacement there, and underwriting Sudan's human rights abuses (Askouri 2007; Hurst 2006; Junger 2007; Manji and Marks 2007; Zweig and Jianhai 2005). Finally, China has been faulted for potentially swaying other oil-needy nations, such as India, to disregard international standards when acquiring oil overseas (Chen 2007). As addressed in Max Stephenson and Lisa Schweitzer's chapter on Ogoniland (chapter 3), China is also a major stakeholder in Nigeria, where Northern oil companies have often operated with impunity.[7]

For oil access in low-income nations, China offers low-interest, easy-payment loans without regulatory stipulations, bids the lowest or the highest, forgives debt, provides bilateral trade agreements, and builds schools, hospitals, railroads, bridges, and dams (Gu, Humphrey, and Messner 2008; Guttal 2008; Hanson 2008; Junger 2007; Manji and Marks 2007; Zweig and Jianhai 2005). Yet it remains unclear whether the seeming benevolent offers of assistance mimic Northern offers that fail to alleviate poverty or to meet the catholic demands of affected communities (Widener 2007a, 2009), or whether China's aid actually meets the unmet need of such communities.

Pointing to the former and indicating a potential underlining intent, Guttal (2008, 45, 18) suggests that China's overseas partnerships and practices "have begun to dangerously resemble colonialism," citing a perilous example in which 30,000 Chinese families were relocated to Laos to work in the fields, build large-scale projects, and manage small businesses. For access to Sudan's fields, China vetoes or dilutes UN initiatives to hold Sudan accountable for its ongoing human rights abuses (Chen 2007).[8] Even though China refers to this policy as one of noninterference, it undoubtedly interferes in Sudan's grassroots democratic efforts (Askouri 2007). Given that China also imports its own skilled labor, uses its own supplies, and hires its own service companies when operating overseas, there is evidence that Chinese interests are met first, followed by local interests, if at all.

Furthermore, China's development aid and lending practices,[9] which are offered without demands for political or economic reform, pit them against the compliance and austerity demands of traditional international lenders. Such practices may also weaken already inferior environmental and social criteria, induce a global race to the bottom for lenders, and increase hardship on impacted ecosystems, communities, and workers. For instance, China's lending practices may have influenced the World Bank's 2005 pilot program to offer loans if a nation complies with its own environmental and social assessments and safeguards, rather than the (albeit weak) World Bank ones (Guttal 2008).

Curbed by Latin American and Northern Models

In contrast to its African and Asian operations, China's oil companies appear to be upholding standards within the oil industry in Latin America, where China's needs and competitiveness in science and technology complement the region's political strength, grassroots activism, union activities, and copresence of Northern companies. Indeed, Chinese oil companies appear to be shoring up access and goodwill in Latin America, while shoring up access in parts of Africa and Asia.

In Latin America, the region's semiperipheral, or middle-income, nations, including Venezuela, Brazil, and Mexico, have demonstrated their strength in balancing China's operations, which is primarily in oil and mineral operations, with their own domestic needs. Likewise, Latin America's peripheral, or low-income, nations are opening their doors to China, while presenting these shifts as more equal-sharing and beneficial than former agreements with Northern MNCs or governments.

For example, Bolivia, Venezuela, and Ecuador renegotiated oil terms with China's oil companies to better benefit the state, while Ecuador also encouraged China to invest in an oil refinery on the Pacific coast and an airport in the Amazon (Spencer et al. 2007; Alvaro 2007).[10] In July 2009, China signed a US$1 billion "loan-for-oil deal" with Ecuador whereby Ecuador agreed to a two-year commitment to export approximately three million barrels of oil per month to China ("Ecuador Set to Receive $1 Billion Loan" 2009). In addition, China and Venezuela are negotiating a Pacific-bound oil pipeline, via Colombia (Hutton 2006), as well as building oil refineries together in China ("Venezuela to Sign Deal" 2007). Likewise, Brazil signed an agreement in 2009 to supply oil for Chinese refineries in exchange for a US$10 billion loan for Brazil to develop its own offshore oil fields ("Brazil Agrees to Supply Crude Oil to China" 2009).

Trade relations with China also vary from a free trade agreement with Chile to trade restrictions adopted by Argentina, from trade surpluses with Mexico and trade deficits with Chile and Peru, and from Brazilian joint ventures in China to direct competition with Mexico for the U.S. market (Barbosa 2008; Jenkins, Peters, and Moreira 2008).[11] Arguably, joint ventures and direct competition point to the economic muscle and political will of some Latin American nations, while restrictions on China's operations indicate the power of labor groups.

Latin America's labor organizations are particularly noteworthy. For instance, Argentina's metalworkers' union was pivotal in pushing for safety measures and certificates of origin in agreements with China (Barbosa 2008), while Brazilian unions have clamored for oil sovereignty. In Brazil, the National Committee against Oil and Gas Privatization, supported by the oil workers' union, Federacao Única dos Petroleiros, launched an "oil must be ours" campaign and even occupied the head-quarters of Petrobras in 2008. Their demands included the cancellation of bids to international companies, the end of crude oil exports, an increase in the export of manufactured oil products, and 100 percent national ownership of Petrobras.[12] In addition, the Brazilian national union, Central Única dos Trabalhadores, demanded national indepen-dence in the country's energy policy, including policies on new oil dis-coveries, and for biodiesel and ethanol to be produced on family farms.[13] Though these campaigns targeted the state to stop its privatization efforts, Chinese companies were targeted like any non-Brazilian multi-national. Brazil's agreement in 2009 to supply oil to China in exchange for a loan signifies this balance as well: Petrobras supplies the crude, not a Chinese company.[14]

As a newcomer to Latin America, China is aware of the region's determination to regulate foreign firms. In Ecuador, the state expelled California-based Occidental Petroleum in 2006 for irregular practices, which led the Chinese venture Andes Petroleum to experience field losses in its 40 percent interest in one of Occidental's oil blocks. Ecuador also froze the assets of Odebrecht, a Brazilian construction company, in 2008 for inferior practices on a hydroelectric project, putting foreign firms on further alert.[15]

In addition to the role of the state in setting expectations for China's operations, Northern multinationals have also established protocol when operating first or in adjacent fields. In Ecuador, for example, there are indications that when the Chinese oil consortium Andes Petroleum obtained an existing oil block from Canadian EnCana Corporation,[16] it initially adopted EnCana's community and environmental standards. A consultant who had worked for both North American and Chinese oil companies in Ecuador observed that for the Chinese company, Ecuador "is a test case on how to become an international player, how to become a major, big oil company."[17]

This is not to say that the community or environmental standards are ideal in North or South America—rarely is that the case with the oil sector—but there were early indications that in the Ecuadorian case the Chinese consortium was imitating the standards of the Canadian company. According to the same consultant, "With the Chinese, [their environmental awareness is] more of a reaction to what they perceive as to what they need to do to operate internationally in an international world,"[18] which points anecdotally to China's desire to identify and to meet global norms. In the past, for example, American multinationals have been described as "exporting environmentalism" to Brazilian and Mexican chemical companies (Garcia-Johnson 2000). Yet these more recent experiences in Ecuador also imply that Northern firms may transfer standards, and even consultants, to Chinese competitors when Chinese and Northern companies are operating in a third country with minimal standards of its own.

Whether Northern practices will be maintained, advanced, or weakened over time remains uncertain. By 2009, standards began to slide downward in the Ecuadorian case, according to some in the industry who witnessed the transition from Northern firms to Chinese ones. By then, some of the first- and second-tier managers had left their post to third-tier managers with limited skill and vision relative to their predecessors and to the requirements of the position.[19] Those interviewed in Ecuador suggested that one of the critical differences was how large private companies invested in preventing problems in the oil fields, whether technically, environmentally, or socially, before the problems arrived, while the Chinese, and perhaps state-owned operators in general, adopted a firefighting mentality, of putting out the conflicts as they arose.

In this case, the president of Ecuador, Rafael Correa, may have enabled the slippage of standards when he took office in 2007. As an outspoken leftist leader, Correa, much like Venezuela's leader Hugo Chávez, was committed to oil-financed, social justice initiatives. Correa renegotiated oil contracts to increase the state's share of oil revenues and streamlined the oil bidding process to expand operations, while also shifting state preference toward state-owned oil companies.[20] China's Andes Petroleum heeded Correa's demands, and renegotiated its contracts to maintain operations and friendly relations with the government. However, these changes also signaled to foreign oil companies, whether private or state-owned, that the criteria of Correa's government were the ones to meet, not necessarily those demanded by grassroots groups or NGOs or even those previously set by Northern MNCs.[21]

These sweeping examples are presented here to emphasize how Latin American states are regulating, some hand in hand with labor groups and civil society, and how Northern companies are informing China's global activities. These cases are in contrast to parts of Africa and Asia where authoritarian regimes neglect communities and ecosystems and where Northern firms are minimal or absent. Yet political shifts in Ecuador, Brazil, and Venezuela toward favoring state-owned companies may still bode poorly for affected communities and ecosystems if state-owned firms have fewer resources to invest in protective measurements. Given these multiple transitions and a history of elite failures in the oil sector, bottom-up, grassroots governance and democratic participation where people live, work, and play may become even more critical in directing the practices of state-owned companies. Activism not only pushes state agencies and industries to respond to community complaints (see Buttel 2003), activism pushes for improved standards, demands redress of multifaceted concerns, and serves as a constant observer to ensure that standards are enforced regardless of the company's headquarters and the political leanings of elected officials.

Potential Pan-Pacific Networks

China's epic quest for oil and its disregard of human and labor rights and environmental justice in *some* places identifies the importance of civil society as educators, monitors, and enforcers. To be clear, China's study of the practices and policies of Northern oil companies and international institutions has been noted in this chapter and by others (see Guthrie 2006; Zhang 2004). However, it was the thousands of community- and labor-based organizations, advocacy groups, EJ networks, and conservation NGOs worldwide, which were instrumental in demanding and establishing norms on human, labor, and environmental rights.

Yet, more questions have been raised than answered with regard to how the Chinese state and Chinese citizens will respond to grassroots and NGO mobilization against China's extractive practices overseas. On the environment in particular, Ebel (2005, 48) asks whether China will "be given a free ride, ignored by the NGOs, or will the reverse occur— that is, will China ignore the NGOs?" Contributing to this concern, Chen (2007) suggests that NGOs that confront or condemn China's overseas oil policies exclusively, rather than including China's SOEs in discussion on global standards, will lose an opportunity to inform and improve Chinese practices. In addition, Shirk's (2007) assessment of how Chinese students have demonstrated against international injustices *imposed on* China implies that a distrust of outsiders may include nonlocal communities, activists, and NGOs, which may be interpreted as impeding China's development by constraining its access to the minerals and fossil fuels of others.

To begin to disentangle this conundrum, this section assesses the competing agendas of the conservation and EJ networks in responding to the oil industry, identifies how Northern NGOs pressure China indirectly by demanding higher Northern standards that the Chinese aspire to meet, and suggests that South American organizations are critical to regulating China's oil practices and perhaps even to encouraging China's own activism. To do so requires a descriptive account of linked events and activities in China, Latin America, and the global North.

Bridging Conservancy Campaigns

In China, the country's budding environmental movement remains domestic, with a focus on conservation and limited, localized activism (Economy 2004). China's organizations, and especially its government-organized, nongovernmental organizations, or GONGOs (Economy 2004), are more likely to adopt campaigns that have been enabled or permitted by state authorities than to exert pressure on the government, while few engage in oppositional activities (Tao 2008). For example, Friends of Nature, China's first environmental organization (launched in 1994), focuses on environmental education, tree planting, and wildlife and habitat conservation rather than environmental toxins in workplaces and communities.

Likewise, the presence of The Nature Conservancy (TNC) and World Wildlife Fund (WWF) in China also supports a conservation-centric orientation to the environment. For example, TNC supported China's first national park, Pudacuo National Park, in the southwest Yunnan Province in 2007. In addition to establishing conservation projects worldwide, Northern NGOs provide at least two important services for their Southern partners. First, Northern organizations link China's up-and-coming conservationists to worldwide campaigns, including potential allies in Latin America. Second, they introduce their corporate ties to their Southern partners, who may adopt similar patterns of negotiation rather than confrontation. For example, Ecuadorian NGOs with support from their international partners negotiated a nearly $17 million environmental fund with a multinational oil consortium between 2002 and 2004 (Widener 2007a). If the Ecuadorian NGOs utilize this experience, they could pressure Chinese companies operating in Ecuador to commit to conservation initiatives and environmental research programs, as well as instruct Chinese NGOs to negotiate for similar agreements as well.

As in the Ecuadorian case, Latin American conservation NGOs have had greater experience in meeting with the oil industry, than Chinese oil companies have had in dealing with NGOs. Such a discrepancy could be promising for conservation initiatives. If Latin America's NGOs are capable of applying their Northern experiences to non-Northern oil entities, then they could potentially demand and advance higher standards from a company with limited environmental confidence and experience.

In spite of these important contributions, Northern conservation NGOs have been criticized by environmental activists for adopting corporate-friendly, malleable environmental demands and for collaborating with industry partners for conservation projects at the expense of affected communities.[22]

EJ Advocacy Networks

In contrast to the conservation networks, North-South community-centric networks have mobilized as well to challenge the disproportionate power and direct impacts of the oil industry's practices. Community-centric EJ struggles have been particularly demanding in Latin America (Carruthers 2008). For instance, Ecuadorian communities with the support of American advocacy networks have waged a lawsuit against Texaco, today Chevron Corporation, since 1993 for the inadequate disposal of oil wastewater and subsequent environmental damages and health impacts (Widener 2007b). In another example, activists from Ecuador, Costa Rica, Paraguay, and Mexico held a panel at the 2009 World Social Forum in Belem, Brazil, to raise awareness of their efforts to challenge the petroleum, hydroelectric power, and biofuel practices of Brazilian transnationals in the region.[23] Even though the panel was sponsored by Rosa Luxemburg Foundation, a German-based foundation for political education, this panel demonstrates an increasingly empowered Southern network that is beginning to contest the impacts of Southern-to-Southern extractive practices, not just Northern practices with the support of Northern advocates.

Even in the absence of Northern support, Ecuadorian protestors seized the facilities of Chinese-owned Andes Petroleum in 2006, taking more than forty workers hostage, and temporarily shutting down production in their ongoing demands for employment and social services from the state and oil industry ("Ministries Concerned by Embassy Robbery" 2006; "Chinese Oil Co Faces Resident Protests" 2006; Kerr 2006; Weitzman 2006).[24] These diverse examples are presented here to indicate that until social and environmental demands are met, oil entities, including Chinese SOEs, can expect prolonged tension surrounding their operations in Latin America.

In contrast, direct demonstrations against environmental injustices may be less customary in parts of Africa and Asia where violations may be even greater. In Southeast Asia, for example, demonstrations against the Chinese-financed Arakan-Yunnan Gas Pipeline from Burma to China were held in four Southeast Asian capitals in 2009, but not in Burma or China.[25] Citing this example is not meant to diminish its import, but to acknowledge the challenges grassroots groups face in some countries. Importantly, one of the most vocal organizations against Chinese oil operations in Burma is Arakan Oil Watch, which focuses exclusively on the Burmese state of Arakan, but is based in Thailand and is linked to South America. Arakan Oil Watch is a member of the Oilwatch International network, whose originating and coordinating office is based in Quito, Ecuador.

In China, the domestic role of activist-oriented NGOs is minimal, while their role in confronting the oil industry overseas is nonexistent for the most part. The Natural Resources Defense Council (NRDC), a New York–based environmental NGO, which opened its first international office in Beijing in 2004, represents a more pointed empowerment opportunity for budding Chinese activists than the international conservation NGOs. Accordingly, Greenlaw, an online resource for communities on environmental laws in China that was launched by NRDC and a local association, hosted an environmental forum in Beijing in 2008 that included discussions on climate change, sustainable development, and environmental participation.

Internationally, Chinese NGOs, or GONGOs, participated in the Regional Environmental Forum for Mainland Southeast Asia on how to govern the Mekong in 2002 and in a joint Asian-African conference that ran parallel to African Development Bank meetings in 2007 (Guerrero and Manji 2008). Chinese organizations also attended the 2007 World Social Forum in Nairobi, where Bello (2007) recorded "tense dialogue" between African and Chinese participants due largely to China's increasing presence in resource extraction and its direct competition with small businesses. Yet at this point there have been no organized meetings or forums that I know of between activist-oriented Chinese NGOs and grassroots groups and communities in the Amazon, which could stimulate Chinese activism overseas. As a further indication of their absence in Latin America, Chinese organizations failed to attend the 2009 World Social Forum held in Brazil.

Nevertheless, Northern and Southern NGOs have indirectly pressured China's lending practices and oil operations by demanding higher standards among Northern entities. Consider for example China's 2007 efforts to incorporate social and environmental considerations into its lending policies, based on the Equator Principles,[26] a voluntary agreement among certain banks to finance socially and environmentally responsible projects. It is important to note that the Equator Principles were established in June 2003, following a vociferous campaign by Ecuadorian and German groups against the German lender Westdeutsche Landesbank's support of a controversial oil pipeline project in Ecuador (Widener 2007a, 2009).

Likewise, three of China's largest oil companies—Sinopec Corp, PetroChina Co Ltd, and China National Offshore Oil Company (CNOOC)– are all publicly traded, which opens an additional avenue for international organizations to influence their environmental and social practices. Fidelity Investments, for example, dropped its PetroChina shares, while other shareholders are being pressured to do so, due to a Northern-based human rights campaign against the company's operations in Sudan (Hamilton 2007; Lou and Zhu 2007). In addition, the West-East gas line in China generated enough international pressure that BP withdrew its support (Economy 2004, 208–209). NGOs in the North have acknowledged that the international NGO community has begun to discuss among themselves how to influence and/or monitor China's domestic and overseas operations.[27] According to one international advocate in Ecuador, "China is definitely a behemoth for sure, but I don't think we should just write it off, and say we can't do anything. I just think it hasn't been done yet, so everyone is sort of just testing the waters and seeing."[28] By "everyone," this advocate was referring to Northern as well as Ecuadorian organizations.[29]

These dynamics point to how affected communities in the Amazon are confronting Chinese oil entities in the absence of external support, how Latin American organizations are establishing greater Southern ties to challenge Southern extractors or polluters, and how Northern advocacy groups remain critical in elevating global standards. Collectively, these actions may also encourage China to advance its own high criteria in order to avoid conflict in South America in particular.

Future Networks: Sino-Latino Justice or an Advocacy Vacuum?

Though China's overseas oil expansion is certain, the response of China's NGOs, advocates, scholars, and journalists is not certain. These professionals may adopt either a conservation position or an environmental justice one, maintain a domestic-only lens, become a global watchdog of China's operations, support labor groups, or interpret global challenges as threatening to national development. The latter could provoke a retraction from global engagement or inspire greater nationalism in support of China's economic growth and global influence, which could amplify spatial injustices between the oil supplier and oil recipient.

With candor, Tao (2008, 245) suggests that "Citizens' participation in, and evaluation of, foreign affairs and foreign aid is basically nonexistent in China," while other scholars caution that "Chinese actors are still learning (rapidly) how to build up global governance capabilities in many global governance arenas, and how to balance national interests with regional and global challenges and responsibilities" (Gu, Humphrey, and Messner 2008, 289). From Shirk's (2007) evaluation of mass patriotism in China, however, it would appear that China's activists and professionals may defend China's economic and political interests, rather than challenging China's contributions to global inequities.

This chapter acknowledges China's limited local campaign experience while stressing Latin America's capable role of cultivating the global entry of China's activist communities. Indeed, contact with Latin America's labor unions and grassroots movements, which have been contesting local-, national-, and international-level policies for decades, could promote more strident demands among China's maturing activists, much like Northern activists encouraged and supported grassroots activism in South America decades ago.

Ideally, Pan-Pacific alliances could also fill the fault lines of North–South networks. First, linking environmental degradation and economic deprivation in the South with lifestyle patterns in the North has remained daunting for transnational EJ networks. Second, Northern advocates have pressured Southern groups to market an internationally receptive position (Bob 2005), which forced a focus on Northern issues, rather than domestic ones (Mandle 2000; Moberg 2005; Widener 2007a, 2009).

In contrast, Pan-Pacific networks, running parallel to oil and investment flows, have the potential to represent a more egalitarian exchange of information, resources, and access. Latin American organizations could raise China's capacity and awareness on global environmental issues. Reciprocally, China could contribute cultural and political insights and access to China's SOEs, as well as an emergent body of labor and community activists, who may be receptive to learning from the more established and tested Latin American groups. For Chinese organizations, learning democratic governance, environmental justice, and labor rights from Latin American organizations rather than biased standards from the political and economic elites of the waning Western world may be critical to advancing global and southern justice.

Despite these promises, an ominous vacuum currently exists. There are Chinese oil operators without the consistent copresence of independent Chinese activists, NGOs, scholars, and journalists. Their absence may be due to an orchestrated effort to restrain differences of opinion domestically or to an overwhelming number of domestic struggles that obstruct their ability to mobilize or join international campaigns. They may also exclude themselves from international collaboration if they interpret international opposition as xenophobic or as a concerted effort to restrain China's status as a rising global power. Indeed, Chinese professionals and activists are Chinese citizens, who may interpret global justice as justice for China alone, at the expense of communities and ecosystems where China seeks resources.

Pathways of Opportunity and Prudence

In sum, the strains between China's oil need and the technocrats' business acumen, directed by grassroots controls, state leadership, and Northern standards, have produced two trajectories for China's overseas operations. On the one hand, need steers oil production in parts of Africa and Asia, where petroleum sits below some of the world's worst civil strife and human rights abuses and where China charts its own path with little global oversight. On the other hand, China's corporate elites exercise their international skills and competitive ability to meet the existing, though inadequate, standards in Latin America. However, , the political drive to replace private Northern firms with state-owned companies in parts of South America may diminish the undercurrent of corporate-to-corporate competitiveness that may improve standards rather than diminish them.

To be clear, China is not doing anything much worse or much different then Northern oil practices, except for its flagrant indifference to political, civic, human, and environmental rights in parts of Africa and Asia, where civil society is weakened by authoritarian regimes and where Northern firms operate with caution due to concerns of negative publicity campaigns by environmental and human rights activists. For more than a decade, community demands for employment, healthy environments, and global justice have been presented to Northern multinationals and state leaders worldwide with only limited, and rarely just, remedy. Moreover, it was the practices of Northern multinationals and the policies, austerity measurements, privatization demands, and exclusionary practices of the global North that led nations in the South to cultivate investment and to seek loans from China. China's entry into Africa, in particular, is due primarily to Eurocentric neoliberal policies that pushed for privatization and open markets, contends Chuen (2008), who argues for regulating the rise of global neoliberal practices, rather than targeting China specifically. Chuen's argument is supported here, though in this case an end to fossil fuel use would be even more effective in reducing the spread of conflict and contamination.

Yet China's interpretation of environmental norms and human rights may be the most problematic, and it warrants consideration, especially if China's officials and perhaps its citizens have an anemic barometer on these issues or have a high tolerance for civic abuse and injustice for themselves, and perhaps even more so for others. In this, China represents an anomaly: China's global operations may be governed by a social and environmental commitment that is greater than even their domestic practices, unlike Northern corporations whose standards slip when operating abroad.

A "race to the bottom" is not likely to occur in regions populated by grassroots activists, strong unions, Northern corporations, and populist political leaders, who enable community mobilization and support environmental and economic justice. Civil society will continue organizing in fields, in kitchens, or at international venues to eradicate injustice, to improve environmental health standards, and to demand local employment, just working conditions, community projects, and a participatory role in oil-related decisions. They will do so until effective and enforceable transnational codes that honor environmental and global justice are achieved worldwide or until an alternative to petroleum-based products are identified. But that is a tall order, and many "ifs" ensue. If more political leaders adopt populist and participatory ideology, greater community rights may be realized, independent of the oil producer. If Pan-Pacific networks are formed, even greater and more inclusive standards from the bottom up and from Southern perspectives may be achieved. If transnational advocacy networks continue to pressure MNCs and stockholders, China's SOEs may continue to strive to meet and perhaps exceed Northern standards. As for the final condition, Northern advocates, who have worked to end environmental injustice, to prevent environmental health burdens, and to block the production of toxins, remain significant and supportive actors even when the North is absent from the conflict. Conservationists in the North link China to South America through their regional and national offices, while North–South EJ networks raise global standards, to which the Chinese aim.

Finally, where Northern multinationals and Chinese SOEs share fields or operations there are technology and environmental standard transfers. Yet, this transfer remains tiered and representative of persistent spatial disparities. China is an economic and political power exerting its demands on weaker, yet oil-rich, nations in some places to the ongoing detriment of local ecosystems, communities, and the working poor. Likewise, while there have been standard transfers between Northern MNCs and Chinese SOEs, there have not yet been substantial advocacy transfers to support affected communities and ecosystems in the global South. Indeed, Chinese professionals may simply imitate citizens of colonial empires in the past and neocolonial and neoliberal beneficiaries of today, who fail to link their economic prosperity with the burdens of others.

Notes

I would like to thank Naihua Zhang for her insightful comments on an earlier draft. Portions of this chapter have been presented at the European Consortium for Political Research on Environmental Capacity Development in Transition States and Emerging Democracies, Rennes, France, April 2008, and the Beijing International Conference on Environmental Sociology, Beijing, China, July 2007.

1. On the health impacts of oil exposure, see Hurtig and San Sebastian 2002; O'Rourke and Connolly 2003; Ott 2005; San Sebastian et al. 2001.

2. China operates in and/or imports oil from Algeria, Angola, Australia, Azerbaijan, Bangladesh, Brazil, Burma (Myanmar), Chad, Congo, Ecuador, Ethiopia, Indonesia, Iran, Kazakhstan, Kuwait, Libya, Malaysia, Niger, Nigeria, Oman, Papua New Guinea, Peru, Russia, Saudi Arabia, Sudan, Thailand, Turkmenistan, Uzbekistan, Venezuela, and Vietnam. See Alden and Davies 2006; Andrews-Speed and Vinogradov 2000; Clasper 2005; Ebel 2005; Junger 2007; Naidu and Davies 2006; Widener 2007a; Zweig and Jianhai 2005. On Africa, see Manji and Marks 2007; on South America, see Kurlantzick 2006 and Lafargue 2006.

3. As a latecomer to global oil need and extraction, China has been selecting among fields that may have already been passed over by more established oil companies, which selected larger, finer, and more accessible fields. Due to increased competition, oil companies are also seeking oil in terrain more difficult politically, geographically, and geologically. See Patey 2007 on the departure of U.S.-based Chevron and Canada-based Talisman from Sudan. See http://www .AmazonWatch.org on U.S.-based Occidental Petroleum's exit from U'wa territory in Colombia following transnational campaigning.

4. Shirk (2007) cites three sources—two Chinese and one American—for these figures. See Johnson (2004) on recent community-level resistance to and lawsuits against tax increases, police brutality and arrests, and loss of home ownership in China.

5. In November 2009, the Burmese government confiscated land, which villagers believed would be given to China National Offshore Oil Company (CNOOC). At this time, approximately seventy villagers traveled into Thailand and Malaysia following demonstrations against CNOOC. See the news report by Tin (2009).

6. China's oil companies entered Burma in 2001.

7. On Nigeria, see Kashi and Watts 2008 as well as Okonta and Douglas 2001.

8. Sudan exports about 60 percent of its oil to China; see Hanson 2008.

9. China is both a provider and a recipient of international loans.

10. As of February 2010, it does not appear as if these investment proposals have been realized.

11. Exports from Latin America to China rose seven times between 1999 and 2005, while imports to Latin America tripled during the same period; see Jenkins, Peters, and Moreira 2008.

12. "O Petróleo Tem Que Ser Nosso!," special issue of a newsletter by the National Committee against Oil and Gas Privatization, presented at the World Social Forum, held in Belem, Brazil, January 27, 2009.

13. "Energy, Sustainable Development, Income Distribution, Valorization of Work, and Sovereignty: CUT Proposals," prepared by CUT-Brazil (Central Única dos Trabalhadores), November 2008; obtained at the World Social Forum, Belem, Brazil, January 2009.

14. Southern unions from South Africa, South Korea, Brazil, Argentina, and India met at the 2009 World Social Forum to strengthen Southern alliances and to counter what they perceive as a Northern dominance at the International Labor Organization. Though China was not represented, strong Southern alliances could influence the standards of China's overseas operations.

15. I conducted research on community-oil conflicts in Ecuador on six occasions between 2001 and 2009.

16. In 2005, EnCana sold its Ecuadorian operations to the Chinese consortium, Andes Petroleum, which includes China National Petroleum Corporation and China Petrochemical Corporation; see "China Oil Firm Buys EnCana Assets in Ecuador" 2005.

17. Interview with consultant, conducted in Quito, Ecuador, on May 22, 2007.

18. Interview with consultant, conducted in Quito, Ecuador, on May 22, 2007.

19. Interview with environmental engineer, conducted in Quito, Ecuador, on May 15, 2009.

20. After one year in office, Correa's administration convinced two oil companies, Petrobras and City Oriente, to hand over some or all of their operations to the state. And after two years in office, Correa's administration confiscated the operations of the French oil company Perenco over a tax dispute.

21. Though an advocate of the poor and disenfranchised, Correa's government disfavored public participation that was critical of its commitment to the oil and mining industries. Correa's administration, for example, temporarily suspended the license of Acción Ecológica, an environmental activist organization, and brought in the military to quell community road blockades and oil-facility seizures in a communal expression of discontent with road maintenance and repair. See Moore 2009 on the former and Aguirre 2008 on the latter point.

22. The Nature Conservancy (TNC), Conservation International (CI), and Birdlife International have, or have had, corporate partners, corporate supporters, or board members from within the petroleum industry.

23. This is noted from firsthand knowledge of this event.

24. Such actions, coupled with limited new projects, led to financial losses for Andes Petroleum in the first half of 2007; see Watkins 2007.

25. See Oilwatch Southeast Asia press release, February 14, 2009, http://oilwatch-sea.org/content/blogcategory/22/4/.

26. See http://www.equator-principles.com.

27. Interviews conducted in Miami, Florida, on April 4, 2008, and in Quito, Ecuador, on May 12, 2009.

28. Interview with international environmental advocate, conducted in Quito, Ecuador, on May 12, 2009.

29. At the Inter-American Development Bank Annual Meeting in Miami in April 2008, a representative of a Washington, D.C.–based NGO said the organization had hired a Chinese consultant in order to better address China's increasingly global presence. I was also told that China had indicated it would give up a controversial oil field in Peru, while the Peruvian government was adamant it should explore the field against the objections of environmental groups and affected communities.

References

Aguirre, Milagros. 2008. *Dayuma: Nunca Más!* Quito, Ecuador: Cicame.

Alden, Chris, and Martyn Davies. 2006. A profile of the operations of Chinese multinationals in Africa. *South African Journal of International Affairs* 13(1): 83–96.

Altenburg, Tilman, Hubert Schmitz, and Andreas Stamm. 2008. Breakthrough? China's and India's transition from production to innovation. *World Development* 36(2):325–344.

Alvaro, Mercedes. 2007. Ecuador's president seeks stronger ties with China. *Dow Jones Emerging Markets Reports*, March 29, 2007.

Andrews-Speed, Philip, and Sergei Vinogradov. 2000. China's involvement in Central Asian petroleum: Convergent or divergent interests? *Asian Survey* 40(2): 377–397.

Arakan Oil Watch. 2008. *Blocking Freedom: A Case Study of China's Oil and Gas Investment in Burma*. Chiang Mai, Thailand: Arakan Oil Watch, October.

Askouri, Ali. 2007. China's investment in Sudan: Displacing villages and destroying communities. In Firoze Manji and Stephen Marks, eds., *African Perspectives on China in Africa*, 71–86. Cape Town, South Africa: Fahamu.

Barbosa, Alexandre de Freitas. 2008. China and Latin America: Strategic partnering or latter-day imperialism? In Dorothy-Grace Guerrero and Firoze Manji, eds., *China's New Role in Africa and the South*, 220–237. Nairobi: Fahamu and Focus on the Global South.

Barboza, David. 2008. China tells businesses to unionize. *New York Times*, September 12, 2008, C1, C5.

Bob, Clifford. 2005. *The Marketing of Rebellion: Insurgents, Media, and International Activism*. New York: Cambridge University Press.

Bello, Walden. 2007. Beijing's diplomacy in Africa sparks debate at World Social Forum. February 6. http://www.tni.org/detail_page.phtml?act_id=16192.

Brazil agrees to supply crude oil to China. 2009. *Miami Herald*, February 20.

Buttel, Frederick H. 2003. Environmental sociology and the explanation of environmental reform. *Organization & Environment* 16(3):306–344.

Caldwell, John C. 1986. Routes to low mortality in poor countries. *Population and Development Review* 12(2):171–220.

Carruthers, David V. 2008. *Environmental Justice in Latin America: Problems, Promise, and Practice*. Cambridge, MA: MIT Press.

Chan, Gerald, Pak K. Lee, and Chan Lai-ha. 2008. China's environmental governance: The domestic-international nexus. *Third World Quarterly* 29(2): 291–314.

Chen, Matthew E. 2007. Chinese national oil companies and human rights. *Orbis* 51(1):41–54.

China bans free plastic shopping bags. 2008. *International Herald Tribune*, reported by Associated Press, January 9.

China oil firm buys EnCana assets in Ecuador. 2005. *China Daily* (from Reuters), September 15.

Chinese oil co faces resident protests to Ecuador pipeline. 2006. *Dow Jones Chinese Financial Wire*, November 10.

Chuen, Luk Tak. 2008. Regulating China? Regulation globalisation? In Dorothy-Grace Guerrero and Firoze Manji, eds., *China's New Role in Africa and the South*, 13–16. Nairobi: Fahamu and Focus on the Global South.

Clasper, James. 2005. Oil-slicked diplomacy. *Arena Magazine* 78 (August-September): 41–42.

Ebel, Robert E. 2005. *China's Energy Future: The Middle Kingdom Seeks Its Place in the Sun*. Washington, DC: CSIS Press.

Economy, Elizabeth C. 2004. *The River Runs Black: The Environmental Challenge to China's Future*. Ithaca, NY: Cornell University Press.

Ecuador set to receive $1 billion loan from China—report. 2009. Reuters, August 17. http://www.reuters.com/article/idUSN1737545720090817.

Enderle, Georges. 2000. Ethical guidelines for the reform of state-owned enterprises in China. In Oliver F. Williams, ed., *Global Codes of Conduct: An Idea Whose Time Has Come*, 196–208. Notre Dame, IN: University of Notre Dame Press.

Fishman, Ted C. 2005. *China, Inc.: How the Rise of the Next Superpower Challenges America and the World*. New York: Scribner.

Garcia-Johnson, Ronie. 2000. *Exporting Environmentalism: U.S. Multinational Chemical Corporations in Brazil and Mexico*. Cambridge, MA: MIT Press.

Gu, Jing, John Humphrey, and Dirk Messner. 2008. Global governance and developing countries: The implications of the rise of China. *World Development* 36(2):274–292.

Guerrero, Dorothy-Grace, and Firoze Manji, eds. 2008. *China's New Role in Africa and the South*. Nairobi: Fahamu and Focus on the Global South.

Guthrie, Doug. 2006. *China and Globalization: The Social, Economic, and Political Transformation of Chinese Society*. New York: Routledge.

Guttal, Shalmali. 2008. Client and competitor: China and international financial institutions. In Dorothy-Grace Guerrero and Firoze Manji, eds., *China's New Role in Africa and the South*, 17–36. Nairobi: Fahamu and Focus on the Global South.

Hamilton, Josh P. 2007. Berkshire reduces holdings in PetroChina. *International Herald Tribune*, October 11.

Hanson, Stephanie. 2008. *China, Africa, and Oil*. Council on Foreign Relations report. http://www.cfr.org/publications/9557.

Hurst, Cindy. 2006. *China's Oil Rush in Africa*. Washington, DC: Institute for the Analysis of Global Security.

Hurtig, Anna-Karin, and Miguel San Sebastian. 2002. Geographical differences in cancer incidence in the Amazon basin of Ecuador in relations to residence near oil fields. *International Journal of Epidemiology* 31:1021–1027.

Hutton, Will. 2006. *The Writing on the Wall: Why We Must Embrace China as a Partner or Face It as an Enemy*. New York: Free Press.

Jenkins, Rhys, Enrique Dussel Peters, and Mauricio Mesquita Moreira. 2008. The impact of China on Latin America and the Caribbean. *World Development* 36(2):235–253.

Johnson, Ian. 2004. *Wild Grass: Three Stories of Change in Modern China.* New York: Pantheon Books.

Junger, Sebastian. 2007. Enter China, the giant. *Vanity Fair,* July, 126+.

Karl, Terry Lynn. 1997. *The Paradox of Plenty: Oil Booms and Petro-States.* Berkeley: University of California Press.

Kashi, Ed, and Michael Watts. 2008. *Curse of the Black Gold: 50 Years of Oil in the Niger Delta.* Brooklyn, NY: powerHouse Books.

Kerr, Juliette. 2006. Protests against Chinese company's oil operations end in Ecuador. *Global Insight Daily Analysis,* November 13.

Kurlantzick, Joshua. 2006. China's Latin leap forward. *World Policy Journal* 23(3):33–41.

Lafargue, Francois. 2006. China's strategies in Latin America. *Military Review* 86(3):80–84.

Lee, Ching Kwan. 2007. *Against the Law: Labor Protests in China's Rustbelt and Sunbelt.* Berkeley: University of California Press.

Lou, Ying, and Winnie Zhu. 2007. PetroChina feels Sudan heat as Fidelity sells shares. *International Herald Tribute,* Bloomberg News, May 16.

Mandle, Jay R. 2000. The student anti-sweatshop movement: Limits and potential. *Annals of the American Academy of Political and Social Science* 570:92–103.

Manji, Firoze, and Stephen Marks, eds. 2007. *African Perspectives on China in Africa.* Cape Town, South Africa: Fahamu.

Meintjes, Garth. 2000. An international human rights perspective on corporate codes. In Oliver F. Williams, ed., *Global Codes of Conduct: An Idea Whose Time Has Come,* 83–99. Notre Dame, IN: University of Notre Dame Press.

Ministries concerned by embassy robbery. 2006. *China Daily,* November 14.

Moberg, Mark. 2005. Fair trade and Eastern Caribbean banana farmers: Rhetoric and reality in the anti-globalization movement. *Human Organization* 64(1):4–15.

Moore, Jennifer. 2009. Swinging from the Right: Correa and social movements in Ecuador. *Upside Down World,* May 13. http://upsidedownworld.org/main/content/view/1856/49/.

Naidu, Sanusha, and Martyn Davies. 2006. China fuels its future with Africa's riches. *South African Journal of International Affairs* 13(2):69–83.

Okonta, Ike, and Oronto Douglas. 2001. *Where Vultures Feast: Shell, Human Rights, and Oil in the Niger Delta.* San Francisco: Sierra Club Books.

O'Rourke, Dara, and Sarah Connolly. 2003. Just oil? The distribution of environmental and social impacts of oil production and consumption. *Annual Review of Environment and Resources* 28:587–617.

Ott, Riki. 2005. *Sound Truth and Corporate Myths: The Legacy of the Exxon Valdez Oil Spill.* Cordova, AK: Dragonfly Sisters Press.

Patey, Luke A. 2007. State rules: Oil companies and armed conflict in Sudan. *Third World Quarterly* 28(5):997–1016.

Poking holes in China's plan to ban plastic bags. 2008. *Los Angeles Times*, January 26, A3.

Pollution in China: Something in the air? 2007. *The Economist*, September 29, 47.

Renner, Michael. 2002. *Worldwatch Paper #162: The Anatomy of Resource Wars*. Washington D.C.: Worldwatch Institute.

Ribet, Steven. 2007. Horrors of Hongwei. *The Standard: China's Business Newspaper*, June 16.

Richerzhagen, Carmen, and Imme Scholz. 2008. China's capacities for mitigating climate change. *World Development* 36(2):308–324.

San Sebastian, M., B. Armstrong, J. A. Cordoba, and C. Stephens. 2001. Exposures and cancer incidence near oil fields in the Amazon basin in Ecuador. *Occupational and Environmental Medicine* 58:517–522.

Shirk, Susan L. 2007. *China: Fragile Superpower*. New York: Oxford University Press.

Spencer, Starr, Carla Bass, Ronald Buchanan, Mary Powers, and Jens Gould. 2007. Latin American oil nationalists may turn pragmatic. *Platts Oilgram News* 85(4)[January 5]:1.

Tao, Fu. 2008. The position of civil society organisations in China today. In Dorothy-Grace Guerrero and Firoze Manji, eds., *China's New Role in Africa and the South*, 238–245. Nairobi: Fahamu and Focus on the Global South.

Tin, Ba Saw. 2009. Junta confiscates land in Arakan State. *The Irrawaddy*, November 18. http://www.irrawaddy.org/article.php?art_id=17241.

Tyrnauer, Matt. 2008. Industrial revolution, take two. *Vanity Fair*, May, 142+.

UNEP and Beijing sign pact for green 2008 summer Olympics. 2005. *Environment News Service*, November 18.

Venezuela to sign deal to build three refineries in China: Chavez. 2007. *Platts Commodity News*, March 26.

Watkins, Eric. 2007. Ecuador taking measures to increase oil production. *Oil & Gas Journal* 16(July):31.

Weitzman, Hal. 2006. Protestors pour trouble on Ecuador's oil producers. *Financial Times* (North American ed.), March 3.

Widener, Patricia. 2007a. Benefits and burdens of transnational campaigns: A comparison of four oil struggles in Ecuador. *Mobilization: An International Quarterly* 12(1):21–36.

Widener, Patricia. 2007b. Oil conflict in Ecuador: A photographic essay. *Organization & Environment* 20(1):84–105.

Widener, Patricia. 2009. Global links and environmental flows: Oil disputes in Ecuador. *Global Environmental Politics* 9(1):31–57.

Zhang, Jin. 2004. *Catch-up and Competitiveness in China: The Case of Large Firms in the Oil Industry*. London: RoutledgeCurzon.

Zweig, David, and Bi Jianhai. 2005. China's global hunt for energy. *Foreign Affairs* (Council on Foreign Relations) 84(5):25–38.

9

Resisting Environmental Injustice through Sustainable Agriculture: Examples from Latin America and Their Implications for U.S. Food Politics

Alison Hope Alkon

Food is at the heart of projects, policies, and movements resisting environmental injustice across the global South. Such activism often aims to resist the globalization of industrial models of agriculture. More specifically, activists argue that the technological advances of the Green Revolution established a capital-intensive agricultural system. To procure these technologies, governments across the global South borrowed heavily from the World Bank and International Monetary Fund (IMF). However, these institutions' lending policies demanded the privatization of many services, preventing national governments from making such advances available to small farmers or to those who do not have secure rights to the land they cultivate. This trajectory, activists argue, has led to the increased consolidation of land ownership while undermining the abilities of agrarian peoples to produce food.

Activists envision an alternative to these environmental injustices in the concept of food sovereignty, the right of people to control their own food and agriculture systems (Via Campesina 2002). Actions in pursuit of food sovereignty have taken a wide variety of forms, including programs promoting small-scale, environmentally sustainable farming, local and national policies designed to increase food access, and national and transnational social movements calling for an alternative agricultural system that benefits small farmers and landless peoples. These multiple strategies call into being a variety of participatory norms—methods of involvement in a social setting and resulting social roles. Those seeking food sovereignty participate as producers and consumers of foods grown outside of the transnational industrial food system, as citizens of cities and states whose policies promote food access and local control, and as protesters executing direct actions challenging the transnational industrial agricultural system.

In the United States, racially and economically marginalized communities have begun to articulate a somewhat parallel demand for food justice. The concept of food justice challenges an industrial food system structured by racial and economic inequality, which results in lack of access to healthy, affordable, culturally appropriate food among low-income people and people of color. U.S. federal policies, according to this movement's analysis, have stripped low-income communities and communities of color of the ability to produce their own food. The growing U.S. food justice movement further claims that national and local policies have created incentives for grocery stores to abandon low-income and minority urban neighborhoods, thereby ensuring that processed, high-calorie food is more affordable than produce. The U.S. food justice movement's community-based response to this analysis demands not only increased food access, but a food system rooted in environmental sustainability and social justice. In articulating this goal, activists bring together the environmental justice movement's attention to how race and class affect access to environmental benefits and the sustainable agriculture movement's emphasis on alternative modes of production, distribution, and consumption (Alkon and Norgaard 2009). Despite an analysis highlighting national policy, the U.S. food justice movement tends not to push for legislation. The neoliberal context in which the food justice movement operates has led to norms of participation that encourage low-income people and people of color who lack food access to become entrepreneurs, providing healthy food in their communities. Such projects have taken the form of farmers' markets and farm stands, school and community gardens, cooking and nutrition classes, and support for home-based businesses offering prepared foods.

In this chapter, I draw on six case studies from Latin America to map potential connections between the U.S. food justice movement and transnational struggles for food sovereignty.[1] Much of the firsthand research on the latter comes from activist-scholars associated with the nonprofit Institute for Food and Development Policy, better known as Food First. These scholars highlight the efforts of networks of small farmers, nongovernmental organizations, social movements, and governments to develop alternative strategies that work toward more sustainable and just forms of agriculture, and of social life. In viewing their case through the lens of the U.S. food justice movement, I tie the production, distribution, and consumption of food to both national policies and the transnational political economy. I also underscore a parallel emphasis on local

knowledge and local control. Finally, I compare the food justice movement's emphasis on entrepreneurial strategies, which restrict participatory norms to market behaviors, with the multiple scales and strategies
embraced by those working for food sovereignty in Latin America. This
analysis highlights the ways that transnational forces are experienced
through the policies of local, national, and remote governments, the
international political economy, and national and transnational social
movements, producing diverse strategies aimed at food sovereignty. From
this analysis, I speculate on the potential and promise of a joined-up
movement for food sovereignty and justice worldwide.

Denied Access to the Means of (Food) Production

In the United States, federal policies have stripped many marginalized
communities of their abilities to produce food. Examples include the U.S.
Department of Agriculture's discrimination against African-American
farmers (Gilbert, Sharp, and Felin 2002), the relocation of Native
Americans from their ancestral territories (Norgaard 2005), and the
incorporation of New Mexican land grants into national parks (Kosek
2006; Peña 2005). In the first case, federal policies threatened the
economic solvency, and thus food sovereignty, of black farmers. In the
latter two, U.S. government agencies directly restricted access to land,
making self-sustenance impossible.

In the global South, scholars and movement intellectuals tend to highlight three processes of globalization as responsible for denied access to
food production. Both the technological developments of the Green
Revolution and the neoliberal push toward privatization amplified the
concentration of agricultural wealth in the hands of large farmers. The
latter have manifested themselves in a number of IMF and World Bank
policies and programs, but those working for food sovereignty tend to
highlight structural adjustment and market-led land reform. Activists
argue that these programs result in increased consolidation of Latin
American agriculture, creating environmental inequalities by constraining small landholders and landless peoples from producing food.

The Green Revolution
Envisioned by U.S. agronomist Norman Borlaug and financed by U.S.
foundations, the Green Revolution sought to increase crop yields in order
to meet the food needs of rising populations. It found a home within the
political climate of the late 1960s, when many in the developed world

believed that the so-called modernization of poor nations could inhibit the spread of communism (Rostow 1990). In opposition, dependency and world-systems perspectives favored the replacement of imports with domestically produced goods (Wallerstein 1974). Both theories, however, envisioned a mechanized, industrial form of agriculture (Holt-Giménez 2006). The Green Revolution developed new cultivars of staple foods that responded well to mechanized irrigation and chemical fertilizers and pesticides that, with funding from the World Bank and U.S. Agency for International Development, were exported around the world (Lappé et al. 1998).

Despite the Green Revolution's tremendous increases in production, world hunger in the global South, with the exception of China, rose 11 percent between 1970 and 1990 (Lappé et al. 1998).[2] Critical social scientists argue that Green Revolution technologies favored larger farms that could afford new seeds, chemical fertilizers, and irrigation systems, or that could obtain credit. These farms then out-competed small landholders, widening existing socioeconomic inequalities (Hewitt de Alcántara 1976; Jennings 1988; Pearse 1980). At the same time, increasing dependence on chemical inputs stripped soils of their fertility, which in turn created increased need for chemical fertilizers (Altieri 1995). While some continue to trumpet the Green Revolution's technical advances and push for further developments, those working for food sovereignty claim that it has exacerbated global environmental inequalities (Rosset et al. 2006; Holt-Giménez 2006; Lappé et al. 1998; Altieri 1995). As in Lewis's research on Ecuador (chapter 5), the foreign foundations that funded the Green Revolution ignored the local social and political contexts in which they worked. Thus their seemingly well-intended goal of feeding the world exacerbated existing environmental inequalities.

Structural Adjustment Programs

The large-scale infrastructure projects called for by both proponents of modernization and import substitution required financing beyond the capacity of the underdeveloped economies of the global South. Originally designed to finance the rebuilding of Europe after World War II, the IMF and World Bank filled this role (Mikesell 1994). In the 1970s, many countries, especially in Latin America, borrowed liberally from these institutions. Latin American debt quadrupled between 1975 and 1983, rising to half the value of the region's gross domestic product (Marichal 1989). The economic recession of the late 1970s and 1980s increased interest rates. In 1982, Mexico became the first nation to default on its debt, and others seemed certain to follow suit (Pastor 1987). In response, the banks stopped lending money and refused refinancing. Billions of dollars worth of loans came due.

Responding to what has since become known as the Third World debt crisis, the IMF and World Bank instituted a policy of structural adjustment. In order to receive new loans, or to refinance existing loans, debtor governments would have to agree to implement a set of neoliberal programs and policies. Common elements of such programs include drastic cuts to government social expenditures such as education and health services, lifting import restrictions and price controls, privatizing any state-owned enterprises, and deregulating markets (Chossudovsky 2003; Finch 1985). Such structural adjustment programs are the ideological opposite of food sovereignty, in that market mechanisms are dictated by transnational fiscal policy rather than local control. Additionally, structural adjustment policies tended to result in increased concentration of land and capital in the hands of transnational corporations and national elites (Chossudovsky 2003; Smith, Acuna, and Gamarra 1994).

With regard to agriculture, structural adjustment programs led to the elimination of any government price supports or subsidies that increased access to Green Revolution technologies. In Mexico, for example, the national government was forced to terminate its practice of providing farmers with access to crop insurance, subsidized seed and fertilizer, low-interest loans, marketing assistance, and high guaranteed prices (Holt-Giménez 2006; Stone 2009). In place of its previous emphasis on food self-sufficiency, the government encouraged export crops (Stone 2009). Moreover, Mexican farmers, and farmers throughout the global South, were forced to compete domestically with U.S. export commodity crops subsidized by the U.S. Farm Bill and often available below the cost of local production (Vorley 2001). This demonstrates that it is not only demand and consumption from the global North, but also remote national policies, that can strengthen environmental inequalities, echoing Stephenson and Schweitzer's insight (chapter 3) that while multinational firms play often primary roles, the drivers of transnational environmental inequality are interlocking and complex.

Market-Led Land Reform

Together, the Green Revolution and structural adjustment programs created an increasingly marginalized class of small farmers and landless peoples throughout the global South, while clustering land and capital in increasingly few hands. Indeed, critics of the Green Revolution assert that it was supported by international lending agencies and U.S. foundations as a technical alternative to social movement efforts to create land reform (Rosset, Patel, and Courville 2006; Holt-Giménez 2006). Efforts toward land reform, however, continued, and by the 1990s, organized grassroots land occupations had occurred in places as varied as Brazil, Zimbabwe, Thailand, and South Africa. These actions pressured the World Bank to pursue its own version of land reform.

The World Bank's land reform policies are led by the market rather than the state or social movements, and emphasize productive efficiency rather than justice (Deninger 1999). They are based on the assumption that rural agrarian poverty persists because individuals do not have clear and sufficiently secure property rights (Borras 2006; Borras and Saturnino 2004). Rather than expropriating privately owned land as demanded by social movements, this approach mandates that landless peoples pay market prices to willing sellers (Borras 2006). Loans are available for such purchases, but often not for infrastructure improvements necessary to make such lands productive. This is one key reason why Brazil's program, for example, had high dropout rates. Sauer's (2006) study of its beneficiaries revealed that many formerly landless people abandoned the program because they could achieve neither subsistence nor profit. They were once again landless, and were now also mired in debt. Scholars studying market-led agrarian reform efforts often argue that they are not a means toward greater food sovereignty (Rosset, Patel, and Courville 2006).

Purchasing Replacements

Unlike many goods, food is essential to human life, and those without access to land must purchase it. In the United States, low-income communities and communities of color often live in so-called food deserts replete with liquor stores and fast-food establishments, but containing few or no grocery stores. Poor rural communities are often located far from supermarkets, and the nearest are generally high priced and lack variety and quality (Jackson 2005). Moreover, U.S. commodity subsidies guarantee that processed foods will be more affordable than fresh produce (Pollan 2006).[3] Poor communities often depend on government commodity foods, which tend to be low in nutrients (Pollan 2006). For food justice advocates, the inability to purchase food is rooted in U.S. policies such as urban renewal, the federal highway program, and the farm bill (McClintock 2008; Pollan 2006; Guthman 2007).

In the global South, many small farmers and landless peoples who can no longer produce their food migrate to urban areas, helping to create what Davis (2006) poetically calls a *Planet of Slums*. Others are pushed toward migration to the United States and Europe, where they continue to experience high rates of hunger (Wirth, Strochlich, and Getz 2008). Still others attempt to continue farming on increasingly marginal lands, creating environmental damage through massive soil erosion (Holt-Giménez 2006; Stonich 1994).

Prior to structural adjustment, food purchasing in the global South could largely be done through domestic markets. Nations such as Mexico (Stone 2009) and Haiti (Quigley 2009) maintained federal policies that kept them largely food self-sufficient. The mandated elimination of such programs, and the opening of markets to outside commodities, increasingly ties formerly agrarian people's food needs to transnational commodity markets. Often, subsidized commodity crops from the United States and Europe undercut the cost of local production. But when transnational prices rise, the global poor have little protection, creating the risk of massive hunger. This occurred during the world food crisis beginning in 2007, in which the price of food staples rose rapidly. Analyses of the highly debated causes of this crisis include increased oil prices (Magdoff 2008), financial speculation (Lappe 2009), the increased use of crops for biofuels (Elliot 2008), and what Jaroz (2009) refers to as the feedgrain-lifestock complex. The global food crisis is largely a crisis of distribution rather than production. According to Josette Sheeran, the head of the UN's World Food Program, "There is food on shelves but people are priced out of the market" (quoted in Borger 2008).

As a result of this vulnerability, food rebellions erupted throughout the global South (Holt-Giménez and Patel 2009). The United Nations and wealthy governments offered billions in aid, but have not acknowledged any link between transnational monetary policies and food shortages. Indeed the U.S. Congress blocked a proposal to make some food aid in cash, rather than U.S.-produced commodities, in order to support local production (Hanley 2008).[4] Governments in the global South have instituted temporary food subsidies, price controls, and export bans, but no long-term reforms.

Against this backdrop of structural limitations, a variety of interrelated movements, networks, policies, and projects have emerged that posit ecologically and economically sustainable agriculture as a means to social and environmental justice. Each pursues the goal of food sovereignty, positing both food access and the ability to define food and agriculture systems as human rights. Additionally, each contains a politics of knowledge privileging the lived experiences of marginalized farmers and landless peoples. They differ, however, in the scale at which they work and the norms through which individuals and communities can participate. In nations that have embraced the globalization of agriculture, some projects create spaces of resistance and social networks that may someday fuel direct opposition to it. For now, individuals participate as producers and consumers of local, sustainably raised food. In nations that have instituted or lean toward socialism, local and national policies can themselves be drivers of food sovereignty and justice, creating participatory norms of citizenry rather than consumption. Finally, social movements engage in direct actions such as land occupation and protests in order to advocate for food sovereignty both within and beyond national borders.

Resistance as Everyday Practice: *Campesino a Campesino* and *El Ranchero Solidario*

At the community level, several projects consist of producers and consumers creating everyday alternatives to the agricultural system dictated by the Green Revolution and international lending agencies. *El Movimento Campesino a Campesino* (the farmer-to-farmer movement) is comprised of small farmers from Central America and Mexico who develop sustainable agricultural practices and share their knowledge with one another. *El Ranchero Solidario* (Solidarity Ranch), on the other hand, helps farmers establish more secure livelihoods through the collective, local distribution of their crops. Together, they create alternatives to the chemically intensive farming regimes and export-oriented marketing strategies enabled and dictated by the Green Revolution and structural adjustment. As in the United States, the Mexican government's deep embeddedness in the above-described transnational policies of privatization fosters participatory norms that work within market-exchange relations.

From Farmer To Farmer

The Campesino a Campesino movement (MCAC) began in Chimaltenango, Guatemala, in the 1970s. There, a retired soil conservationist employed by a U.S. NGO experimented with agroecological techniques, raised his crop yields, and sought to share his success with his Mayan neighbors. Despite years of low yields and debt incurred in the purchase of soil amendments, these Mayan farmers were initially reluctant. Eventually, several agreed to try small experiments on their own land and found similar success. They began to teach additional neighbors through the pedagogically horizontal techniques of demonstration and experimentation.

As Holt-Giménez (2006) describes in his in-depth study of the movement, Chimaltenango's campesinos have accumulated a vast amount of agroecological knowledge. With help from NGOs like Oxfam and World Neighbors, they have spread their model of farmer-led agricultural development to other parts of Guatemala and Mesoamerica. Regional farmers responded well to the instruction of such *promotores*, who continuously created new knowledge and new teachers through workshops and exchanges. In contrast to the example offered by Lewis (chapter 5), as well as the U.S.-based foundations that funded the Green Revolution, this demonstrates the important supportive role that organizations based in the global North can play when they highlight the knowledge and skills of local people.

Success enabled Guatemalan campesinos to compete with their former *patrones*. In the early 1980s, the Guatemalan Army "disappeared" several prominent promotores, while others fled. International NGOs drew on their transnational networks to help some promotores find work in other parts of the region. Two such men became nonprofit extension agents in the Mexican town of Vicente Guerrero, where structural adjustment programs had recently eliminated state assistance to small farmers. Collectively, campesino teams began to establish school gardens, communal orchards, and other community agricultural development projects emphasizing collective local consumption rather than export. From Mexico, Campesino a Campesino extended to Nicaragua and Cuba.

Unlike the Green Revolution, in which technological development was led by U.S. scientists and diffused through state extension networks (Rogers 1969), and the IMF and World Bank's structural adjustment programs, in which outside consultants mandate on-the-ground practices, MCAC's pedagogy and methodology privilege the knowledge of "local farmers in the development of their own agriculture" (Holt-Giménez 2006, 79). Practically, this consists of teaching campesinos to experiment, rapidly recognize successes, and work as extension agents in passing on their new knowledge (Bunch 1996). Campesinos tended to view professional extension agents with suspicion because of their technocratic jargon, emphasis on helping banks recover loans, and lack of farming experience (Holt-Giménez 2006). As demonstrated by the following quote from the president of a cooperative in Pochuape, Nicaragua, they regard promotores quite differently. "The Mexicans are campesinos just like us," he said. "We understand each other. They have shown us what we can become" (quoted in Holt-Giménez 2006, 16). Such bonds are not only generated by cultural similarity but by a pedagogy that fuses research, training, and education. Thus, the promotores are always learning along with those who attend workshops, and, armed with their own place-based ecological knowledge, the learners are always teaching as well. For this reason, Holt-Giménez (2006) regards campesino pedagogy not only as a methodology, but as a practice of cultural resistance against the reliance on outside, expert knowledge and drive toward privatization that characterize the globalization of agriculture. Although emphasis on local knowledge has often been associated with insular strategies (Harvey 1996), here it becomes essential to the creation of transnational networks. Such an emphasis on local knowledge also informs the U.S. food justice movement's creation of local alternative food systems through farmers' markets and community gardens, highlighting the possibility for increasing transnational alliances.

Solidarity Ranch

While the Campesino a Campesino movement is primarily concerned with production, *El Ranchero Solidario* maintains a similar approach toward distribution. El Ranchero Solidario is a cooperative grocery store owned by fifty-two farm families in the town of Anáhuac in Chihuahua, Mexico. Until the 1980s, farmers in this area sold much of their grain to the National Food Staples Company (CONASUPO), a government distribution agency that set prices for staple foods. Although smaller farms lacked access to this market, they benefited indirectly from its price floors. CONASUPO was disbanded under the structural adjustments mandated by the IMF and World Bank in exchange for refinancing Mexico's defaulted loans. Transnational corporations such as Cargill and Gruma became the region's primary purchasers and distributors (Stone 2009).

El Ranchero Solidario seeks to enrich the livelihoods of its members, who receive first priority to sell their goods there, as well as other local farmers. Co-op members set prices in accordance with the Chicago Stock Exchange, reflecting ongoing ties to the global market. However, because the co-op itself does not seek to make a profit, it can pay farmers the bulk of those prices while offering competitive rates to consumers. Thus, the co-op provides its members with a more reliable income than other area farmers. For its owner families, the co-op takes on the role abdicated by the government-dismantled National Food Staples Company.

This income precludes the need for U.S. migration. Structural adjustment programs, and later NAFTA, opened Mexican markets to subsidized U.S. inputs, making farming a difficult economic proposition. These political and economic processes have fueled migration to the United States. However, unlike many farmers in the area, all fifty-two co-op owner families and their children have stayed in Anáhuac. According to one farmer and co-op member, "Most of the people who go to the U.S. make more money, but they're not happy. To be happy, you have to be in our own land" (quoted in Stone 2009). El Ranchero Solidario allows its member owners to maintain control of their system of food distribution, and thus, their food sovereignty and livelihood.

In addition to providing income for farmers, the co-op supplies groceries to approximately 1,000 customers per day. Goods include produce, eggs, meat, cheese, flour, corn, and other staples. It also carries bread and cookies from a nearby Mennonite village, organic amaranth from Teotihuacán, and Oaxacan fair trade coffee grown "in solidarity with the Campesino a Campesino movement" (quoted in Stone 2009). The co op attempts to appeal to a broad base of customers through such diverse products, which allows it to succeed economically.

Like the U.S. food justice movement, the work of El Movimento Campesino a Campesino and El Ranchero Solidario is constrained by state policies that favor the export-oriented and input-intensive agriculture enabled by the Green Revolution and mandated by the IMF and World Bank. Such policies confine the norms of participation embedded in these programs to everyday economic practices of production and consumption—such as agroecological techniques and local distribution—that do not embody political opposition to the globalization of agriculture. And yet, these programs help their participants develop what Holt-Giménez (2006) calls "structural literacy" in which ordinary people learn to see their own circumstances as the result of transnational social, environmental injustices.[5] Thus, projects such as Campesino a Campesino and El Rancho Solidarity may help to develop the critical consciousness and social networks through which actors may eventually confront their political and economic constraints. In the next two examples, government policies support food sovereignty. Thus, they represent a vision of what Campesino a Campesino and El Rancho Solidarity might someday become.

Sustainable Agriculture as Policy: Belo Horizonte and Cuba

In the examples above, as well as the U.S. food justice movement, national governments have tended to support market-driven forms of agriculture associated with neoliberal globalization and increased environmental injustice. In a few cases, however, national and local governments have countered that trend. The first example below describes how the city government in Belo Horizonte, Brazil, has created agricultural programs to support small farmers and increase food access. Additionally, barred from Green Revolution technologies by the collapse of the Soviet Union and the U.S. embargo, Cuba has created a system of organic and low-input agriculture that maintains human and ecological health.

Beautiful Horizon

Brazil has the second highest rate of economic inequality of any nation in the world. This statistic explains why, despite its status as the world's fifth largest economy and being a major agricultural exporter, 46 million Brazilians do not have enough to eat (Wade 2004). One percent of landowners control nearly half the arable land. High malnutrition rates accompany high rates of infant mortality (Ondetti 2008). Against this backdrop, Belo Horizonte, Brazil's third largest metropolitan area, has declared food a right of citizenship. Moreover, its efforts to guarantee this right have been largely participatory. Former mayor Patrus Ananias began by assembling twenty representative citizens, labor leaders, and church officials to comprise a city agency that would design a new food system (Lappé 2009). The city government works in partnership with the private and nonprofit sectors to institute strategies aimed to help farmers provide affordable produce.

For example, the government leases twenty-five prime city locations to farmers at low prices in exchange for the ability to set produce prices below market rates. Busy locations ensure numerous customers, and thus farmer profits, while patrons benefit from low prices. Additionally, farmers leasing the most sought-after spots during the week must agree to sell food in the city's poor *favelas* each weekend. During her visit to Belo Horizonte, noted food writer Frances Moore Lappé described meeting one of these farmers: "A farmer in a cheerful green smock, emblazoned with 'Direct from the Countryside,' grinned as she told us, 'I am able to support three children from my five acres now.'" As at *El Ranchero Solidario,* when the intermediary does not seek to earn a profit, the producers earn more while the consumers pay less.

Perhaps what is most striking about Belo Horizonte's food policy is not that the government is involved in food pricing, but the city's explicit regard for food as a human right. According to Adriana Aranha, the city's Hunger Program director, "We believe the status of citizen surpasses that of consumer. . . . Quality food for all is a public good" (quoted in Lappé and Lappé 2002). Because it aims to increase food access as well as local control of the food system, Belo Horizonte's approach reflects the concepts of food justice and food sovereignty. Proponents of this city's program argue that it moves beyond charity models and emergency feeding programs, establishing the government's authority to ensure that all citizens are adequately fed. Such government intervention directly confronts the market-oriented logic of structural adjustment described earlier in this chapter. This demonstrates that when local governments are supportive of food sovereignty, they can foster norms of participation that highlight citizenship and human rights. In the United States, the food justice movement has similarly named food as a human right, but has not developed the kind of policy or government support seen in Belo Horizonte.

Although Belo Horizonte's government is involved in food pricing, it does not aim to eliminate market exchange as a means of food distribution. Indeed many of this city's programs, according to Aranha, are aimed at "helping to keep the market competitive." To this end, city officials announce various supermarkets' prices of forty-five commodities in the newspapers and over the radio, enabling customers to find low-cost items. This is complicit with the neoclassical economic assumption that proper information regarding prices ensures competition and thus market functioning. Although it counters the logic of a neoliberal food system by asserting a role for the state in the prevention of hunger, Belo Horizonte's notion of *food citizenship* does not oppose strategies that make use of market mechanisms.

Despite their success at the local level, proponents of Belo Horizonte's food program recognize that hunger is tied to wider structural inequalities in land ownership and employment. Aranha remains hopeful, however, that Brazilian President Luiz Ignacio Lula de Silva's national antihunger program will begin to address these larger inequalities. The president may find a model of national policy promoting food sovereignty in Cuba.

Socialist Agriculture in Cuba
Cuba's embrace of local, low-input agroecology was the result of crisis. Before the 1959 revolution, land was concentrated in the hands of

foreign companies and domestic elites, and was dedicated to producing sugar for export. Farmworkers lived in poor conditions, largely in shacks without running water, and nearly half were illiterate. After the revolution, the government nationalized much of the land, keeping the majority under state control while turning nearly a third over to worker cooperatives. However, reliance on export-oriented agricultural strategies continued, as socialist countries purchased Cuban sugar under stable and preferential terms (Alvarez et al. 2006). The Soviet Union financed Cuba's embrace of Green Revolution technologies (Funes et al. 2002).

In 1989, the collapse of the Soviet Union created a food crisis. Cuba had imported two-thirds of its foodstuffs, and nearly all of its fuel and machinery. Industries were forced to close and public goods, such as transportation and power plants, worked at minimum capacity. The crisis was worsened when, in 1992, the United States tightened its embargo by blocking shipments of food and medical supplies. Seeking to increase production while coping with limited inputs, the Cuban government reorganized its agricultural economy. Large portions of state-owned land were given to cooperatively organized farmers, increasing local control. Government research and extension focused on promoting biodiversity rather than specialized monocultures, and in developing low-cost inputs that could be produced on the farm such as compost and biological pest controls. Campesinos who had farmed prior to the introduction of Green Revolution technologies played an important role in this research, as did promotores from the Campesino a Campesino movement. Additionally, Cuba promoted urban agriculture and community gardens, and opened farmers' markets where producers could sell surplus (Alvarez et al. 2006). Yields fell initially, but recovered soon afterward and Cuba has maintained high standards of living and life expectancy and low rates of diet-related diseases (Amador and Peña 1991). For this reason, Rosset and Borque (2002, xv) triumphantly describe recent Cuban history as "the overcoming of a food crisis through self-reliance, smaller farms, and agro-ecological technology."

In practice, the Cuban agricultural sector mixes state, cooperative, and private ownership. The number of state-owned farms has decreased since the revolution, with parallel increases in locally managed cooperative and family farms. The latter often remain part of cooperative associations through which they access credit and other services. Additionally, state enterprises can enter into partnerships with foreign capital, and have begun to do so. Levins (2002), however, argues that these transformations in land ownership reflect reorganization within socialism rather than a departure from it. Cuban agriculture maintains its opposition to wage labor and the primacy of economic considerations (also see Enriquez 2004). Moreover, the move toward local land management aligns with the concepts of food sovereignty and food justice.

As in the United States, Cuba's organic farming movement consists of more than just farmers. The Cuban Organic Farming Association was developed during the Agrarian University of Havana's First National Conference on Organic Agriculture, and seeks to develop consciousness, projects, research, teaching and networking on the topic of organic agriculture. The university offers MA and PhD programs in agroecology, as well as a popular correspondence course offering certification to national farmers. In 1995, the first Cuban delegation visited Vicente Guerro to participate in a Campesino a Campesino workshop, and Mexican promotores led a workshop in Havana the following year. Since then, Cuba's National Association of Small Farmers has become a strong supporter of the Campesino a Campesino movement, and thousands of small farmers have participated in their agroecology trainings. This demonstrates the practice of transnational alliances between market-based, state-based, and social movement advocacy for food sovereignty.

In his study of the Cuban organic farming movement, Funes (2002, 22) declares that its "principles run counter to the vicious globalization promoted by neo-liberalism." Despite, or perhaps due to its forced marginalization by the global economic system, Cuba's state policies have established and supported a system of organic agriculture that promotes food sovereignty and human and ecological health. Such an approach, supporters claim, has been economically solvent, but not motivated by profit (Levins 2002). However, recent murmurings from both the U.S. and Cuban governments suggest that the end of the embargo may be within sight. Whether such a political realignment pushes Cuban agriculture toward the neoliberal, market-dominated approaches that activists see as obstacles to their food sovereignty remains to be seen.

In the United States, government policies subsidizing industrial farming result in processed foods being significantly cheaper than local produce, often confining sustainable agriculture to an elite niche market. This presents a challenge to the U.S. food justice movement, which must work to make such produce both available and affordable to low-income communities and communities of color, while also seeking to provide adequate returns for struggling farmers. In Belo Horizonte and Cuba, on the other hand, government policies promote sustainable agriculture, enabling locally grown produce to become the basis of popular diets.

Because local production is key, governments must support local land-use management and encourage farmers' agroecological knowledge. In both Belo Horizonte and Cuba, food remains a commodity to be bought and sold. However, this city and nation work to ensure food access, contesting the market-led approach advocated by the IMF and World Bank. Thus they encourage new participatory norms for food sovereignty in which sustainable agriculture speaks to citizens rather than consumers.

Demands for Food Sovereignty: The MST and La Via Campesina

The transition from programs increasing food sovereignty at the local level to broad policies guaranteeing it will require the participation of social movements demanding food as a human right and democratic participation in food and agricultural systems. Perhaps the best known of such movements is Brazil's *Movimento dos Trabalhadores Rurais Sem Terra* (Landless Workers Movement, or MST). The MST is widely associated with the establishment of encampments on privately owned but unused land. They also work in concert with La Via Campesina (literally "the peasant way" but more often translated as "the international peasants' movement"), creating transnational advocacy for food sovereignty and opposition to the environmental injustices resulting from the globalization of agriculture. While the U.S. food justice movement operates mainly through entrepreneurial strategies at the local level, these national and transnational movements offer a variety of scales, approaches, and participatory norms.

The Landless Workers Movement
The MST was officially founded in 1984, following the fall of the Brazilian military regime. It is best known for its *festas*, or parties, where landless families collectively occupy privately owned but unoccupied and unused land. Brazilian law requires that land serve a social function, and authorizes the government to expropriate land not doing so for the purpose of agrarian reform. After a festa, the MST attempts to legitimize settlements using this law. The movement claims almost two million members, and has successfully created more than a thousand settlements (Wolford 2007). The MST, and the constellation of national and transnational forces it seeks to address, create participatory norms that encompass many aspects of members' lives, creating everyday economic, educational, and political practices through which individuals and communities can pursue their demand for food sovereignty.

The everyday realities of MST settlements are quite different from those established through the World Bank's market-led agrarian reform (Martins 2006). MST squatters do not incur debt because, while beneficiaries of the market-led program must buy their land, these activists demand and seize it. And while those acquiring land through the World Bank have difficulty obtaining the infrastructure necessary to manage a farm, MST settlers can access credit or other agricultural services through the National Confederation of Agrarian Reform Cooperatives. Sometimes described as the economic arm of the MST, this organization helps maintain the economic solvency, and thus sustainability, of MST settlements (Martins 2006). Moreover, while structural adjustment policies dictate the application of expert knowledge from the global North, MST settlers maintain local control over land management through a collective model of planning and farm production. They participate in frequent assemblies in which they discuss problems and make proposals. All of the settlements' major political and economic decisions are made democratically, including the reinvestment and distribution of profits.

Observers of the MST highlight its dedication to education, which it posits as an essential link between agrarian reform and broader social change. The movement operates six hundred elementary and twenty high schools, as well as vocational and political training schools serving more than 500,000 adults. Their pedagogy seeks to honor both youth and adult students' lived experiences by incorporating the movement's lessons and struggles into their curricula (Martins 2006). A study of recently settled farmers in four regions of Brazil revealed that 87 percent did not attend school past the fourth grade (Ondetti 2008). Although this study includes only MST members living in settlements, it suggests that MST schools must teach basic reading and writing skills alongside structural literacy.

Beyond land reform, the MST seeks to participate in the formation of political alternatives to neoliberalism that emphasize employment, education, housing, food, and health (Martins 2006). Supporters describe the movement's Popular Project as a democratic and participatory space in which networks of MST members engage in dialog with professors, politicians, technicians, students, and priests. The MST then seeks to gain publicity for their political vision through popular protest. For example, in 1998, almost 6,000 workers marched across the country in protest against then-president Cardoso's support for the market-led agrarian reform advocated by the World Bank. And while they tend to view President Luiz Ignacio Lula de Silva as an ally, a second march in 2005 was designed to pressure him into stronger support for the MST's goals.

The Peasant Way

The MST's demands for land reform are articulated largely at the national level, because it is the Brazilian government that has the authority to expropriate and redistribute land. However, recognizing that neoliberal models of agriculture are imposed from beyond national borders, the MST has joined a transnational social movement opposing the economic liberalization of agriculture, and advocating for an alternative model based on small-scale farms, peasant agriculture, inclusion, and social justice. Founded in 1993, La Via Campesina has gained global recognition for its participation in direct actions opposing corporate globalization. Members of this organization have been visible at protests against the meetings of international monetary institutions such as the IMF and World Bank. Beyond opposition, La Via Campesina has also participated in transnational meetings such as the World Food Summit and the World Social Forum.

Recognizing that neither individual farmers nor national peasant movements have the capacity to pressure international monetary institutions and to transform the global political order, La Via Campesina is a transnational network consisting of 148 organizations from 56 countries. Rafael Alegria, who served as Operational Secretariat from 1996 to 2004, describes the importance of a transnational response:

From the Via Campesina's point of view, the neo-liberal model is causing the collapse of this . . . peasant economy. It is destroying natural resources, and the environment. It is also undermining our own peasant movements from around the world. For this reason, it is very important that we have an international organization like the Via Campesina. . . . Creating a global response is the very reason for the Via Campesina's existence. (quoted in Desmarais 2007, 33)

La Via Campesina promotes transnational organization in order to amplify the voices of its diverse national, regional, and local constituent movements.

To build unity within this diversity, the Via Campesina has developed strict processes and policies aimed at holding the international organization accountable to its members. The Via Campesina is divided into eight regions, each of which elects one man and one woman to a sixteen-member International Coordinating Commission. Additionally, every few years, delegates from all regions gather to determine the movement's general direction, policies and strategies. Thus far, four meetings have been held on four different continents. International gatherings are preceded by regional ones, in which coordinators survey the interests and positions of their constituents. This model is designed to privilege local knowledges and to ensure that the transnational movement's work remains grounded in local realities.

What binds the members of La Via Campesina is not just a set of organizational policies, but a shared opposition to the Green Revolution technologies and neoliberal policies they believe have created food crises throughout the global South. Indeed it is this movement that coined the term *food sovereignty*, and it maintains an ongoing discussion as to its meaning. Generally, though, the movement's rhetoric contends that food sovereignty favors small-scale family and collective farms and peasant agriculture, and prioritizes sustainable production and access to local markets. International trade is reserved for surpluses remaining after local populations are fed (Rosset 2003, Rosset and Borque 2001, Desmarais 2007). Thus La Via Campesina offers a model of a global agricultural system in direct opposition to the market-led approach enabled by the Green Revolution and advocated by the IMF and World Bank. Moreover, La Via Campesina posits land reform as necessary to food sovereignty, and seeks to support its members' various efforts to achieve this. Additionally, the movement has been a strong, vocal opponent of genetically modified foods and of the patenting of seeds. These technologies, movement leaders argue, represent a continuation of the Green Revolution, and will produce further ecological degradation and increase corporate control over global agriculture (Desmarais 2007). The U.S. food justice movement, as well as the Campesino a Campesino movement and El Rancho Solidario, offer models of resistance within global industrial agriculture. But it is La Via Campesina's notion of food sovereignty, combined with its new structures of collective action and broad participatory norms, that create direct opposition to industrial agriculture.

Food Justice and Food Sovereignty

The six examples described in this chapter provide evidence of the diversity of interconnected resistances, oppositions, and alternatives to the environmental injustices created by Green Revolution technologies and the neoliberal IMF and World Bank monetary policies in Latin America. Like the U.S. food justice movement, they highlight how small farmers and landless peoples have been deprived of the ability to grow food, and how adequate, appropriate, affordable food is not available for purchase. Additionally, actors involved in the Latin American projects, policies, and movements described above share the U.S. food justice movement's regard for place-based local knowledge, particularly that of farmers, as essential to agroecological production. Deploying a pedagogy that treats the everyday life experiences of their constituents as important, actors in both the food justice and food sovereignty movements seek to empower communities to take control of their food and agricultural systems.

However, one key difference between the two is that the neoliberal context in which the U.S. food justice movement operates fosters participatory norms encouraging marginalized peoples to become entrepreneurs in the emerging "green economy." Although there are exceptions, most organizations train low-income people and people of color to grow, process, and cook food as a form of "green economic development." The examples from Latin America, on the other hand, have more varied relationships with market economies, leading to a wider variety of ways to participate. Farmers in the Campesino a Campesino movement, for example, do aim to sell their products, but do so after their own community's food needs are met. The emphasis on self-sufficient production disrupts the World Bank and IMF assumption that food should be grown in order to be sold. Despite calls for food to be treated as a human right, the U.S. food justice movement's primary focus on entrepreneurship supports a logic that treats food primarily as a commodity.

In this regard, the discourses and practices of those working for food sovereignty in Latin America shed light on the role of government in providing food. For the U.S. food justice movement, this insight may help to resolve a tension between the needs of producers and consumers. In U.S. food movements generally, the desire to provide more income for farmers is often at odds with the goal of providing affordable food. Organizations supporting sustainable agriculture in wealthy communities have largely prioritized the former (Allen 2004). For food justice activists, this remains a largely unacknowledged contradiction. El Ranchero Solidario and Belo Horizonte provide an alternative to this dilemma. State and cooperative organizations play the role of nonprofit intermediaries, buying from farmers and selling to consumers. In the former, prices are close to market rates while state funding enables Belo Horizonte to trade access to public lands for reduced food costs. Even in socialist Cuba, the market remains an important player in determining food prices and policies, though in this case, farmers' profits are a less visible concern.

In the U.S. food justice movement, nonprofit organizations have at times played this role, helping to connect farmers and consumers.

However, the funding structure of nonprofit organizations generally demands that after some kind of incubator period, programs become economically solvent. Food justice activists in the United States have not lobbied for the kind of state involvement seen in Belo Horizonte and Cuba. Indeed, recognizing that the U.S. government largely steps in on the part of agribusiness, food justice activists tend to argue against government intervention. But the example from Belo Horizonte indicates that, even within a nation enmeshed in market-led agricultural policies aimed at harnessing the technological advances of the Green Revolution, there may be opportunities to pressure state and local policymakers to support programs favoring food justice and food sovereignty. Such ongoing state funding may help U.S. movements to simultaneously expand food access while providing adequate returns for farmers. It is worth noting that this strategy is quite different from U.S. movements' emphasis on eliminating intermediaries by encouraging direct relationships between producers and consumers.

Moreover, the various examples from Latin America posit their own food disenfranchisement—both lack of land tenure and lack of access to affordable, appropriate food—as the result of particular forces of globalization. Like the U.S. food justice movement, some efforts function as everyday resistance within states embracing the globalization of agriculture. Others, however, directly challenge state policies that favor this political economic order, creating participatory norms of direct action rather than alternative forms of production and consumption. The MST, for example, confronts an inequitable land tenure system worsened by market-led agrarian reform (Sauer 2006; Wolford 2007). Their land occupations directly oppose World Bank and IMF policies aimed at privatization, while their protests pressure state actors to create a more equitable agricultural system. The MST is also a member of La Via Campesina, and through this alliance they participate in protests against international monetary institutions while sharing their experience with landless peoples worldwide. This combination of national and transnational targets represents the movement's understanding that the effects of globalization are amplified by and experienced through state policies. Given that the U.S. food justice movement regards federal policy as responsible for environmental injustices within the food system, it is striking that their tactics are generally not aimed at policy change. However, as with Campesino a Campesino, the U.S. food justice movement's programs may help to build the structural literacy and grassroots power necessary for such an undertaking.

Finally, in their focus on the U.S. policies that have certainly contributed to inequalities within the food system, food justice scholars and
movement intellectuals largely ignore the role of neoliberal globalization
and its tendency to increase environmental injustices. The U.S. food
justice movement's analysis largely overlooks the Green Revolution,
which has allowed increasingly small numbers of corporate farmers to
produce increasingly large yields of a few commodity crops. Additionally,
the movement tends not to name the neoliberal trend away from entitlement programs—such as welfare or food stamps—as a source of unequal
food access. Indeed, many in the U.S. food justice movement have
adopted the right-wing interpretation of such programs as promoting
dependency and complacency, and posit entrepreneurial approaches as
a more empowering alternative.

The U.S. sustainable agriculture movement (sometimes called the food
movement), on the other hand, does recognize globalization as a key
creator of an ecologically destructive food system. Supporters of this
movement have been one of developed countries' key constituencies in
protests against the World Bank and IMF, and have rallied against
present-day Green Revolution technologies such as genetically modified
seeds. Yet, the primary response of the sustainable agriculture movement
has been to encourage their mainly wealthy supporters to attempt to
"opt out" of the global food system and support local, organic, small-
scale family farmers instead. U.S. policies and neoliberal trade agreements, as well as economies of scale, tend to ensure that such food is
more expensive than that produced by corporations embracing Green
Revolution technologies. The sustainable agriculture movement tends
to prioritize support for farmers over increasing food access, and thus
fails to link its analysis of globalization to the environmental injustices
it produces. Moreover, while supporting local food systems has many
positive effects for communities that can afford to do so, the movement's
emphasis on "the local" is complicit with globalization in that it tends
to weaken the state by undermining support for the federal entitlement
programs on which many food-insecure people depend (Swyngedouw
2004). Such an approach prevents U.S. food movements from envision-
ing the kinds of state support seen in Belo Horizonte and Cuba,
which may make food justice and food sovereignty widely available
realities.

Environmental injustices may be overcome if the U.S. food justice
movement connects to transnational efforts to create food sovereignty in
the global South. The Via Campesina is able to link peasant movements

from around the world, in part, because they share a common analysis of the Green Revolution and neoliberal monetary policies as responsible for their lived realities. Constituent movements then maintain individual analyses of how national and local policies interact with these transnational processes in order to create particular conditions. In looking beyond borders, as well as to national policies, the U.S. food justice movement may recognize the role of globalization in creating the environmental and spatial injustices it faces, as well as commonalities between its own circumstances and those confronted by small farmers and landless peoples in the global South. Such an analysis could eventually drive the creation of a joined-up movement for food justice and food sovereignty worldwide.

Notes

The author thanks Eric Holt-Giménez and the staff of Food First! for their help conceptualizing this chapter, and for undertaking much of the primary research on which it is based.

1. Though the movement for food sovereignty is truly global, I am particularly focused on Latin America. Given critiques in the literature that food justice activism relies on entrepreneurial strategies complicit with capitalism (Guthman 2008), I am particularly interested in whether and how conditions play out differently among states that wholeheartedly embrace neoliberalism and those that seem to be moving left.

2. Worldwide, hunger actually declined 16 percent during this time. However, the stark decline in China was due not to the import of Green Revolution technologies, but to changes in land tenure.

3. As governed by the commodity title of the U.S. Farm Bill.

4. It is U.S. policy that all food aid be purchased from U.S. farmers, and packaged and shipped by U.S. companies. This costs approximately 50 percent of the money allocated (Quigley 2009).

5. In this way, it very much parallels Mills's (1959/2000) classic sociological imagination.

References

Alkon, Alison Hope, and Kari Marie Norgaard. 2009. Breaking the food chains: An investigation of food justice activism. *Sociological Inquiry* 79(3):289–305.

Allen, Patricia. 2004. *Together at the Table: Sustainability and Sustenance in the American Agrifood System*. State College: Pennsylvania State University Press.

Altieri, Miguel. 1995. *Agroecology: The Science of Sustainable Agriculture*. New York: Perseus Books.

Alvarez, Mavis, Martin Borque, Fernando Funes, Lucy Martin, Armando Nova, and Peter Rosset. 2006. Surviving crisis in Cuba: The Second Agrarian Reform and sustainable agriculture. In Peter Rosset, Raj Patel, and Michael Courville, eds., *Promised Land: Competing Visions of Agrarian Reform*, 225–248. Oakland, CA: Food First Books.

Amador, Miguel, and Manuel Peña. 1991. Nutrition and health issues in Cuba: Strategies for a developing country. *Food and Nutrition Bulletin* 13(4). http://www.unu.edu/unupress/food/8F134e/8F134E08.htm.

Borger, Julian. 2008. Feed the world? We are fighting a losing battle, UN admits. *The Guardian*, February 26. www.theguardian.co.uk.

Borras, Saturnino M., Jr. 2004. *La Via Campesina: An Evolving Transnational Social Movement*. Transnational Institute Briefing Series No. 6. Amsterdam: Transnational Institute.

Borras, Saturnino M., Jr. 2006. The underlying assumptions, theory, and practice of neoliberal land policies. In Peter Rosset, Raj Patel, and Michael Courville, eds., *Promised Land: Competing Visions of Agrarian Reform*, 99–128. Oakland, CA: Food First Books.

Bunch, Ralph. 1996. *People-Centered Agricultural Development: Principles of Extension for Achieving Long-Term Impact*. London: Overseas Development Institute.

Chossudovsky, Michel. 2003. *The Globalization of Poverty and the New World Order*. Hayward, CA: Global Research.

Davis, Mike. 2006. *Planet of Slums*. New York: Verso.

Deninger, Klaus W. 1999. Making negotiated land reform work: Initial experience from Colombia, Brazil and South Africa. *World Development* 27(4): 651–672.

Desmarais, Annette. 2007. *La Via Campesina: Globalization and the Power of Peasants*. London: Pluto Press.

Elliot, Kim. 2008. *Biofuels and the Food Price Crisis: A Survey of the Issues*. Center for Global Development Working Paper No. 151. Washington, DC: Center for Global Development.

Enriquez, Laura. 2004. The role of the small farmer in the retreat from and the reconfiguration of socialism. Paper presented at the Meeting of the American Sociological Association, San Francisco.

Finch, C. D. 1985. *Adjustment Policies and Conditionality*. Washington, DC: Institute for International Economics.

Funes, Fernando, Luis Garcia, Martin Borque, Nilda Perez, and Peter Rosset. 2002. *Sustainable Agriculture and Resistance: Transforming Food Production in Cuba*. New York: Food First Books.

Gilbert, Jess, Gwen Sharp, and M. Sindy Felin. 2002. The loss and persistence of black-owned farms and farmland: A review of the research literature and its implications. *Southern Rural Sociology* 18:1–30.

Guthman, Julie. 2007. Can't stomach it: How Michael Pollan et al. made me want to eat Cheetos. *Gastronomica: The Journal of Food and Culture* 7(3):75–79.

Guthman, Julie. 2008. Neoliberalism and the making of food politics in California. *Geoforum* 39(3):1171–1183.

Hanley, Charles J. 2008. "'We blew it' on global food, says Bill Clinton." Associated Press. *San Francisco Chronicle*.

Harvey, David. 1996. *Justice, Nature, and the Geography of Difference*. New York: Wiley-Blackwell.

Hewitt de Alcántara, Cynthia. 1976. Modernizing Mexican agriculture. Geneva: United Nations Research Institute for Social Development.

Holt-Giménez, Eric. 2006. *Camesino a Campesino: Voices from Latin America's Farmer to Farmer Movement for Sustainable Agriculture*. Oakland, CA: Food First Books.

Holt-Giménez, Eric, and Raj Patel. 2009. *Food Rebellions: Crisis and the Hunger for Justice*. Oakland, CA: Food First Books.

Jackson, Jennifer. 2005. *Nutritional Analysis of Traditional and Present Foods of the Karuk People and Development of Public Outreach Materials*. Happy Camp, CA: Karuk Tribe of California.

Jaroz, Lucy. 2009. Energy, climate change, meat and markets: Mapping the coordinates of the current world food crisis. *Geography Crisis* 3(6):2065–2083.

Jennings, Bruce. 1988. *Foundations of International Agricultural Research: Science and Politics in Mexican Agriculture*. Boulder, CO: Westview Press.

Kosek, Jake. 2006. *Understories: The Political Life of Forests in Northern New Mexico*. Durham, NC: Duke University Press.

Lappé, Frances Moore. 2009. The city that ended hunger. *Yes Magazine*. www.yesmagazine.org.

Lappé, Frances Moore, Joseph Collins, and Peter Rosset, with Luis Esparza. 1998. *World Hunger: Twelve Myths*. New York: Grove Press.

Lappé, Frances Moore, and Anna Lappé. 2002. *Hope's Edge: The Next Diet for a Small Planet*. New York: Tarcher.

Levins, Richard. 2002. The unique pathway of Cuban development. In Fernando Funes, Luis Garcia, Martin Bourque, Nilda Perez, and Peter Rosset, eds., *Sustainable Agriculture and Resistance: Transforming Food Production in Cuba*. Oakland, CA: Food First Books.

Magdoff, Fred. 2008. "The World Food Crisis: Sources and Solutions." *Monthly Review*. www.monthlyreview.org. Accessed June 5, 2009.

Marichal, Carlos. 1989. *A Century of Debt Crises in Latin America*. Princeton, NJ: Princeton University Press.

Martins, Monica Dias. 2006. Learning to participate: The MST experience. In Peter Rosset, Raj Patel, and Michael Courville, eds., *Promised Land: Competing Visions of Agrarian Reform*, 265–276. Oakland, CA: Food First Books.

McClintock, Nathan. 2008. *From Industrial Garden to Food Desert: Unearthing the Root Structure of Urban Agriculture in Oakland, California*. ISSC Fellows Working Papers, Paper ISSC_WP_32. Oakland, CA: Institute for the Study of Social Change.

Mikesell, Raymond F. 1994. *The Bretton Woods Debates: A Memoir*. Princeton, NJ: Department of Economics, Princeton University.

Mills, C. Wright. 1959/2000. *The Sociological Imagination*. 40th anniv. ed. Oxford: Oxford University Press.

Norgaard, K. 2005. *The Effects of Altered Diet on the Health of the Karuk People Karuk Tribe of California*. Happy Camp, CA: Karuk Tribe of California. Filed November 2005 with Federal Energy Regulatory Commission on Behalf of the Karuk Tribe in the Klamath River Project relicensing process.

Ondetti, Gabriel. 2008. *Land, Protest, and Politics: The Landless Movement and the Struggle for Agrarian Reform in Brazil*. State College: Pennsylvania State University Press.

Pastor, Robert. 1987. *Latin America's Debt Crisis: Adjusting to the Past or Planning for the Future?* Lafayette, LA: Lynne Rienner.

Pearse, Andrew. 1980. *Seeds of Plenty, Seeds of Want: Social and Economic Implications of the Green Revolution*. Oxford: Clarendon Press.

Peña, Devon. 2005. *Mexican Americans and the Environment: Tierra y Vida*. Tucson: University of Arizona Press.

Pollan, Michael. 2006. *The Omnivore's Dilemma: A Natural History of Four Meals*. New York: Penguin.

Quigley, Bill. 2009. *30 Years Ago Haiti Grew All the Rice It Needed. What Happened? Counterpunch*. http://www.counterpunch.com.

Rogers, Everett. 1969. *Modernization among Peasants: The Impact of Communication*. New York: Holt, Rinehart and Winston.

Rosset, Peter. 2003. Moving forward: Agrarian reform as part of food sovereignty. In Peter Rosset, Raj Patel, and Michael Courville, eds., *Promised Land: Competing Visions of Agrarian Reform*, 301–322. Oakland, CA: Food First Books.

Rosset, Peter, and Martin Borque. 2001. Lessons of Cuban resistance. In Fernando Funes, Luis Garcia, Martin Borque, Nilda Perez, and Peter Rosset, eds., *Sustainable Agriculture and Resistance: Transforming Food Production in Cuba*. New York: Food First Books.

Rosset, Peter, Raj Patel, and Michael Courville. 2006. *Promised Land: Competing Visions of Agrarian Reform*. Oakland, CA: Food First Books.

Rostow, Walt W. 1990. *The Stages of Economic Growth: A Non-Communist Manifesto*. Cambridge: Cambridge University Press.

Sauer, Sérgio. 2006. The World Bank's market-based land reform in Brazil. In Peter Rosset, Raj Patel, and Michael Courville, eds., *Promised Land: Competing Visions of Agrarian Reform*, 177–191. Oakland, CA: Food First Books.

Smith, William, Carlos H. Acuna, and Eduardo A. Gamarra. 1994. *Latin American Political Economy in the Age of Neoliberal Reform: Theoretical and*

Comparative Perspectives for the 1990s. Miami: University of Miami Iberian Studies Institute.

Stone, Dori. 2009. *Beyond the Fence*. Oakland, CA: Food First Books.

Stonich, Susan. 1993. *I am Destroying the Land!: The Political Ecology of Poverty and Environmental Destruction in Honduras*. Boulder: Westview Press.

Swyngedouw, Eric. 2004. *Glocalisations*. Philadelphia: Temple University Press.

Via Campesina. 2002. *Food Sovereignty*. Flyer distributed at the World Food Summit +5, Rome. http://www.viacampesina.org.

Vorley, Bill. 2001. *The Chains of Agriculture: Sustainability and the Restructuring of Agri-Food Markets*. London: IIED Publications.

Wade, Robert. 2004. Is globalization reducing poverty and inequality? *International Journal of Health Services* 34(3):381–414.

Wallerstein, Immanuel. 1974. *The Modern World-System, I: Capitalist Agriculture and the Origins of the European World-Economy in the Sixteenth Century*. New York: Academic Press.

Wirth, Cathy, Ron Strochlic, and Christy Getz. 2009. *Hunger in the Fields: Food Insecurity among Farmworkers in Fresno County*. Davis, CA: California Institute for Rural Studies. http://www.cirsinc.org.

Wolford, Wendy. 2007. Neoliberalism and the struggle for land in Brazil. In Nik Heynen, James McCarthy, Scott Prudham, and Paul Robbins, eds., *Neoliberal Environments: False Promises and Unnatural Consequences*. New York: Routledge.

10

Going Beyond the State to Strengthen the Rule of Law: Local Activists, Transnational Networks, and Gold Mining in Bulgaria

Barbara Hicks

We have become used to seeing large international corporations investing in resource extraction in developing countries, and we often see transnational environmental justice issues as efforts of local communities in these cases to prevent the investments or control the effects of production on their natural and social environments and economy. These sorts of investments also started appearing in the postcommunist transition countries in the 1990s. Coming at a time of major economic and political transformation, the projects have taken advantage of and become entangled in transition politics. This chapter seeks to understand what factors influence whether local residents are able to protect their economic, environmental, and communal interests by shaping or preventing these projects.

While at one level this chapter is a case study of external investment in resource extraction in postcommunist states, its findings are applicable to other countries as well. Phrased more generally, the research question would be: What are effective strategies for local communities seeking environmental justice in the face of major transnational investments in small or mid- to low-income countries with weakly institutionalized state decision-making procedures and weak rule of law? The states of comparative interest here range from semiauthoritarian to democratic, but they usually have enough of a participatory political process and a sufficient measure of general accountability to the public that their governments cannot simply crush citizens with outright force, as can more repressive states. While they may face selective repression, local communities' greatest challenges in these states generally lie in having their voices considered and in ensuring that the state follows its own prescribed practices and standards or that it develops reasonable practices where there are none. These conditions are typical of transitional regimes of various types and many developing countries.

The varied trajectories of the three cases examined in this chapter suggest a couple of paths to acquiring a voice, and ultimately environmental justice, for local communities in countries with weak participatory practices and inconsistent rule of law. Above all, a strong majority of local residents must be united and steadfast in their opposition, and they need to develop a core organization or leadership that can devise strategies, communicate with external actors, and maintain resistance over time. While local opposition may be a necessary condition for success in confronting a tangle of corporate and government interests favoring rapid resource exploitation, such opposition is often not sufficient on its own to reverse or revise investment decisions. In more repressive systems, isolated local resistance can be put down by physical force; in less repressive systems, a variety of selective punishments and incentives can make it difficult to maintain resistance. The recourse for local groups is to tap into existing networks of environmental or civil rights organizations that can reach actors on the national and transnational levels. These organizations provide not only contacts and exposure that break local isolation and increase pressure on investors and the state from other sources, but also legal, scientific, and organizing advice at the domestic level and sometimes resources. Finally, this comparison shows that the particular combination of strategies and frames and their likelihood of success are contingent on timing and specific features of the case.

Local Dynamics in the Context of Institutional Transition

Bulgaria is a good example of a country in political and economic transition toward liberal democracy and a liberal version of capitalism. Governed by the Soviet-type model of state socialism and the same ruler for thirty-five years, Bulgaria remained a stalwart Soviet ally from the end of World War II until the revolutions of 1989. The country developed rapidly along the lines of the Soviet model until the late 1970s, when both living standards and economic growth stagnated. The Bulgarian Communist Party was rather repressive and effective in preventing the development of independent civic and political groups until Gorbachev's reforms in the second half of the 1980s. Although Todor Zhivkov, the country's aging leader, vacillated wildly in his discussion of reforms in the Gorbachev period, little true change came from above. Toward the end of the 1980s independent groups and unions started to form, among them *Ekoglasnost*, an environmental group with its roots in opposition to Romania's industrial and canalization policies in the Danube delta.

One of the more visible civil society actors, *Ekoglasnost* took a lead in pressing for greater change as reform accelerated in the Soviet Union and elsewhere in Eastern Europe, while Zhivkov's regime remained entrenched in its ways. Regime change came to Bulgaria in 1989 by means of an internal coup led by the Foreign Minister Petr Mladenov, a more reformist communist, on November 10, the day after the fall of the Berlin Wall. The ruling party quickly arranged elections for June 1990, despite protests by the opposition that there was not enough time to organize and campaign. The elections gave the newly renamed Bulgarian Socialist Party (BSP) a slight edge. The postcommunists were not able to maintain a stable government in the face of protests and strikes, and by the end of the year the BSP formed a government of national unity with the opposition groups gathered under the Union of Democratic Forces.

The political transition in Bulgaria was prolonged by the fact that the old regime was brought down by an insider, by the relative balance between the former communists and the opposition for the first decade of postcommunist rule, and by a period of grand coalition. At the same time, the economic transition led to the rapid growth of private businesses and privatization processes that were not at all even or transparent. The liberalization of the economy was prolonged by internal politics and the geographic misfortune of being cast of the Yugoslav wars of succession and the economic blockade on Serbia. Partial liberalization tends to intertwine the state and new private sector, creating incentives and opportunities for entrepreneurs and certain state actors to stall further reforms and the establishment of a clear rule of law in the economy (Hellman 1998; Barnes 2007; Tzvetkova 2008). For Bulgaria, the result of these political and economic trajectories has been a set of tight relationships between certain business and financial circles and specific political parties (Ganev 2006; Konstadinova 2007). Despite a consistent string of multiparty elections and constitutional, institutional, and legal reforms, these relationships remain strong and they limit the autonomy of governmental institutions, transparency and accountability, and the rule of law (Engelbrekt 2007; Barnes 2007; Ganev 2006; Schönfelder 2005).

Compared with other postcommunist and semideveloped countries, Bulgaria's accession to the European Union makes it one of the set of countries *more* likely to have developed the institutional and legal framework necessary to ensure public participation in decision making regarding environmentally sensitive projects and, more generally, the rule of law. In the EU accession process, prospective members must adopt EU law, including environmental standards and participatory procedures, when making decisions about investments that will have environmental impacts. The accession process also reinforces democracy, institutional accountability, and the rule of law. Bulgaria's progress on these measures was slow, leading to the country being left out of the first round of postcommunist accession. Even when Bulgaria joined three years later, persistent weaknesses in these areas led the EU to add unprecedented conditions to the accession agreement. The record both during accession and since has been decidedly mixed. Elections occur regularly and ballots are not fraudulent. However, there are shortcomings in media access during elections and in governance. In fact, the EU has acted on the conditions attached to Bulgaria's entrance. Faced with intractable corruption on an EU-supported highway project and after several warnings and pressures to improve financial and institutional accountability, the EU froze infrastructure fund flows (under the Instrument for Structural Policies for Pre-Accession or ISPA program) to Bulgaria in January 2008. When after six more months, the government still failed to address crime and corruption satisfactorily, the European Commission cut off financial assistance and withdrew the accreditation of two Bulgarian government agencies to manage EU funds. This measure was unprecedented, although it was foreseen by the special conditions attached to the accession agreements with Bulgaria and Romania. Despite these enormous losses, the government was unable or unwilling to right its house enough to unfreeze the funds through 2008. The EU did unblock some of the funds in May 2009 after Bulgaria had adopted a Conflict of Interest Act and revised both the Public Tenders Act and the Road Act (Sofia News Agency 2009b). Bulgaria still ranked last in absorption of ISPA funds in the fall of 2009 (Sofia News Agency 2009a) and was threatened with the loss of more infrastructure aid well into 2010 for not being able to initiate and complete projects within the allowable time frame (*Sofia Echo* 2010). This ongoing struggle demonstrates both the possibility and limitations of EU influence over domestic institutions, accountability, and the rule of law (see also Noutcheva and Bechev 2008).

Three Cases of Foreign Investment in Gold Mining

Bulgaria has been a significant site of gold mining at least since the days of ancient Thrace. Through the centuries, gold mining has been conducted underground in traditional fashion. Under Soviet-influenced communist rule, exploration and exploitation of gold resources continued, leaving in their wake many studies and a good deal of contamination.

As the country faced economic crisis during the blockade on Yugoslavia and Bulgaria's own transformation to capitalism, several of the state mining companies became insolvent. Foreign investors moved in, establishing partnerships and targeting the most lucrative holdings. The three cases studied here comprise the set of major foreign initiatives in the gold sector. All of these investments started in the early years of the millennium, hit their first major phases of activism and resistance in 2005–2006, and have followed differing trajectories since.

Examining three different cases in the same country over the same period allows one to hold national institutional factors constant while studying how other factors shape the decision-making process both on their own and in the way they relate to national institutions. If the dynamics and outcomes of these three cases vary, then they cannot be explained primarily by national institutions and laws. The paths of the cases highlight local factors, strategies of different actors, involvement of transnational actors, contingencies affecting how national institutions treated these cases, and decisions of the companies undertaking the investments.

Following the July 2009 elections, the new Bulgarian government asserted its intention to increase transparency and accountability in institutional decision making, including in the use of EU funds. A new Minister of Environment and Water with experience in two previous governments came in as well. While it is still too early to determine whether Bulgarian politics is indeed becoming more institutionalized or whether the government is simply using institutions to different ends from its predecessor, some of the most recent developments in the cases here suggest that the government has placed more of an emphasis on adhering to formal processes. The directions the cases are taking are mixed from the vantage point of those opposed to the gold-mining investments and plans for cyanide use. They too, though, are pursuing institutional means to halt or alter the projects.

Chelopech

Chelopech has long been a mining area. The current controversy started with the purchase of mining rights by Dundee Precious Metals, a firm developed for investments in Southeastern Europe with ties to Newmont, Teck Comico, and others major international companies (Panayotova 2008; Panayotova and Kuznetsov 2008). Dundee started its activity in Chelopech in 2003 with environmental remediation, exploration of reserves, and production by existing methods, Phase I of its project

(Marchev 2006). The heart of Dundee's investment (Phase II) focuses on mining the most promising veins and reprocessing old mining waste with cyanide leaching in order to obtain more of the gold, then filling the old tunnels with the solid waste from the processing, thereby rendering the remaining ore permanently inaccessible. The cyanide-laced tailings would be stored in a new pond. As designed, the project seeks to mine the area intensively for several years, after which the known accessible resources will be depleted. Experts in the Cyanide-Free Bulgaria coalition estimate that at the projected rate of 3,000,000 tons of ore per year, the resources available for the planned means of exploitation should be depleted in seven to eight years (Fournadzhiev 2006; A. Kovatchev 2006; P. Kovatchev 2006; Radev 2006). The European Bank for Reconstruction and Development approved a loan for the first phase in 2004 (Popov 2008b; Bacheva 2006), but the project stalled out in March 2006, when the Minister of Environment and Water froze the environmental impact assessment (EIA) process for Phase II. Plans for further development began to move ahead again, when an agreement between the government and Dundee in spring 2008 led to the delayed approval of the EIA at the end of July 2008.

While the proposed project split Chelopech residents from the beginning, with a small majority for the Dundee project, many of the residents of neighboring Chavdar, who would now have a cyanide tailings pond alongside two older tailings ponds, were strongly opposed. They formed a local initiative committee, "Future for Chavdar," and voiced their opposition to the project in public hearings. Still, the project was approved by local authorities and the company continued its Phase I projects and planning for Phase II. Opponents, especially those from Chavdar, voiced their opposition both in local protests and in the hearings mandated by the EIA process, which were held in December 2005. Proponents dominated the meetings, and no significant changes were demanded of or proposed by the company as the hearings finished at the local level.

The EIA process was blocked in March 2006 by Minister of Environment and Water, Dzhevdet Chakarov, not by a rejection of the project but by a "silent refusal" to approve it. The pairing of the project with Dundee's other proposal in Krumovgrad had a good deal to do with the block, because the Krumovgrad proposal had raised more local and political opposition. Although the minister was required to make a decision within ninety days of the public hearings, he did not. The company took the matter to Bulgaria's Supreme Administrative Court and won a ruling against the minister in April 2007. The ruling required that the minister either accept or reject the Chelopech EIA, but he still refused to make a decision. In July 2007 Dundee Precious Metals pressed the European Commission to start infringement proceedings against the Bulgarian government for interfering with market competition (DPM 2007).[1] The proceedings had not been completed, when the company and the Bulgarian government entered intensive negotiations in spring 2008. At issue in these negotiations were not only the environmental concerns and permitting process, but also the financial terms of the contract. According to the original agreement, Bulgaria would receive only 1.5 percent of the profits and a fairly low concession fee. As elsewhere in postcommunist countries (e.g., with the Turquoise Hill investment in Mongolia and the Rosia Montana project in Romania), the terms of the contract, once knowledge of them finally spread, shocked the population at large, raised questions about who would negotiate such a contract and why, and increased political opposition to the investment. During the spring 2008 negotiations between Dundee and the Bulgarian government, the financial issues received the most attention, and the final agreement gave the Bulgarian government a 25 percent stake in the company and increased the concession fee. In return for the changes, the government agreed to unfreeze the EIA process, and on July 30, 2008, the minister approved the Chelopech EIA.

Given the time limits built into each stage of EIA process, as well as some omissions and changes in the plans submitted for review in the EIA process, environmentalists and advocates for local democracy argued that the entire EIA process needed to start again. The new green party Zelenite (formed in 2008), the Cyanide-Free Bulgaria coalition, and a neighboring village all filed complaints to have the EIA process invalidated (Bacheva-McGrath 2008b). This argument was very important to opponents to the project, because a new EIA process would start *after* Bulgaria's accession to the EU, allowing citizens and organizations in Bulgaria recourse to EU institutions. The original processes were initiated after Bulgaria's signature to several European and international conventions and adoption of much of EU law, but prior to accession. The Directorate-General for Environment of the European Commission thus found no grounds to take up the case (2007; Popov 2008a). If the project were to require a new EIA, then both the EIA process and the actual conduct of the project could not violate EU standards. While activists focused on the EIA process, Member of Parliament Maria Kapon introduced a proposal into parliament to ban cyanides as another avenue to stopping pending projects. The latter initiative was not successful, and Dundee seemed on its way to realizing the Chelopech project after ministerial approval of the EIA.

It has been the legal approach that has stalled the Chelopech program for the time being. In November 2009, the Supreme Administrative Court canceled the approval of the EIA on appeal by Cyanide-Free Bulgaria. The Ministry of Environment is appealing that decision, but for now it stands. The grounds for the court's cancellation of the EIA were that there was insufficient evidence that the company was planning to use the best technology, that other communities beyond Chelopech and Chavdar had not been included, and that too much time had elapsed between the conduct of the EIA and ministerial approval (Goranova 2009). In response to the court cases and the prospect of spending several years to get new permits, Dundee announced that it was freezing its investment, threatening to pull out of Chelopech in favor of a project in Namibia (Bivol 2010). However, the company has continued expanding production in Chelopech, while the issue of cyanide use remains contested.

Krumovgrad

Plans for the Ada Tepe mining project located in Krumovgrad were also developed by Dundee Precious Metals under a contract signed in 2003. Although the contract for Ada Tepe was similar to that of Chelopech in terms of financial arrangements, the plans for this project called for an open-pit mine. Three key sociopolitical differences also distinguish these cases. Krumovgrad is not a mining area, like Chelopech, but rather an agricultural region known primarily for tobacco. The tobacco is of high quality, an important export product, and central to the regional economy. Krumovgrad also lies in an area where Bulgaria's Turkish minority is dominant, which changes the political dynamics of the case. Finally, the natural environment of the Krumovgrad area is unique, and plans had been underway for an Eastern Rhodopi Nature Park and the declaration of the area as part of the EU's Natura 2000 program, since 1999, well before the Dundee contract was made (Beshkov 2006; Bacheva-McGrath 2008b).

A strong majority of Krumovgrad residents have resisted the project consistently since it was announced (Beshkov 2006, 2008; Dichev 2008). Their resistance started with the formation of a local initiative group by the name of "Life for Krumovgrad" and protests that drew the attention of environmental groups (Dichev 2006; Bacheva 2006), and of the residents of Popintsi, who sent representatives to support the Krumovgrad opponents to Ada Tepe. Initially, the position of the local government regarding the investment was not clear; those opposed to the project feared local officials were leaning toward approval at an August 2005 public hearing that was packed with the company's supporters and experts and drawing out for hours. Opponents finally started to object. By the end of the meeting, the local officials had adopted a position against the investment. The position of the Krumovgrad Municipal Council was clearly staked out the next month, when it issued a unanimous resolution against the project, collected nearly 10,000 signatures on a petition, and began to lobby leaders of the dominant party in the region to oppose the project (Municipal Council of Krumovgrad 2005; Bacheva-McGrath 2008b).

Very important was the frame that the opponents adopted both in a media release and at that public hearing. In one of its first press releases, the NGO coalition had quoted a Turkish member of the Bulgarian Socialist Party as saying that "we have been resettled all of our lives, and we will not allow ourselves to be resettled again" (Bacheva 2006). At the meeting, after noting that no one agreed with the project,[2] a coalition activist pointed out that the project would force farmers to move, thus violating their rights and freedoms (Dichev 2006; Bacheva 2006). The strength of this frame was in both its historical referent and its contemporary political phrasing. The ethnically Turkish population in the region has been the subject of discrimination, including loss of land, at several times in history (Warhola and Boteva 2003). In most recent memory were the very controversial Bulgarization policies of the Zhivkov regime in the 1980s that had forced approximately 344,000 of Bulgaria's Turkish population to flee temporarily or permanently to Turkey (Angelov and Marshall 2006, 10; Warhola and Boteva 2003). By noting that residents would be forced to move or stop farming, and arguing that the local authorities needed to protect the "rights and freedoms" of the residents, opponents struck at the heart of the identity and claims of the Movement for Rights and Freedoms (MRF), the political party widely recognized as the Turkish ethnic party.[3] This party often functions as a swing party or coalition partner for the larger parties in the political system (Rechel 2008, 2007). Adding to the importance of the general frame that garnered the support of local MRF officials, the party was just assuming control over the Ministry of Environment and Water at the national level.

Throughout the fall of 2005, Life for Krumovgrad and the Cyanide-Free Bulgaria coalition continued to press their opposition to the investment. Activists from nearby prefectures in Greece and the Greek group

Hellenic Mining Watch came to protest; Turkish activists expressed
support but were not able to obtain visas (Bacheva-McGrath 2008b).
The Greek activists also organized a complaint from their government
that Greece's rights under the Espoo Convention had been violated.
Bulgaria had signed the Convention, thereby recognizing the rights of
neighboring countries to be consulted on projects that could have damaging effects on their environment. Turkish groups have long resisted gold-
mining investments and cyanide use in their own country, particularly in
Bergama (Panayotova and Kuznetsov 2008). Both ethnic ties and the
framing so prevalent in Bergama that links living with nature to opposition to mining (Çoban 2004) have resonance in Krumovgrad.

By the end of 2005, the Minister of Environment and Water still had
not ruled on the EIA, and the Vice Minister indicated that the company
should take that fact as a "silent refusal." The Krumovgrad case was
included in the company's charges in the Supreme Administrative Court
the following spring and the decision of that court in April 2007, as well
as in Dundee's appeal to the European Commission to start infringement
proceedings. The two cases, however, were uncoupled during the negotiations in spring 2008. Whereas the company claimed that the negotiations should result in both cases being resolved, the Bulgarian government
said nothing about the negotiations covering Krumovgrad and did not
move to reopen that case. While the minister then approved the Chelopech EIA, the Krumovgrad EIA was not approved. The decoupling was
perhaps foreshadowed by the difference between the informal justification the ministry offered for the "silent refusal" on Krumovgrad in
December, which highlighted local opposition and Greek opposition, and
the economic arguments he was citing regarding Chelopech the next
summer. Some of the movement observers believe that the minister was
willing to sacrifice Chelopech to protect Krumovgrad, an argument consistent with his party's interest in supporting its base. In December 2008,
the ministry asked Dundee to prepare a Compatibility Assessment of its
Ada Tepe project with the Natura 2000 criteria as a prerequisite for the
ministry issuing a decision on the EIA. The outcome of this process was
not clear; the activities of the company are difficult to reconcile to Natura
2000 unless it can argue that there will be a sufficient buffer between
its activities and protected areas. Indeed, the initial study did find problems with parts of the project. The company proposed an alternative
location for waste and tailings, and the report incorporating this change
was completed in June 2009 (DPM 2009). In September 2009, the
Ministry of Environment and Water issued the "Commercial Discovery

Certificate" that confirms a claim and allows the company to develop plans for exploitation of the deposit. The president of Dundee, Jonathan Goodman, interpreted the move as evidence that the new prime minister has the will to alter the investment climate in Bulgaria (Katanska 2009). The Compatibility Assessment and the Certificate, however, are only the starting point of a new EIA process that must take place under EU criteria. Most recently, Dundee has proposed a project that does not use cyanide-based technology.

Popintsi

About 50 kilometers from Chelopech lies Popintsi, a small town in central Bulgaria populated mainly by families who have lived in the town for generations. Many of the town's residents have worked in mining in the region and sometimes abroad (Panayotova 2008; Fournadzhiev 2008; Marchev 2006). The gold-mining project for Popintsi was proposed by the Canadian firm Euromax Resources, registered in Bulgaria as Martern, which had bought the exploration rights to Petelovo Hill from the state. The hill sits directly above the town, and the resources in the hill had long been mapped by Bulgarian and Soviet geologists. As had Dundee in the other cases, Martern bought the previous studies for very low fees and in 2003 proceeded to gain permits for exploration and extraction of gold and copper. The low quantity of gold per ton of ore in Popintsi makes cyanide leaching the only profitable technology for obtaining gold. From the beginning, Martern planned an open-pit mine with cyanide processing.

The residents of Popintsi were united in opposing the project. Not willing to have the hill destroyed and the town's water supply threatened by cyanide and other waste for whatever returns the project might bring—and at the planned rate of exploitation there would only have been employment for five years—they prevented the company from developing the project. As Martern prepared to drill boreholes for further exploration and mapping of the resources, residents of the town blocked the road to the hill. They knew that once the company drilled, it could claim a finding and the right to exploit the resources. The company tried to move the drills up at least four times, usually in the middle of the night. Four times the residents took to the hill to block the drills. Immediately the message went around and residents went up the hill. The final time the company tried to get the drills up, residents camped on the hill day and night for several days. Despite tension and threats, the blockade held.

In addition to the blockade, the people of Popintsi held a referendum on the project. Fully 97 percent of the residents rejected the project on July 10, 2006 ("Balkan Gold Up-Date" 2006, 11). The strategy of pressing for a referendum was encouraged by the Cyanide-Free Bulgaria coalition. The actions of the residents drew some media attention, and the coalition members mobilized to help publicize the case, bringing news of the resistance to the transnational networks of activists, mentioning the Popintsi case in their own discussions with the press, and going with representatives of the local group to Sofia for an interview with a TV news program. Media attention was then piqued by the mysterious stabbing of a key activist in July, who sustained three stab wounds near his heart and refuses to reveal who attacked him. It is not clear whether the stabbing was related to his opposition to the project (Panayotova and Kuznetsov 2008; Dichev 2008), but the very mystery of the case fuels suspicions and dislike of the company. President Parvanov and local representatives to parliament visited the road camp after the referendum and incident. Following the blockade, the referendum, this incident, and the ensuing media and political attention, the company ceased its activity in the area. No new project has been proposed since then.

Formal organization in this case was very thin, since most activity took place through local networks. However, many residents did form the Popintsi (sometimes called Petelovo) Initiative Committee (Daskalov 2006; Dichev 2008). Ties with national environmental groups facilitated publicizing the case and were a source of information about other cases. The closest ties were with Green Balkans, a general conservation NGO located in the nearby city of Plovdiv and a member of the Cyanide-Free Bulgaria coalition. Still, the key actions of blocking the hill, presenting their case to the president, and finally organizing a local referendum were planned and taken by local residents.

Links among the Cases

While each of these cases has its own dynamics, they are to varying degrees linked. The Chelopech and Krumovgrad projects have the same foreign investor, Dundee Precious Metals, who gained concession rights to Chelopech and the licensing rights to Krumovgrad in its buyout of the bankrupt Navan Mining. The EIA processes for both projects took place in the same time period; both were effectively stalled by the refusal of the Minister of Environment and Water to make final decisions; and Dundee filed a complaint to the European Commission in July 2007 naming both cases. Negotiations between Dundee and the Bulgarian government led to an oral agreement in March 2008 to restructure shares and fees at Chelopech and unblock the EIA process. While the government said nothing about the Krumovgrad project in announcing the Chelopech agreement, the company expressed the expectation that the second project would be addressed as well. Opponents also fear the cases are linked by larger long-term plans to process ore from all of Dundee's holdings in Bulgaria and Serbia at Chelopech.

Although the Popintsi project was proposed by an entirely different foreign firm—Euromax as Martern—at issue was the same principle of cyanide-leaching processes in gold mining as well as the same procedural matters surrounding the sale of exploration licenses and previous surveys and the conduct and content of the EIA. The Popintsi site is also not far from Chelopech, and new mining there would affect the same river basin. That the Martern investment occurred in the same time period as Dundee's investments in Chelopech and Krumovgrad meant that failure to stop or change the investment at Popintsi could weaken resistance in the other cases. From the vantage point of local activists, this case was linked to the Dundee cases as well. The local initiative committee from Popintsi was an early and stalwart supporter of the Krumovgrad residents and has supported several of the Cyanide-Free Bulgaria coalition's initiatives.

Even a new proposal in Kardzhali (alternatively spelled Kurdzhali), put forward by the Bulgarian firm Gorubso, is seen by opponents of the other projects as a test case for cyanide use in gold mining (Bacheva-McGrath 2008a; Dichev 2008; Fournadzhiev 2008; Radev 2008). In the Kardzhali case, a national firm that is already processing gold and has used cyanide for processing lead and zinc, wants to reprocess the leftover gold ore with cyanide leaching (Dichev 2008). Kardzhali is a large urban area, already contaminated, and situated in a region that tends to flood. These conditions make it a very dangerous place for the extensive use of cyanide and storage of cyanide-tainted waste. Still, in October 2009 the new Minister of Environment and Water, Nona Karadjova, approved the EIA for the project on the grounds that the current plant no longer had room to store hazardous materials (Enchev 2009). The municipal government, Cyanide-Free Bulgaria, and the Greens immediately announced their plans to appeal the decision (Borisova 2009).

The more immediate links among the cases are also reflected in their ties to the broader development and application of national and EU law. Each of these cases is theoretically subject to the same institutions, laws, and standards as the other cases. As the institutions within Bulgaria compete for influence and autonomy, their positions and decisions with respect to any of these cases can establish precedents applicable to the other cases regarding the interpretation and implementation of regulations and standards as well as process and institutional jurisdiction. At this early point of Bulgaria's EU membership, decisions regarding these cases also establish the government's interpretations of EU law and processes. Finally, the interests of neighbors link the cases. Chelopech and Popintsi are both located near small rivers that feed into the Maritsa, which flows into Greece and Turkey. Krumovgrad is also very close to the Greek border. International agreements to which Bulgaria is a party require that neighbors are allowed input into decisions entailing environmental risks to them.

Strategic Action in the Local, National, and International Arenas

The politics surrounding these projects involved actors and strategies on different levels. While local action is central in cases of environmental justice, especially in investments in point resources, campaigns to change or reverse decisions that have negative impacts on local environments are often more effective if they are waged on several levels, utilizing networks of movement organizations and institutional leverage on key decision makers, in this case the Bulgarian government and the investors. The three cases examined here did involve multiple levels of strategy, albeit to differing degrees. The contexts, actors, and decisions in the cases are summarized in table 10.1.

Over the last two decades, theorists of social movements have expanded on the rich body of work analyzing domestic determinants of movement formation to incorporate external influences on the structure of social movements and their opportunities for mobilization (Giugni 1998; McAdam 1998). In particular, they have built on the insights of international relations scholars examining transnational "epistemic policy communities" and their influence on states both from within and through international institutions (Risse-Kappen 1994, 1995). Some authors have examined the generation of transnational values or "civil society" and the transmission of norms and related policy (especially environmental norms) from this transnational community to the domestic level (McCormick 1989; Kamieniecki 1993; Wapner 1995; Boli and Thomas 1999; Florini 2000; Lewis 2000). However, much of the work on transnational influence has sought to explain the rapidly developing dynamics of transnational social movement networks. Of particular

Table 10.1
Summary of gold-mining cases

	Chelopech	Krumovgrad	Popintsi
Contextual factors			
History of mining	Yes	No	Yes
Environmental conditions	Polluted, mining contamination	Parts natural, other parts with agricultural pollutants	Mining contamination
Resident opinion	Split, plurality for	Vast majority against	Vast majority against
Political/economic factors	Mining infrastructure	Ethnic minority; agricultural	Deposit in mountain above town
Investor/date of proposal	Dundee Precious Metals	Dundee Precious Metals	Euromax/Martern
Local-level actors			
Organized opposition	Weak in Chelopech, strong in Chavdar	Strong, political mobilization	Strong, direct action, referendum
Positions of local officials	For	Against	Against
Local firms	For	Not relevant	Not relevant
Movement actors			
National issue groups	Cyanide-Free Bulgaria (CFB)	CFB major campaign	CFB support after local initiative
National general groups	None beyond CFB	Nature park mobilization	Green Balkans early advice
Transnational organizations and networks	Central and East European Bankwatch (CEEB)	CEEB, Greek and Turkish opposition, European Parliament	Not mobilized, some publicity about the blockade

Table 10.1
(continued)

	Chelopech	Krumovgrad	Popintsi
National actors and institutions			
Institutional decisions under 2005–2009 government	Ministry of Environment froze decision; government negotiated continuance; EIA approved	Ministry of Environment froze decision, requested compatibility study with Natura 2000; new government accepted Compatibility Assessment for Natura 2000, awarded Certificate of Discovery	President and MP visit, no decisions at national level
Political parties	Not central actors	MRF local pressing national	Not mobilized
Courts and tribunals under 2005–2009 government	Supreme Administrative Court ordered minister to decide on EIA; he did not obey; unblocked EIA rejected by Supreme Administrative Court; new government appealing	Supreme Administrative Court ordered minister to decide on EIA; he did not obey	No decisions at national level; local prosecutor ordered exploration stopped (ignored, prosecutor replaced)
Transnational actors and arenas			
Arenas that influence the state	Environmental media, EU Commissioner for the Environment pressing public participation, European Commission considering infringement case	Environmental media, EU Commissioner for the Environment pressing public participation, Bulgarian and Greek activists pressing European Parliament, European Commission considering infringement case	Environmental media
Arenas that influence investors	EBRD	EBRD	International media
Outcome to date	Company declared a freeze on its activity, but continues to expand production, still negotiating future changes to the project	EIA to restart; company proposed a new project without cyanides	Investor stopped

interest to local movements for environmental justice are examinations of how groups in one country can mobilize external groups to provide pressure back on their government, either directly or through other governments or international institutions (Princen 1994; Princen, Finger, and Manno 1994; Smith 1997, 2000; Smith, Chatfield, and Pugnucco 1997; Kriesberg 1997; Keck and Sikkink 1998; Tarrow 1998, 2005; Della Porta and Kriesi 1999; Passy 1999; Reimann 2001; Carmin and Hicks 2002). With globalized investment and production and several pressing transnational environmental effects of human activity, the transnational networks of NGOs, international institutions, and the interaction of the two have become crucial resources for strengthening local voice and power.

A particularly dense set of networks has developed in the European Union, spurred on by the strengthening institutions and widening policy scope of the EU. Several authors in the transnational social movement literature have focused more specifically on these social movement links across the European Union and ties to EU institutions (Imig and Tarrow 1999; Marks and McAdam 1999; Carmin, Hicks, and Beckmann 2003; Petrova and Tarrow 2007; Vachudova 2008). With complex decision-making processes that involve the European Commission, the European Parliament, and committees and agencies working across these institutions and the Council of the European Union, and with the differing importance of specific member states and political parties in all of these institutions, movement actors can find several paths of influence into different decision points. Moreover, the existence of a body of law to which all member states have agreed and procedures (albeit slow and sometimes weak) for addressing states' failures to comply with that law gives the EU institutions, other member states, NGOs, firms, and citizens avenues of leverage on individual states and firms.

Both general transnational networks and, especially, networks and institutions in the European Union have been important actors and resources for local groups and Bulgarian NGOs striving to influence decisions in the three gold-mining cases. Thus, the strategies for opposing these investments have involved actors and actions on multiple levels from the local village to international institutions.

Local-Level Actors

Local actors have been involved in all three of the Bulgarian cases. The mobilization of opponents to the projects, their interactions with local officials, and their ties to national actors have varied, and this variation has been central to the courses of decision making about the projects. Above all, unity seems crucial to the ability of a local community to have any say in whether or how the project continues. The splits in views in Chelopech gave the firm, its local supporters, and national officials openings to shape the course of decision making in ways that isolated opponents from any influence over the shape of the project. While local unity is necessary to assert influence in the process, it may not be sufficient. Chavdar's residents were originally strongly against the planned investment in Chelopech, but they could not block the decision to proceed.

In addition to unity, local actors also need effective organization and well-timed actions and interventions into the decision-making processes of the political system or company. The residents of Popintsi were able to stop the company before it could reach the legal status of having "discovered" (by drilling boreholes) depositories and thus claim the right to exploit its findings. The strong stance by the residents of Krumovgrad early in the decision-making process set in motion a number of strategies. Green Balkans and other environmental groups mobilized the Cyanide-Free Bulgaria coalition (originally called Cyanide-Free Rhodopi for the Rhodopi mountains in which Krumovgrad is located). The coalition and the local resistance group were crucial in pressing local officials of the MRF party to oppose the project.

Part of the organization and strategy of local groups has to be to find allies beyond their area, especially at the national level and possibly at the transnational levels. These allies can be movement or nongovernmental actors who can mobilize technical and legal expertise in the decision-making process; political parties; or even institutions seeking to establish certain precedents, define standards, reinforce law, or simply strengthen their autonomy and position in the political system.

Movement Actors at the National Level

Environmental movement actors working at the national level can provide local residents with a variety of resources and assistance in their activism. They are sources of information about technical, legal, and political processes; and their links to other environmental NGOs outside the country, to international organizations, and to national and international media can support local citizens with the means to pressure both their governments and the investors. Environmental groups in Bulgaria developed in the last half of the 1980s, played a central role in the popular mobilization that prompted and accompanied the elite changes ending the communist regime, and have continued to press for more active civic participation in decision making throughout the transition period, albeit with a lot of turnover in groups (Cellarius and Staddon 2002).

The NGO community has engaged local and other actors in these gold-mining cases in the form of the Cyanide-Free Rhodopi/Bulgaria coalition. The coalition was originally formed by a handful of environmental NGOs of varying size and specialization: Environmental Association "Za Zemiata," Federation "Green Balkans," Balkani Wildlife Society, Eko-forum, Center for Environmental Information and Education (CEIE), and Ekoklub 2000, as well as the Initiative Committees in Krumovgrad (Life for Krumovgrad) and Popintsi, and independent experts concerned with the potential effects of the projects. Other groups have joined since, but these founding groups remain at the core of the coalition.

By organizing a campaign—often an issue campaign—at the national level, environmental NGOs can assist local groups in organizing, identifying potential points around which to mobilize, and initiating action. A campaign also helps individual localities leverage their cases to issues of national importance by linking them to broader causes. Furthermore, the connections provided by a campaign allow local groups to utilize NGO knowledge about and links into governing institutions. The Cyanide-Free Bulgaria campaign has served these purposes for all three gold-mining cases, although NGO engagement on behalf of Chelopech and Krumovgrad has been more long-standing and farther reaching, in part because of the different local dynamics and relatively quick success of the Popintsi case.

One of the strongest roles of movement actors in cases of transnational investment is their ability to mobilize their connections to transnational-level actors and develop strategies to put pressure on both the state and the investor. More than one of the organizations in the coalition has close ties with Central and East European Bankwatch, a nongovernmental network headquartered in Brussels that tracks investments by international financial institutions. Bankwatch, in turn, has ties to some EU representatives and offices. Both the coalition and Bankwatch have mobilized allies and pressed the concerns about the Chelopech and Krumovgrad investments in transnational arenas, particularly in the NGO community, the environmental media, and international institutions.

National Political Actors and Institutions
In addition to movement actors, several other actors affect the outcome of investment decisions with environmental implications—key among

them are various governing institutions, political parties, and courts. In the three cases under examination here, the local groups have relied heavily on the advice and (limited) access of movement actors to official institutions. Only in Krumovgrad have direct local ties to national-level political actors been a major factor.

The central institution involved in the processes studied here has been the Ministry of Environment and Water. The role of the ministry in the EIA process has put it on the front line of decision making regarding these investments. The process has not been smooth. The ministry's Supreme Environmental Expert Council is charged with issuing opinions on EIA cases, and the politics around the staffing of this council and its decisions have been controversial. The NGO community pressed to have a voice on council appointments in order to strengthen its independence from government interests, and two NGO members, Dimitur Vassilev and Andrei Kovatchev, were appointed to the council. The council approved the EIA for Chelopech in February 2006. However, the council's decisions are only recommendations to the minister, and another level of political struggle ensued after the council's decision. The minister returned the EIA to the council for reconsideration, and it was approved again at the end of March. At the height of the mobilization against the approval of the projects in March 2006, when protests were occurring outside the ministry, the NGO representatives were barred from entering and Vassilev was even arrested. Rather than approve the EIA after the second decision from the council, the minister froze the process.

The ministry, however, has to negotiate authority with other interested institutions. The Economy Ministry has been an advocate for these projects, to the point of engaging in public criticism of the Ministry of Environment (see, for example, *Sofia Echo* 2007). These struggles can rise to cabinet level, and the prime minister balances various government interests in deciding on a course of action. It is likely that the EU infringement case and growing EU pressure on Bulgaria more generally to strengthen accountability and the rule of law led the government to negotiate with Dundee over Chelopech, despite the obstruction from the Ministry of Environment.

Officials from the major political parties, particularly the Bulgarian Socialist Party and parts of the former Union of Democratic Forces,[4] have at varying times promoted or enabled the investments in question. Neither camp has taken a clear stance in support of public participation in decisions regarding these projects. The one party that has been involved, the Movement for Rights and Freedoms, has also not taken a

uniform position. However, the position of local officials in Krumovgrad
has been clear and, despite some internal party differences, seems to have
influenced the Minister of Environment and Water, a member of that
party. The informal tactics and ad hoc decisions of the minister with
regard to the two flawed EIA processes, rather than application of
scientific or procedural standards or development of precautionary principles, reflects the underinstitutionalization of governance in this period.
The outcome of allowing one case to go ahead with less than satisfactory
environmental safeguards, however, may have allowed the wedge in the
door to broader cyanide use and manipulation as the new EIA process
goes forward. With this precedent it may be harder to protect Krumovgrad in the future.

Besides working to influence political parties, local groups and their
supporters in the movement lobby members of parliament directly. The
local groups and movement organizations have developed ties with
several representatives, and a few members of parliament have introduced measures to ban cyanides or called for investigations. However,
these efforts have not brought major legal changes or reversal of the
decisions of executive institutions. In one case, the parliament's Commission on the Environment was able to get some information from the
Ministry of Environment in response to an inquiry, information that the
civic organizations had been unable to obtain (Bacheva 2006).

Until recently, the courts have not been major actors in these cases.
When asked about their role as potential defenders of rule of law in 2006
and 2008, most environmental activists were skeptical (Bacheva 2006;
Dichev 2008; Vassilev 2008). Still, Cyanide-Free Bulgaria and local communities have filed several "signals" to prosecutors' offices for investigation[5] and cases in various courts. These signals have generally remained
uninvestigated. (Prosecutors' offices have a great deal of discretion in
deciding whether to initiative investigations, particularly given the large
number of potential cases in their logs.) In 2005, the residents of Popintsi
were able to get an order from the chief prosecutor declaring the concession illegal and ordering a stop to exploration, but the order was ignored
and the chief prosecutor was later replaced (Daskalov 2006). From the
other side, Dundee filed and won a case with the Supreme Administrative
Court, but the court's decision had no discernable effect on the development of the case. Had the rule of law been stronger, the ruling in
Dundee's favor would have brought action, but so also might have the
initiatives of local groups and the coalition to address flaws in the processes of selling concessions and studies and in local consultation both

before and during the EIA processes. The latest ruling of the Supreme Administrative Court rejecting the Chelopech EIA for violations of the EIA timeline and consultation guidelines may be a sign of change, but it is too early to tell. One other set of obstacles to clear legal paths and the rule of law are contradictions in the law itself, which increase the discretion of both the courts and other institutional actors. For example, Bulgaria's environmental laws do not require an EIA to get a permit for exploration, whereas the Law on Underground Resources does require an EIA for such a permit (Bacheva 2006).

Transnational Actors and Arenas
Several transnational actors and arenas have been involved in these gold-mining cases, largely through the efforts of the NGO coalition. Bulgaria and other postcommunist countries have undergone a fourth transition of transnationalism (see Orenstein, Bloom, and Lindstrom 2008a for a recent argument to this effect) intertwined with their political and economic transitions and their transition to independent statehood—in some cases, renewed or new nation-states, in others independence from the oversight of the USSR. This argument about the growth of transnationalism and its interaction with other areas of change can be extended to many developing countries as well. Transnational actors of all sorts—corporations, financial institutions, international organizations, transnational nongovernmental organizations—are often involved in investment decisions and the politics around them. For Bulgaria, the European Union with its extensive body of law, oversight mechanisms, and resources, is the most important of these actors. As Vachudova (2008) points out, the EU intensifies the effects of other transnational actors. Still the timing of the contracts and original EIA processes, completed before Bulgaria's accession to the EU, and the reliance of the EU on national institutions to carry out EU policies, have limited the direct power of Brussels to influence outcomes in these cases.

Activism at the transnational level can affect decision making through two main channels: by influencing the decisions of the state in which the investment is situated and by influencing the investor. Because the primary transnational arena of importance to the Bulgarian state during the period since these investment controversies arose has been the European Union, the coalition has been very active in bringing the issues surrounding these investments, particularly the Chelopech and Krumovgrad cases, to the attention of various EU institutions. The coalition has established contacts with the European Parliament, the European Commission, and the latter's Directorate General for Environment, including the Commissioner for the Environment from 2004 to 2009, Stavros Dimas (from Greece), who visited Bulgaria and pressed for respect of the public participation guidelines of the Aarhus convention. European Members of Parliament, particularly Dutch Green Party member Els de Groen, have also advanced the interests of civic and environmental groups. Part of the coalition's strategy has also been to encourage neighboring Greece to pursue its interests through the EU. One could argue that the coalition has been more effective at building its connections to transnational actors and bringing transnational pressure to bear on the state than it has been at mobilizing strong participation in actions at home, a pattern that is not unique in postcommunist Central and Eastern Europe (Petrova and Tarrow 2007, 88).

Besides bringing pressure to bear on the state from international organizations, movement activists also have connections to the international media. For the most part, the coalition has only been able to bring these cases to the attention of the networks of transnational NGOs, which increases pressure on the Bulgarian government only slightly. The blockade and stabbing in Popintsi, followed by the president's visit, however, threatened to attract attention beyond the Bulgarian media and the transnational NGO network, and this potential was probably the deciding factor in Euromax's pullout from the project.

In addition to mobilization strategies that aim to influence the Bulgarian government's handling of cases in various capacities, local opponents and their allies use direct action in arenas that influence the investor, primarily international media and financial institutions. Coalition efforts to have the Chelopech and Krumovgrad projects added to Oxfam's very visible "No Dirty Gold" campaign, as was the Rosia Montana project in Romania, did not pan out. However, the movement and its transnational allies have sought to pressure the companies through other channels. In particular, the Bankwatch network has been vigilant about tracking support for the projects (and other environmentally risky projects in the postcommunist region) in international financial institutions. Bankwatch has engaged the European Bank for Reconstruction and Development repeatedly on its support for these projects. Although Bankwatch recognized that the first phase of the Chelopech project focused on necessary remediation and improvement of production processes, the network has been adamant about not extending support to the second phase or to Dundee's plans for Krumovgrad (CEEB 2005; Popov 2008b). At this point the EBRD has not offered support for the more controversial second phase or for the Krumovgrad project, and Bankwatch's persistence in monitoring investments, attending meetings, and raising objections may be at least part of the reason for what appears to be the EBRD's cooled enthusiasm for the projects.

The Quest for Environmental Justice in Transition States

The varied trajectories of these cases in the same institutional setting and time frame suggest that local unity and organization, whatever its initiation, is necessary to obtain environmental justice. At least in this context of weak rule of law and underinstitutionalized democracy and public participation, environmental claims against the projects by activists at the national level have not been sufficient to force reconsideration or adjustments to the project when there has not been unified and persistent opposition at the local level. Despite a concerted campaign at the national and European levels, support from activists in neighboring countries, studies explaining the particularly dangerous geological, meteorological, and human settlement conditions, controversy over arsenic leaching from existing activity at the mine, and even opposition of the neighboring village of Chavdar, the proposed project in Chelopech was not stopped under the former government. The population of Chelopech is divided but more in favor of the project, at least in the opinions that have been expressed openly. Moreover, while the financial terms of the investment were adjusted, the environmental concerns raised in the initial EIA process remained unaddressed. Only in November 2009 did the clear violations of the EIA process lead the Supreme Administrative Court to require a new EIA. Despite the new government's concern to demonstrate its adherence to EU law and procedure, the Minister for Environment is appealing that decision, albeit through due institutional channels of appeal. Bulgarian environmentalists have had the same experience with other sorts of investments (e.g., ski resorts in the Pirin and Rila National Parks)—their ecological and legal arguments, no matter how strong, cannot carry the day if the local population is not opposed to the project and not willing to act on this opposition.

While unified local action is necessary to press environmental concerns, it is often not sufficient to ensure that institutions take up those concerns. The case that came the closest to a pure victory for local resistance—Popintsi—still had some assistance from regional and national environmental organizations in raising media awareness at home and abroad and in strategizing about the referendum. The other case of strong local opposition—Krumovgrad—is not yet settled. If the project is rejected, the will of the vast majority of residents, that outcome will owe a good deal to the mobilization and assistance of the Cyanide-Free Bulgaria coalition, the pressure by local officials inside the political party Movement for Rights and Freedoms, and perhaps the attention at the European level, heightened by proximity to Greece, by the fact that the European Commissioner for the Environment during the crucial period of activism was both sympathetic to the project's opponents and Greek, and by the campaign for a Natura 2000 nature park in the area. The door, though, may still be ajar. The new government has recognized Dundee's proposed changes to address the problems pointed out in the Natura 2000 Compatibility Assessment and granted the company a Commercial Discovery Certificate. While these are not good signs for opponents, the need to restart the EIA process under EU law is also a major obstacle for the company.

Even with strong local opposition and the support of national and external groups, timing of activism and the linking of cases to broader issues are crucial. Had Martern been able to drill in Popintsi, the company could have made a stronger claim to "discovering" gold and hence ownership. Had Cyanide-Free Bulgaria coalition members not supported local opponents to mining in Krumovgrad at the meeting when local leaders of the Movement for Rights and Freedoms were still undecided, neither local residents nor the environmental movement might have had the leverage necessary to press the Minister of Environment and Water later to freeze the EIA process. The coalition's ties to transnational networks and knowledge of European institutions and laws facilitated support from Greek activists and intensified the pressure on the government from European sources. When it comes to timing, clearly earlier input and mobilization are preferable. However, mobilizing early requires information and a predictable procedural course around which to mobilize.

If environmental justice is to be achieved and harmful investments put off for good, not just temporarily, the strategy of environmental activists has to strengthen the hand of national actors that guarantee procedures and rights. Such a strategy may involve developing local political connections to ensure the integrity of participatory processes. Arousing the national media as a watchdog over institutional practices or as a way of putting pressure on key political actors is usually a central strategy of those seeking to strengthen the rule of law. And, where national institutions are weak or corrupted, strategies that bring transnational pressure to bear on both the state and the investor can help to establish more legitimate decision-making procedures. The national movement can develop such strategies across individual cases and must do this when the cases are linked, because investors could have strong legal and political grounds to use one case as precedent for another and convincing economic rationales for continuing with linked projects once one of the projects has been started.

Ultimately, each case is shaped to a great deal by its contingencies in strategies, timing, and framing. In order for patterns of contingencies and their outcomes to become regularized and predictable enough to facilitate strategizing, political decision-making processes and the application and enforcement of standards, laws, and regulations must be institutionalized. In the Krumovgrad and Chelopech cases, the ad hoc decisions by the Minister of Environment, although providing immediate relief to opponents, did nothing to strengthen institutional processes and standards for decision making. Institutionalization is necessary not only for consistency across locales, but also for consistency across time. Decisions made to stop or alter a particular investment do not necessarily set the lines of participation and environmental justice in the country or even in that locale. The potential for recurrence once a particular investment is stopped or adjusted is real, as we have seen with Chelopech. Firms can hold permits, land, or shares, and bide their time; or they can sell them to other firms who then initiate new investment processes. Whether citizens can obtain environmental justice will depend largely on whether earlier rounds strengthened the institutions that ensure rights or whether the coalition that stopped or changed an investment project remains intact and develops effective strategies for subsequent rounds (and cases). Decision making in these cases under the new government suggests some regularization of institutional procedure and continued challenges by the opposing coalition, but it is too early to tell whether these processes have actually strengthened citizens' recourse to law to protect their rights.

In Bulgaria, there is a long way to go in strengthening the institutions that can ensure a rule of law, including the integrity of investment, EIA, and participation procedures—all of which are necessary to guarantee environmental justice. Given the political trajectory in the early transition period, the resulting balance of two main opposing camps, the ties between each of these camps and circles of businesses and banks that benefit from their rule and support them (a pattern replicated by other parties as they entered the political scene), and very limited progress in fighting corruption, the hope for environmental justice seems to go through external channels. The most effective channels through which to apply external pressure on decision makers are various EU institutions, international financial institutions offering funding for environmentally destructive investments, transnational media outlets, and transnational movement organizations targeting both the state and the corporations. Although it is still early to assess the new government, its sensitivity to censure by the EU (and the international community more generally) seems to have been a major factor in prompting more regular institutional processes, which may bring some improvement in the rule of law over time. The EU, however, is no panacea for opponents of these projects. Business interests exert strong influence in the EU (the use of cyanide in gold mining, for example, is not forbidden by EU regulations), so moving politics up to that level provides no guarantee that citizens' interests will prevail. Furthermore, the EU only has limited direct leverage over national institutions, as demonstrated by the EU's need to withhold structural funds and the failure of that penalty to bring the Bulgarian institutions and their practices into line. Ultimately, most local groups who wish to oppose or alter investment plans in order to ensure equitable environmental outcomes will have to develop strong ties and a complex strategy on multiple levels.

Notes

I would like to thank the scholars and activists in Bulgaria who took the time to help with this project, as well as Diana Hinova for research assistance and David Alexander for early bibliographical work.

1. Infringement proceedings are one of the main tools used by the European Commission to ensure fair competition in the EU's single market. The European Commission investigates allegations of infringement of its own accord or at the request of a member state and can decide to bring proceedings against a member state at the Court of Justice of the European Communities (formerly known as the European Court of Justice). Usually the commission attempts to resolve the issue before it goes to court. If a case is not resolved before it is heard, the Court of Justice can order a resolution of the case and, on second hearing if the commission finds noncompliance, fine the state for infringement.

2. The coalition estimated that 90 percent of the Krumovgrad residents were opposed to the project, a figure borne out by the 10,000 signatures collected on the Municipal Council's petition in 2005 (Beshkov 2008).

3. Bulgarian law does not allow ethnic parties, so the MRF campaigns on a platform of rights and freedoms for all Bulgarians and allows everyone to join. Still, its membership is largely Turkish and most ethnic Turks support the party.

4. The dominant party in the ruling coalition after the July 2009 elections, Citizens for the European Development of Bulgaria (GERB), was formed only at the end of 2006 and identifies as rightist and pro-European. The right side of the political spectrum has fragmented in the last two election cycles. The Union of Democratic Forces continues as a smaller party, while splinters of the old party and new forces have formed new center-right and right parties.

5. Signals are complaints with some corroborating evidence. The evidence does not have to meet the standard necessary for a trial, but it must arouse sufficient doubt about the case to cause the prosecutor's office to investigate.

References

Angelov, Angel, and David F. Marshall. 2006. Introduction: Ethnolinguistic minority language policies in Bulgaria and their Balkan context. *International Journal of the Sociology of Language* 179(May):1–28.

Bacheva, Fidanka. 2006. CEE Bankwatch, Za Zemiata. Interview, June 13, Sofia, Bulgaria.

Bacheva-McGrath, Fidanka. 2008a. CEE Bankwatch. Interview, July 9, Blago-evgrad, Bulgaria.

Bacheva-McGrath, Fidanka. 2008b. CEE Bankwatch. Personal e-mail communication, August 16.

Balkan gold up-date. 2006. *Stability Pact Watch Bulletin* 11:7–8.

Barnes, Andrew. 2007. Extricating the state: The move to competitive capture in post-communist Bulgaria. *Europe-Asia Studies* 59(1):71–95.

Beshkov, Stoyan. 2006. Associate professor. Interview, June 12, Sofia, Bulgaria.

Beshkov, Stoyan. 2008. Associate professor. Interview, June 26, Sofia, Bulgaria.

Bivol, Alex. 2010. Dundee Precious freezes Bulgarian project, switches attention to Namibia. *Sofia Echo*, January 25. http://sofiaecho.com/2010/01/25/ 847309 _dundee-precious-freezes-bulgarian-project-switches-attention-to-namibia.

Boli, John, and George N. Thomas, eds. 1999. *Constructing World Culture: International Non-Governmental Organizations Since 1875.* Stanford, CA: Stanford University Press.

Borisova, Albena. 2009. Sblusuk: Zlato i Cianidi—Konstantin Dichev, "Zeleni Balkani." *Dnevnik*, December 2. http://www.dnevnik.bg/ekobiznes/2009/12/02/ 824339_sblusuk_zlato_i_cianidi_-_konstantin_dichev_zeleni/?ref=rss.

Carmin, JoAnn, and Barbara Hicks. 2002. International triggering events, transnational networks, and the development of the Czech and Polish environmental movements. *Mobilization* 7(2):304–324.

Carmin, JoAnn, Barbara Hicks, and Andreas Beckmann. 2003. Leveraging local action: Grassroots initiatives and transboundary collaboration in the formation of the White Carpathian Euroregion. *International Sociology* 18(4): 703–725.

CEEB [Central and East European Bankwatch]. 2005. NGOs issue paper on EBRD Project: Ada Tepe gold mine in Bulgaria. http://www.cyanidefreerhodopi .org/cfradmin/files/IP_Ada_Tepe_10_05.pdf.

Cellarius, Barbara A., and Caedmon Staddon. 2002. Environmental nongovernmental organizations, civil society, and democratization in Bulgaria. *Eastern European Politics and Societies* 16(1):182–222.

Çoban, Akyut. 2004. Community-based ecological resistance: The Bergama movement in Turkey. *Environmental Politics* 13(2):438–460.

Daskalov, Georgi. 2006. Popintsi Initiative Committee. Interview, June 14, Plovdiv, Bulgaria.

Della Porta, Donatella, and Hanspeter Kriesi. 1999. Social movements in a globalizing world: An introduction. In Donatella della Porta, Hanspeter Kriesi, and Dieter Rucht, eds., *Social Movements in a Globalizing World*, 1–22. New York: St. Martin's Press.

Dichev, Konstantin. 2006. Green Balkans Federation. Interview, June 14, Plovdiv, Bulgaria.

Dichev, Konstantin. 2008. Green Balkans Federation. Interview, July 10, Plovdiv, Bulgaria.

Directorate-General for the Environment, European Commission. 2007. Letter from the Head of the Unit for Communication, Legal Affairs and Civil Protection to the Center for Environmental Information and Education, November 26.

DPM [Dundee Precious Metals]. 2007. Media release: DPM files formal complaint with the European Commission against Bulgaria. http://biz.yahoo.com/iw/ 070606/0262922.html.

DPM [Dundee Precious Metals]. 2009. Krumovgrad Gold Project. December 1. http://www.dundeeprecious.com/Operations/Bulgaria/KrumovtradProject/ default.sapx.

Enchev, Milen. 2009. Ekoministurut Razreshi Cianidnoto Proizvodstvo na "Gorubso Kurdjali." *Dnevnik*, October 23. http://www.dnevnik.bg/ekobiznes/ 2009/10/23/804438 _ekoministurut_razreshi_cianidnoto_proizvodstvo_na/?ref=rss.

Engelbrekt, Kjell. 2007. Bulgaria's EU accession and the issue of accountability: An end to buck-passing? *Problems of Post-Communism* 54(4):3–14.

Florini, Ann M. 2000. *The Third Force: The Rise of Transnational Civil Society.* Washington, DC: Carnegie Endowment for International Peace.

Fournadzhiev, Georgi. 2006. Consultant. Interview, June 12, Sofia, Bulgaria.

Fournadzhiev, Georgi. 2008. Ecoforum. Interview, July 5, Sofia, Bulgaria.

Ganev, Venelin I. 2006. Ballots, bribes, and state building in Bulgaria. *Journal of Democracy* 17(1):75–89.

Giugni, Marco G. 1998. The other side of the coin: Explaining crossnational similarities between social movements. *Mobilization* (San Diego, CA)3(1): 89–105.

Goranova, Kalina. 2009. Cudut Otmeni Ovos na Chelopech Maining. *Dnevnik*, November 11. http://www.dnevnik.bg/pazari/2009/11/11/814501_sudut_otmeni _ovos _na_chelopech_maining/?ref=rss.

Hellman, Joel, S. 1998. Winners take all: The politics of partial reform in post-communist transitions. *World Politics* 50(2):203–234.

Imig, Doug, and Sidney Tarrow. 1999. The Europeanization of movements? A new approach to transnational contention. In Donatella della Porta, Hanspeter Kriesi, and Dieter Rucht, eds., *Social Movements in a Globalizing World*, 112–133. New York: St. Martin's Press.

Kamieniecki, Sheldon, ed. 1993. *Environmental Politics in the International Arena: Movements, Parties, Organizations, and Policy*. Albany: State University of New York Press.

Katanska, Tsvetelina. 2009. Zlatodobivnata Dundi Poluchi Udostoverenie za Tugovsko Otkritie v Krumovgrad. *Dnevnik*, October 15. http://www.dnevnik.bg/ pazari/ 2009/09/15/785113_zlatodobivnata_dundi_poluchi_udostoverenie_za/?ref =rss.

Keck, Margaret E., and Kathryn Sikkink. 1998. *Activists beyond Borders: Advocacy Networks in International Politics*. Ithaca, NY: Cornell University Press.

Konstadinova, Tatiana. 2007. The impact of finance regulations on political parties: The case of Bulgaria. *Europe-Asia Studies* 59(5):807–827.

Kovatchev, Andrei. 2006. Balkani Wildlife Society. Interview, June 12, Sofia, Bulgaria.

Kovatchev, Petko. 2006. CEIE. Interview, June 12, Sofia, Bulgaria.

Kriesberg, Louis. 1997. Social movements and global transformation. In J. Smith, C. Chatfield, and R. Pugnucco, eds., *Transnational Social Movements and Global Politics: Solidarity beyond the State*, 3–18. Syracuse: Syracuse University Press.

Lewis, Tammy L. 2000. Transnational conservation movement organizations: Shaping the protected area systems of less developed countries. *Mobilization* (San Diego, CA) 5(1):105–123.

Marchev, Milan. 2006. Bulgaria may lose $350 million in foreign investment. *AmCham Bulgaria Magazine*, August-September, 10–13.

Marks, Gary, and Doug McAdam. 1999. On the relationship of political opportunities to the form of collective action: The case of the European Union. In Donatella della Porta, Hanspeter Kriesi, and Dieter Rucht, eds., *Social Movements in a Globalizing World*, 97–111. New York: St. Martin's Press.

McAdam, Doug. 1998. On the international origins of domestic political opportunities. In Anne N. Costain and Andrew S. McFarland, eds., *Social Movements and American Political Institutions*, 251–267. Lanham, MD: Rowman & Littlefield.

McCormick, John. 1989. *Reclaiming Paradise: The Global Environmental Movement*. Bloomington: Indiana University Press.

Municipal Council of Krumovgrad. 2005. Resolution No. 329. From Protocol N17/16.09.2005. Translated and archived at http://www.cyanidefreerhodopi .org/index.php?articleid=106.

Noutcheva, Gergana, and Dimitar Bechev. 2008. The successful laggards: Bulgaria and Romania's accession to the EU. *Eastern European Politics and Societies* 22(1):114–144.

Orenstein, Mitchell A., Stephen Bloom, and Nicole Lindstrom. 2008a. A fourth dimension of transition. In Mitchell A. Orenstein, Stephen Bloom, and Nicole Lindstrom, eds., *Transnational Actors in Central and East European Transitions*, 1–18. Pittsburgh: University of Pittsburgh Press.

Orenstein, Mitchell A., Stephen Bloom, and Nicole Lindstrom, eds. 2008b. *Transnational Actors in Central and East European Transitions*. Pittsburgh: University of Pittsburgh Press.

Panayotova, Nevena. 2008. Freelance investigative journalist. Interview, June 26, Sofia, Bulgaria.

Panayotova, Nevena, and Denis Kuznetsov. 2008. Gold: The Balkan trail. A series of investigative reports archived at http://www.i-scoop.org/index .php?id=24&tx_ttnews[tt_news]=630&tx_ttnews[backPid]=17&cHash=9dea06 ebdd&MP=24-42.

Passy, Florence. 1999. Supranational political opportunities as a channel of globalization of political conflicts: The case of the rights of indigenous peoples. In Donatella della Porta, Hanspeter Kriesi, and Dieter Rucht, eds., *Social Movements in a Globalizing World*, 148–169. New York: St. Martin's Press.

Petrova, Tsveta, and Sidney Tarrow. 2007. Transactional and participatory activism in the emerging European polity: The puzzle of East-Central Europe. *Comparative Political Studies* 40(1):74–94.

Popov, Daniel. 2008a. CEIE, National Coordinator for Bulgaria for CEE Bankwatch. Interview, June 30, Sofia, Bulgaria.

Popov, Daniel. 2008b. Introduction of cyanide leaching at the Chelopech gold and copper mine. CEE Bankwatch Network NGO Issue Paper, prepared for the EBRD Annual Meeting, Kiev, May 2008.

Princen, Thomas. 1994. NGOs: Creating a niche in environmental diplomacy. In Thomas Princen and Matthias Finger, eds., *Environmental NGOs in World Politics: Linking the Local and the Global*, 29–47. London: Routledge.

Princen, Thomas, Matthias Finger, and Jack Manno. 1994. Transnational linkages. In Thomas Princen and Matthias Finger, eds., *Environmental NGOs in World Politics: Linking the Local and the Global*, 217–236. London: Routledge.

Radev, Radi. 2006. Association Ecoforum. Interview, June 12, Sofia, Bulgaria.

Radev, Radi. 2008. Association Ecoforum. Interview, July 5, Sofia, Bulgaria.

Rechel, Bernd. 2007. State control of minorities in Bulgaria. *Journal of Communist Studies and Transition Politics* 23(3):352–370.

Rechel, Bernd. 2008. Ethnic diversity in Bulgaria: Institutional arrangements and domestic discourse. *Nationalities Papers* 36(2):331–350.

Reimann, Kim D. 2001. Building networks from the outside in: International movements, Japanese NGOs, and the Kyoto Climate Change Conference. *Mobilization* (San Diego, CA) 6(1):69–82.

Risse-Kappen, Thomas. 1994. Ideas do not float freely: Transnational coalitions, domestic structures, and the end of the Cold War. *International Organization* 48(2):185–214.

Risse-Kappen, Thomas, ed. 1995. *Bringing Transnational Relations Back In: Non-State Actors, Domestic Structures, and International Institutions.* Cambridge: Cambridge University Press.

Schönfelder, Bruno. 2005. Judicial independence in Bulgaria: A tale of splendour and misery. *Europe-Asia Studies* 57(1):61–92.

Smith, Jackie. 1997. Characteristics of the modern transnational social movement sector. In Jackie Smith, Charles Chatfield, and Ron Pugnucco, eds., *Transnational Social Movements and Global Politics: Solidarity beyond the State*, 42–58. Syracuse: Syracuse University Press.

Smith, Jackie. 2000. Social movements, international institutions, and local empowerment. In Kendall W. Stiles, ed., *Global Institutions and Local Empowerment: Competing Theoretical Perspectives*, 65–84. New York: St. Martin's Press.

Smith, Jackie, Charles Chatfield, and Ron Pugnucco, eds. 1997. *Transnational Social Movements and Global Politics: Solidarity beyond the State.* Syracuse: Syracuse University Press.

Sofia Echo. 2007. Warning on Dundee involvement in Bulgaria. July 2. http://www.sofiaecho.com/article/warning-on-dundee-involvement-in-bulgaria/id_23434/catid_23.

Sofia Echo. 2010. 500M Euro in ISPA funding hanging by a thread for Bulgaria. January 18. Translated from Dnevnik.bg and available at http://sofiaecho.com/2010/01/18/ 843528_500m-euro-in-ispa-funding-hanging-by-a-thread-for-bulgaria.

Sofia News Agency. 2009a. Bulgaria ranks last in EU by ISPA funds absorption. October 12. http://www.novinite.com/view_news.php?id=109389.

Sofia News Agency. 2009b. European Commission unfreezes EUR 115 M in Bulgaria ISPA aid. May 12. http://www.novinite.com/view_news.php?id=103551.

Tarrow, Sidney. 1998. *Power in Movement: Social Movements, Collective Action, and Politics.* New York: Cambridge University Press.

Tarrow, Sidney. 2005. *The New Transnational Activism.* New York: Cambridge University Press.

Tzvetkova, Marina. 2008. Aspects of the evolution of extra-legal protection in Bulgaria (1989–1999). *Trends in Organized Crime* 11(4):326–351.

Vachudova, Milada Anna. 2008. The European Union: The causal behemoth of transnational influence on postcommunist politics. In Mitchell A. Orenstein, Stephen Bloom, and Nicole Lindstrom, eds., *Transnational Actors in Central and East European Transitions*, 19–37. Pittsburgh: University of Pittsburgh Press.

Vassilev, Dimitur. 2008. Environmentalist. Interview, June 28, Sofia, Bulgaria.

Wapner, Paul. 1995. Politics beyond the state: Environmental activism and world civic politics. *World Politics* 47(3):311–340.

Warhola, James W., and Orlina Boteva. 2003. The Turkish minority in contemporary Bulgaria. *Nationalities Papers* 31(3):255–279.

11

Politics by Other Greens: The Importance of Transnational Environmental Justice Movement Networks

David Naguib Pellow

The race, class, gender, and national inequalities and ecological violence that are at the core of global capitalism underscore a point that many participants in environmental movements often overlook: social inequalities are the primary driving forces behind ecological crises. That is, we should no longer view race, class, and other inequalities as the most important variables in a general model that might explain environmental injustice. Rather they are also the most important factors for theorizing the overall predicament of ecological unsustainability. Social inequalities are, therefore, not just an afterthought of an environmentally precarious society; they are at its root.

There are times when we must be reminded of the inescapable interdependence among human societies and of those interdependencies we experience with broader ecosystems. Thus a close observation of the myriad forms of institutional violence among human communities always reveals the associated violence visited on ecosystems. Therefore social movements confronting human rights abuses—particularly in the global South—tend to also confront questions of ecological abuse because the domination over people is reinforced and made possible by the domination of ecosystems. But the interdependencies that human and nonhuman systems share underscore that no one is exempt from the far-reaching impacts of institutional and ecological violence. Thus radical transformative democratization of societies is a critical component in the global effort to achieve environmental sustainability and social justice.

In this chapter I investigate the phenomenon of transnational environmental justice (EJ) movements, specifically considering the work of activists, organizations, and networks that constitute this political formation. Linking environmental justice studies, environmental sociology, ethnic studies, and social movement theory in new ways, and drawing on interviews and archives, I ask how social movements challenge environmental inequalities across international borders. I argue that transnational EJ movement networks do this (1) by disrupting the social relations that produce environmental inequalities, (2) by producing new accountabilities vis-à-vis nation-states and polluters, and (3) by articulating new visions of ecologically sustainable and socially just institutions and societies.

Environmental Sociology and Social Inequalities

In this first section of the chapter I consider sociological theories of environmental conflict and link them to theories of social inequality. I begin with Ulrich Beck's "risk society" thesis, which contends that late modern society is marked by an exponential increase in the production and use of hazardous chemical substances, producing a fundamental transformation in the relationship among capital, the state, civil society, and the environment. What this means is that the project of nation building and the very idea of the modern nation-state are undergirded by the presence of toxins—chemical poisons—that permeate every social institution, human body, and ecosystem. This toxic modern nation-state also depends on the subjugation of ecosystems and certain human populations designated as "others"—those who are less than deserving of full citizenship. This process attenuates the most negative impacts of such a system on elites. Toxic production systems produce privileges for a global minority and externalize the costs of that process to those spaces occupied by devalued and marginal "others"—people of color, the poor, indigenous communities, and global South nations. The study of such inequalities, of course, is the foundation of the field of environmental justice and inequality studies (Agyeman, Bullard, and Evans 2003).

Thus, according to Beck, advanced capitalism creates wealth for some and imposes risks on others, at least in the short term. In the long run, however, the problem of widespread global ecological harm ends up returning to impact its creators in a "boomerang effect." That is, the risks of late modernity eventually haunt those who originally produced them (Beck 1999). In that sense, Beck acknowledges environmental inequality in the short term, while also maintaining a global, long-range view of what becomes, to some extent, a democratization of risk. Beck confirms the enduring problem of what other scholars have termed the "metabolic rift"—the disruptions in ecosystems that capitalism produces because of its inherent tendency to expend natural resources at a rate that is greater than the ability of ecosystems to replenish those materials

(Foster 2000). These rifts are linked to and reinforce social dislocations and inequalities that siphon wealth upward and restrict the economic and political capacities of the working classes and communities of color. Thus environmental harm is necessarily intertwined with the institutional violence that constitutes race, gender, and class hierarchies.

Building on these ideas from within environmental sociology, I now turn to theoretical developments from within the field of ethnic studies. For well over a century, a number of scholars and public intellectuals have used words like *poison* and *toxic* in speech and writings about racism. This is a powerful way to capture the harm racism does to both its victims and perpetrators or beneficiaries. Many authors have described racism as a *poison* that reveals deep contradictions and tensions in this nation, which have periodically erupted in violence, revolts, and wars over the years. Critical race theorists Lani Guinier and Gerald Torres make use of this terminology in their book *The Miner's Canary*. They write:

The canary's distress signaled that it was time to get out of the mine because the air was becoming too *poisonous* to breathe. Those who are racially marginalized are like the miner's canary: their distress is the first sign of a danger that *threatens us all*. It is easy enough to think that when we sacrifice this canary, the only harm is to communities of color. Yet others ignore problems that converge around racial minorities at their own peril, for these problems are symptoms warning us that we are all at risk. (Guinier and Torres 2002, 11; emphasis added)

Guinier and Torres also introduce a concept they term "political race," which "encompasses the view that race . . . matters because racialized communities provide the early warning signs of *poison* in the social atmosphere" (Guinier and Torres 2002, 12; emphasis added). In other words, political race forces us to think beyond specific instances of culpability and discrimination to produce a broader vision of justice for society as a whole. These concepts push us to rethink and challenge racism because it "threatens us all," not just the people of color who may be its primary targets. The concept of political race begins with an emphasis on race and moves to class, gender, and other inequalities, so while the principal emphasis is on race, this model is also inclusive of other categories of social difference.

The toxic metaphor for racism—and class and gender domination, for that matter—parallels Beck's "risk society" model in many ways. For example, racism, class and gender domination, and pollution are ubiquitous and deeply embedded in our institutions, our culture, and our bodies. Moreover, while the production of race, gender, and class hierarchies and toxic chemicals results in widespread harm across human communities and ecosystems, they both can also operate like a boomerang and eventually circle back to impact all members of society through uprisings, social unrest, and other conflicts. Finally, they are also powerful symbols for organizing resistance movements and for bringing people together across social and spatial boundaries. These concepts are helpful for thinking about the power and potential of transnational EJ movements.

Transnational Social Movements for Global Environmental Justice

While the primary focus of this chapter is on antitoxics struggles, it must be said that the movement for global environmental justice and human rights casts a much broader net. This includes struggles against extractive industries, transboundary pollution and waste flows, free trade agreements, and—more importantly—the ideological and social systems that reinforce such practices, including racism, capitalism, patriarchy, and militarism. For example, hydroelectric dams have catalyzed many communities around the globe where people are fighting water privatization and external control of that most fundamental element on the planet. In response to the massive human rights abuses and environmental impacts associated with large dams, a highly influential and effective international movement emerged to force changes in current dam-building practices. In addition to organizations of dam-affected peoples, this arm of the EJ movement includes numerous allied environmental, human rights, and social activist groups around the world. International meetings in recent years have brought together dam-affected peoples and their allies to network and strategize, and to call for improvements in planning for water- and energy-supply projects. Every year, community and activist groups from around the world show their solidarity with those dispossessed by dams on the International Day of Action, a global event organized to raise awareness about the impacts of dams and the value of dam-free and undammed rivers (McCully 2001).

Groups like the International Campaign for Responsible Technology are primarily focused on the social, economic, and ecological impacts of the global electronics industry, from mineral and water extraction for the production of electronics products, to their manufacture, sale, consumption, and disposal. In other words, this particular global EJ network adopts a lifecycle approach to the problem, following the materials and their effects on people and ecosystems (Smith, Sonnenfeld, and Pellow 2006). Many of these EJ movement networks articulate a critique of broader ideological systems of socioenvironmental hierarchy that give life and legitimacy to global environmental injustice. Without such critical guiding frameworks, these movements would be limited in their political power and vision.

Numerous transnational social movement organizations (TSMOs) concerned with EJ and human rights issues focus their efforts on a range of state and industrial sectors. Taken together, these global organizations and networks constitute a formidable presence at international treaty negotiations, within corporate shareholder meetings, and in the halls of congresses and parliaments. Even so, they are only a part of the broader global movement for environmental justice. Arguably the most important components of that movement are the domestic local, regional, and national organizations in the various communities, cities, and nations in which scores of environmental justice battles occur every day. Those groups provide the front-line participants in the struggles for local legitimacy within TSMOs and their networks. Together, the numerous local grassroots organizations and their collaborating global networks produce and maintain a critical infrastructure of the transnational public sphere.

Social movements must mobilize resources—funds, technology, people, symbols, ideas, and imagination—to achieve their goals. Transnational social movements are rarely successful if we narrowly define success as a major change in a specific policy within a nation-state (Keck and Sikkink 1998). But they are increasingly relevant in international policy debates, because they seek not only to make changes in international law and multilateral conventions, but also to change the terms and nature of the discourse within these important debates. These conventions include, for example, the Montreal Protocol (on the production of ozone-damaging chemicals), the Kyoto Protocol (concerning global climate change), the Basel Convention (on the international trade in hazardous wastes), and the Stockholm Convention (on the production and management of persistent organic pollutants). In each of these cases, TSMOs are often a critical source of knowledge for governments seeking information about environmental and social justice concerns, and their presence raises the costs of failing to act on certain issues, thus increasing the possibility of government accountability. In a global society where a nation-state's reputation can be tarnished in international political and media venues, transnational social movements can have surprisingly significant impacts. When movements disseminate information to the point that it becomes a part of common wisdom, such "popular beliefs . . . are themselves material forces" (Gramsci 1971, 165). That is, meaning systems can support or challenge systems of structural and material control. This is a critical point because, as cultural studies scholars and urban political ecologists have argued, social movements are struggling over cultural meaning systems as much as they are fighting for improved material conditions and needs (Moore, Kosek, and Pandian 2003).

In other words, the "natural" environment becomes a symbol of meaning for human communities. It can become a symbol of our attachment to—or contempt for—nature, and as a political or cultural tool for mobilizing against people whom hegemonic actors consider inferior and unimportant. The history of the genocide of Native peoples in the United States and the continued practices of environmental racism are just two examples of associating despised human "others" with landscapes and ecosystems that are also targets of extraction, pollution, or selective valuation. On the other hand, for the same reasons, ecosystems play a cultural role in the mobilization of social movements in favor of protecting nonhuman nature from risks associated with industrialization. As Moore, Kosek, and Pandian (2003) argue, nature is a terrain of power, through which we discursively and materially advance various meanings, agendas, and politics. Thus transnational EJ movement networks challenge environmental inequality by confronting the social forces that produce these outcomes and by arguing for new relationships of accountability vis-à-vis state and corporate actors.

Boomerang Effects

Recall that Beck's "risk society" and Guinier and Torres's "miner's canary" speak to the relational and interdependent character of industrial chemicals and social inequalities through the phenomena of boomerangs. Research on transnational social movement networks reveals that these formations produce their *own* boomerang effects as well. That is, when local governments refuse to heed calls for change, transnational activist networks create pressure that "curves around local state indifference and repression to put foreign pressure on local policy elites. Thus international contacts amplify voices to which domestic governments are deaf, while the local work of target country activists legitimizes efforts of activists abroad" (Keck and Sikkink 1998). It is the interaction between repressive domestic political structures and more flexible structures in other nations that produces this boomerang.

In their influential book *Activists beyond Borders*, Keck and Sikkink (1998) explore the significance of the work of transnational social movement networks. These groups of activists in two or more nations have, for decades, successfully intervened in and changed the terms of important global and national policy debates, pushed for regulation of activities deemed harmful to social groups, and influenced states to embrace practices that might improve the lives of residents in any given nation. Transnational movement networks often do this by gathering critical information and strategically making it available to publics, governments, media organizations, and other movements in order to force change. These movement networks also achieve such goals through mobilizing support for boycotts, letter-writing campaigns, and other forms of protest that shine a spotlight on objectionable institutional practices with the goal of halting or transforming them. Transnational movements frequently take advantage of the multiple geographic scales at which these networks operate and sidestep the barriers that nation-states in one locale may create in order to access the leverage available from within other states—the boomerang. Transnational EJ movements also use the boomerang to challenge the power that states and corporations enjoy over vulnerable communities, thus confronting the race, gender, and class inequalities that produce environmental injustices.

What Goes Around Comes Around

Guinier and Torres underscore the importance of "political race" through the metaphor of the "miner's canary," which symbolizes the role of people of color whose oppression is a sign of a poisonous social atmosphere that ultimately threatens all of society, not just those communities that suffer directly from racism. That is, racism creates its own boomerang effects that reveal systems of interdependence and accountability that impact people from all racial and class strata (albeit unevenly). Wars, revolts, uprisings, and social movements spawned, in part, by demands for racial, gender, and class justice against systems of oppression are among the many examples of such a boomerang effect. While mobilizing the boomerangs of transnational social movements, environmental justice activist networks also draw on analyses of race, class, and gender inequality to unmask the drivers of environmental injustice and to frame a vision of a more sustainable and socially just world.

There are multiple boomerang effects evident in EJ struggles, and I examine two of them here. The first is the way social movements use transnational activist networks to leverage power across international borders to target states and corporations. The second is the boomerang effect of racial, gender, and class inequalities and how such hierarchies often harm both beneficiaries and targets/survivors. After presenting a case study in which both boomerangs are in play, I then offer a conceptual framework for thinking through the kinds of social and political accountabilities and interdependencies these stories reveal, and their implications for social movements' dreams of freedom and invigorating new political formations.

Something Toxic from Denmark: Mozambique's Battle with Foreign Pesticides

This story begins in 1998, in Mozambique's capital city of Maputo, where a Danish international development agency (Danida) funded an effort to incinerate nine hundred tons of obsolete toxic fertilizer and pesticide stocks. This case underscores two major examples of global environmental inequality: the massive export of pesticides, which often leads to surplus obsolete pesticide stocks lying unsecured in warehouses, vacant lots, and fields in global South nations; and the massive export of incineration technology to these nations.

Mozambique has a population of nineteen million people, 70 percent of whom live off the land. Located in Southeastern Africa, it is the world's ninth poorest nation. The country is slowly rebuilding itself after five centuries of brutal colonization by Portugal, followed by seventeen years of civil war, which resulted in the deaths of one million persons. Former independence fighters with the group FRELIMO won the country's first democratic elections in 1994, and UN peacekeeping forces finally departed one year later. Since that time, Mozambique has enjoyed relative peace. Even so, the average Mozambican's life expectancy is just forty years and the citizenry experience grinding poverty on a daily basis. The U.S. ecological footprint is 23.7 acres per capita—and a sustainable footprint in that nation would be 4.6 acres. Mozambique represents the other end of the scale, with an ecological footprint of 1.3 acres per capita. Unfortunately, the reason for this lighter footprint is because there is so much poverty and so little industrialization occurring in Mozambique ("Rich Nations Gobbling Resources at an Unsustainable Rate" 2004). Despite this harsh reality, new civil society organizations are emerging and thriving there, and the first signs of new civil society growth in Mozambique sprang forth from a struggle for environmental justice.

A Toxic Discovery: Mozambique as a Risk Society
In 1998, in Maputo, community activist Janice Lemos read a story in
Metical—an independent local newspaper—about Danida's effort to
fund the incineration of obsolete toxic fertilizer and pesticide stocks in
a cement factory in the southern city of Matola. Danida sought to donate
a hazardous waste incineration facility that would be housed in the
cement factory, which the aid agency would also pay to have retrofitted
for the operation. Ms. Lemos wrote to the newspaper for more information about the cement kiln incinerator proposal, but none was available.
She then contacted Greenpeace International's headquarters in the Netherlands, where someone informed her that two U.S.-based antitoxics
activists would soon be visiting South Africa, and they might be able to
travel to Maputo and Matola if Mozambican community leaders would
invite them. With the help of Greenpeace and Oxfam Community Aid
Abroad, Lemos and fellow concerned residents met with the U.S. activists
Ann Leonard (then with the group Essential Action) and Paul Connett
(a St. Lawrence University chemistry professor and renowned expert
on and opponent of incineration), as well as with Bobby Peek, a South
African toxics expert and activist (with the Environmental Justice
Networking Forum).

The visiting activists were quite concerned because they possessed
documentation that cement kiln incinerators produce a range of deadly
toxins such as dioxins and furans. In fact, scientists estimate that 23
percent of the world's newly created dioxin comes from cement kiln
incinerators alone (Puckett 1998). Prior to their arrival, the visiting activists were able to access documents about Danida's plans and had additional information about the proposed project. EJNF's Bobby Peek
stated, "Whether or not anybody actually became concerned about the
issue . . . we strongly felt that we had the moral obligation to pass on
what we knew about the plan, and the real risks of cement kiln incineration. They had the right to know. As we feared, almost nobody had heard
about the project at all" (Puckett 1998, 25). This lack of public knowledge was particularly disturbing because Danida has a policy of "actively
involving individuals, non-governmental organizations and associations
and businesses formally and informally in formulating and implementing
environmental policies" (Neilsen 1999). Yet few people in Maputo or
Matola had heard anything about the project from Danida. In fact, the
foreign visitors were the *only* people at the meeting who had seen a copy
of the short environmental impact assessment (EIA) Danida had prepared. Moreover, the report was written in English, although the official

language of Mozambique is Portuguese. One local activist remembered that "only a few of us could manage to read the report and . . . do a brief analysis" (Lemos 2004). Connett denounced the entire project. He stated: "In the United States or Canada, those proposing a new toxic waste facility would be obliged to fully discuss all of the alternatives, all of the risks, and would have been required to hold several public hearings before decisions could be made about a particular disposal method. The environmental assessment and public involvement in this project is a sham" (Puckett 1998, 25). For its part, Danida conducted an EIA that concluded no serious environmental impacts would result from the incineration of the pesticides (Mangwiro 1999).

The visiting activists also informed the Mozambican citizens of the questionable record of Waste-Tech Ltd., a South African firm that was to be contracted for the Danida effort. At that time, Waste-Tech Ltd. was seeking to import foreign waste into South Africa—a clear violation of the law there—and was the subject of an investigation by the South African Human Rights Commission concerning possible abuses in the case of two incinerators it had located in close proximity to an economically depressed community. The firm was also confronted with other legal investigations being conducted by the South African Department of Water Affairs and Forestry.

Mauricio Sulila, one of the local community leaders from Maputo present at the meeting, later told a reporter: "When we explained [to others attending the gathering] that the government had decided the factory would burn toxic waste, they became terrified" (Lowe 2003). Local people already suspected the presence of toxic materials at the site because, as Sulila recalled, earlier flooding in the area prompted residents to pump the water into a nearby swamp where, soon afterward, "someone ate a fish caught in this swamp and died" (Lowe 2003). The terror that people experienced at the news of a toxic threat underscores risk society theorists' findings that the dangers of modern industrial pollutants often instill fear and dread among exposed communities (Erikson 1995).

At the meeting with U.S. and South African activists, local residents and community leaders founded an organization to address the problem of environmental hazards in the area. Mr. Mazul, one of the attendees who was also an artist, explained that, since the citizens had been kept in the dark by the Danish and Mozambican authorities at the Environment Ministry, the group should be named *Livaningo*, which translates to "all that sheds light" in Shangaan, one of many languages spoken in that region of the country. Mauricio Sulila was appointed the group's general secretary. Janice Lemos and her sister Anabela joined the group's leadership as well. The development of an activist organization in Maputo also reflected the symbolic or cultural dimension of environmental justice politics. This dimension facilitates people's expression of their sense of concern and care for ecosystems in ways that allow them to convert that sentiment into political action. The use of the word *Livaningo* for the new EJ organization was a perfect example. Embodied in this single name lies an acknowledgment of the local culture, the story of how this community came to be under siege, and an intent to make transparent and improve their situation. "All that sheds light" is also an ecological metaphor for the power of the sun and the power of an organized community.

Action and Networking at Multiple Scales
Soon after its first meeting, Livaningo grew and enjoyed some influence with the local and national governments. They organized public gatherings and meetings, brought their concerns to local residents and businesses, and made strategic use of the independent press. They also held some of the first public demonstrations in postrevolution Mozambique. Sulila explained, "It is important to say that Livaningo was the first organization in Mozambique to really challenge the government" (Pellow 2007, 174). Livaningo was eventually able to secure the services of a firm that conducted an independent environmental assessment of the project. Anabela Lemos proudly recalled that the firm's "conclusion was completely what we thought from the beginning: under no condition should the cement factory be turned into an incinerator" (Lemos 2004).

However, the organization faced numerous hurdles in its efforts to oppose the incinerator. For example, the Mozambican government refused to consider Livaningo's independent environmental assessment. Activists then tried to secure an audience with the Danish embassy in Maputo, but they were refused. In the fall of 1998, members of the Danida board of directors visited Maputo, but rejected Livaningo's request for a meeting. In response, the activists elevated the struggle and went to the source. Aurelio Gomes of Livaningo and Bobby Peek of the EJNF in South Africa traveled to Denmark to address the Danish Parliament about Danida's pesticide incineration project. As Gomes stated on arrival in Denmark, with regard to Danida's earlier refusal to meet with them, "This won't prevent us from voicing our concerns, therefore we've come to Copenhagen today to provide the Danish government with information to justify the immediate halt and rethinking [of the incineration effort]" (Basel Action Network 1998). Although the Parliament granted them an audience, its members made no effort to intervene in the conflict. Despite this rebuff, this was a critical moment in the development of a transnational EJ collaboration, because Mozambican, U.S., South African, and Danish activists were working together in close coordination. Allies such as Greenpeace International and the Joint Oxfam Advocacy Program (JOAP, Mozambique) donated the funding support for these activities. Mauricio Sulila remembered:

That was great . . . After that, the Mozambique government opened up the door a little. We explained to them that we will not give up, we will not be intimidated. We continued to make pressure, to make noise, to hold international meetings and meetings at the local level. We were working with several organizations, especially Greenpeace Denmark. JOAP's support was fantastic. Say we need to do a demonstration in two days, they were able to provide funds to advertise in the newspaper. When we needed to travel to Denmark, JOAP funded us. It's not a lot of money, but it is at the right time, when we really need it. (Lowe 2003)

When asked later how Livaningo organized so effectively on an international scale, Anabela Lemos stated,

It is mostly through the Internet. But whenever we campaign, we make some noise here in Mozambique, and at the same time we have the international network. When our government told us to stop complaining, we went to Denmark and we spoke to the people *there*, and we realized that, as a result, they started to listen to us *here*. So we realized then that we couldn't just do a campaign here, but instead we had to work both ways, here in Mozambique and in Denmark. (Lemos 2004)

Activists with Greenpeace Denmark were critical to the campaign's success as well. While the Danish government initially refused accountability for the pesticides, Danish activists took responsibility for their nation's involvement in this conflict. Greenpeace Denmark staff member Jacob Hartmann commented on the inconsistency involved in his government's embrace of the Basel Convention on Transboundary Hazardous Wastes (which prohibits wealthy OECD nations from trading or dumping hazardous wastes in poorer non-OECD nations) while also encouraging the incineration of pesticides in Matola: "Considering that Denmark is one of the countries that have taken the lead on this vital treaty, it makes little sense for Denmark to advocate for an elimination of POPs [persistent organic pollutants] globally while promoting new sources of the worst of them in Mozambique" (Puckett 1998, 26). POPs include the most toxic substances known to science such as dioxins, furans, and polychlorinated biphenyls (PCBs), and are common by-products of incineration.

Denmark's Development Minister, Poul Nielsen, denied that his country was seeking to impose incinerators on Mozambique, but activists found this claim suspect, given that Danida had funded a failed incinerator in India in 1986, and because Denmark was considering financial support for garbage incinerators in Zimbabwe and Tanzania in 1998, the year the conflict in Mozambique ignited ("SA Dumping Plan 'Trashed' by NYC" 1998).

Coalition activists consistently called for the pesticide incineration project to be halted, for the pesticides to be exported to a global North nation, for the wastes to be disposed of using nontoxic nonincineration technology, and for all the costs to be borne by the companies that produced the chemicals in the first place ("Mozambique Activists Win Huge Victory" 2000). And although Livaningo activists were only recently beginning civil society organizing on EJ issues, they were familiar with the problem of environmental injustice, since this was something that has been widespread in the region. Anabela Lemos remarked: "In South Africa, always the dumping sites are near the poor people. And we have a waste dump here in the city and there is a concentration of poor people there, so it's the same thing here. The poor, they always get the waste" (Lemos 2004).

Thus, this transnational coalition of environmental justice activists clearly articulated their opposition to Danida's use of local Mozambican ecosystems and communities as waste repositories. Activists channeled these grievances into a vision of environmental justice that communicated an articulation of the symbolic, cultural, and political dimensions of ecosystems—that is, a viewpoint that challenged the dominant perspective of nature as a site of resource extraction and a place for dumping effluence. Thus, they were deeply engaged in disrupting the social relations that produced environmental injustice in their community and sought new relations of accountability locally, nationally, and transnationally.

The Boomerang in Motion

After two years of campaigning, Livaningo had its first major breakthrough. The Mozambican government agreed to a "return to sender" arrangement and allowed the chemicals to be shipped to a global North nation—the Netherlands—for processing and disposal by hazardous waste treatment firms there ("Mozambique Environmentalists Defeat Incinerator Plan" 2000). While the Mozambican government did have to pay some of the costs, Denmark shared the expenses. And, despite EJ activists' hopes that nonincineration technologies would be used, some of the wastes were indeed incinerated in Europe.

Even so, the EJ coalition achieved its primary goal of "return to sender"—exporting the wastes to a global North nation. Livaningo reached out to a broad group of established TSMOs, including the Environmental Justice Networking Forum (South Africa), Essential Action (U.S.), Greenpeace International (Netherlands, Denmark, and Brazil), the Basel Action Network (U.S.), and Oxfam's JOAP (UK), to amplify its voice and augment any leverage it already had in order to achieve one of the most impressive global-local EJ collaborations in the movement's history. The South Africa–based EJNF lent a critical African presence to the struggle. No less important was the legitimacy that Livaningo provided for its international partner organizations and activists who might otherwise be viewed as "outside agitators" in Mozambique. And Greenpeace Denmark provided much needed credibility for Mozambican activists confronting the Danish government. Drawing on local, regional, and international activist support, as well as international law and aggressive movement tactics, the coalition succeeded. These external resources were critical to the campaign, but the local activists' level of determination and commitment to the struggle was what ultimately sustained the effort. As Livaningo's Aurelio Gomes remarked, "We have nothing against Denmark, and hope they have nothing against us. We just want them to understand that here in Mozambique, while we may not be wealthy, we will never compromise our health—that is all some of us have" (Puckett 1998, 26). Likewise, Livaningo activist Anabela Lemos commented, "We just decided that we would not fail, although there were many times when it looked as if all hope was lost" ("Mozambique Environmentalists Defeat Incinerator Plan" 2000).

Although Mozambique is a democracy, it is still a young one. The government is slowly becoming accustomed to the idea of being challenged by civil society groups, whether inside or outside its borders. As Anabela Lemos (2004) commented, "Mozambique is a country where people are scared to speak out, and still today, but it is getting better. We are going through democracy after so many years. We are the only NGO [nongovernmental organization] doing this work. If something is wrong, we speak up, we don't talk just for talking's sake. When we speak, we know we are right and we know we have to say it."

Next Steps for Mozambique: A Broader Vision of Justice and Sustainability

The campaign to halt the incineration project and export the pesticide wastes from Matolo, Mozambique, was successful. This was a pleasant surprise for people throughout the international EJ and NGO community as they witnessed activists from one of the world's poorest nations exert uncommon political leverage.

Since this unprecedented success, Livaningo has used the opportunity to broaden its focus beyond toxics to include other environmental justice struggles in the region. As Livaningo expands its work, it is now pursuing projects aimed at introducing ecologically sound waste management systems in healthcare institutions in Mozambique, in collaboration with international activist groups like Health Care without Harm. They are also working to oppose harmful "development" projects like the Mpanda Uncua Hydroelectric dam on the Zambezi River in Mozambique, in partnership with TSMOs like International Rivers (based in Berkeley, California). Livaningo is also combating oil extraction efforts by trans national corporations in southern Africa, which would pollute the air, land, and water and return few economic benefits to the people of the region.

Livaningo's victory in the pesticide incinerator case is credited with opening a broader political space for other civil society groups and social movements to work in Mozambique on a host of social concerns. Organizations working on HIV/AIDS, human rights, land rights, and global economic justice efforts now enjoy greater support as a result of the political space Livaningo opened. In other words, they secured access into the nation's political process by challenging and transforming the structure itself. As Anabela Lemos (2004) stated,

It is true that we opened things up for people in our nation because we are not scared to speak out and to raise our issues. We think we have the right to do so. And I think that civil society has to get involved, we can't just sit on our hands and complain. If something is wrong, we should work for it. I think people should start to realize that to have big changes we have to give a lot up and we have to sacrifice. . . . You should not be scared. If you are right, then you have the right to speak, and I think it does make a difference.

Thus, the Danida case allowed activists to build on the success of a single environmental justice struggle and expand outward to be inclusive of a greater breadth of environmental and social concerns of civil society. This mobilization also revealed how deeply Mozambique had become a part of the "world risk society" (Beck 1999) through the embrace of ecologically and socially toxic forms of economic development that are rampant throughout southern Africa.

The case of Livaningo also reveals how environmental inequalities reflect a type of sexual violence (Smith 2005), in the way that hegemonic social forces attempt to either impose ecologically harmful practices or extract ecological resources without the consent of affected communities. In other words, Andrea Smith argues that—similar to traditional forms of interpersonal sexual violence—environmental inequality involves a violation of a social body without consent. Whether this involves dumping hazardous wastes, locating a polluting industrial facility near residents, or extracting natural resources, environmental inequalities around the globe routinely involve the absence of community approval. Thus, environmental justice must ultimately embrace an orientation that confronts all forms of inequality and recognizes how capitalism thrives off of hegemonies of humans over ecosystems, whites over people of color, the rich over the poor, men over women, citizens over noncitizens, and heterosexuals over gay/lesbian/bisexuals/transgendered/queer communities. Without integrating these systems of hierarchy into our analyses of the problem, we will fall short of proposing viable solutions.

Discussion and Conclusion

The emergence of a transnational movement for environmental justice and the case of Livaningo allow us to think through questions of social hierarchy and the kinds of accountabilities and interdependencies that constrain and enable social and political change from within vulnerable communities. Here I wish to extend Guinier and Torres's "miner's canary" model of a racial metaphor to examine the miner's canary as a *spatial* metaphor. When global South communities are the targets of international environmental injustice (via hazardous waste dumping, illegal waste trading, or resource extraction from the global North), those spaces *and* the people who occupy them constitute the miner's canary. Thus entire communities, nations, and regions are often viewed as disposable or devalued by more privileged actors on the global stage. When social movements mobilize to demand that imported toxics be returned to their points of origin, the receiving nations of the global North serve as a reminder that environmental racism—like racism, class, and gender inequality more generally—threatens us all. This analysis allows one to theorize and link the boomerang effects of racism, class and gender inequalities, and social movements across international borders. In this way, the "miner's canary" can signal a potential or impending environmental danger that threatens not only members of vulnerable social groups, but also privileged populations living across vast geographic and social borders. This occurs as a result of the boomerang effects that racial, class, and gender inequalities and social movements produce, challenging social hierarchies that create environmental inequality and making hegemonic institutions accountable to vulnerable populations.

The idea of a boomerang effect is productive for theorizing social movements and environmental justice politics because it is a dynamic concept. The boomerang reveals that race, gender, and class inequalities and ecological harm associated with global capitalism are not just oppressive of people of color and ecosystems, but may ultimately be unsustainable and hazardous to those who benefit from that system. These race, gender, and class inequalities are not just an unfortunate by-product of an ecologically unsustainable society; they are at its root. Social inequalities are the principal forces driving ecological crises. Thus no one is exempt from racial, class, gender, and ecological violence, and social movements can present important and disruptive challenges to these social forces.

The boomerang is a metaphor. It is also a reminder of the interdependence among human societies and the unavoidable accountabilities we have to each other. The power of the boomerang returns us to the core of the human-environment and human-human interactions and the reason we should be concerned about the various social dimensions of ecosystems: when we harm ecosystems we also perpetrate harms against other human beings, and vice versa (Harvey 1996; Merchant 1980). When we build relationships of respect and justice within human communities, we tend to reflect those practices in our relationships to ecosystems. Transformative, radical restructuring of societies is required to achieve environmental justice, and creative social movements are an indispensable foundation of that process (Speth 2008).

This chapter links environmental justice studies, environmental sociology, ethnic studies, and social movement theory in new ways, by drawing on key concepts and metaphors from these fields to produce new intellectual space for thinking about environmental politics, transnational movements, and social hierarchies. I began with the question: How do social movements challenge environmental inequalities across international borders? I argued that transnational EJ movement networks do this by disrupting the social relations that produce environmental inequalities, by producing new accountabilities among states and polluters, and by promoting a vision of an ecologically sustainable and socially just society. They achieve these ends by mobilizing bodies, information, and the cultural imaginary.

References

Agyeman, Julian, Robert Bullard, and Bob Evans, eds. 2003. *Just Sustainabilities: Development in an Unequal World*. Cambridge, MA: MIT Press.

Basel Action Network. 1998. Danish development project encouraging toxic waste trade into Mozambique? Press release, October 5. Copenhagen: Basel Action Network.

Beck, Ulrich. 1999. *World Risk Society*. Cambridge: Polity Press.

Erikson, Kai. 1995. *A New Species of Trouble: The Human Experience of Modern Disasters*. New York: Norton.

Foster, John Bellamy. 2000. *Marx's Ecology: Materialism and Nature*. New York: Monthly Review Press.

Gramsci, Antonio. 1971. *Selections from the Prison Notebooks*. New York: International Publishers.

Guinier, Lani, and Gerald Torres. 2002. *The Miner's Canary: Enlisting Race, Resisting Power, Transforming Democracy*. Cambridge, MA: Harvard University Press.

Harvey, David. 1996. *Justice, Nature, and the Geography of Difference*. Boston: Blackwell.

Keck, Margaret E., and Kathryn Sikkink. 1998. *Activists beyond Borders: Advocacy Networks in International Politics*. Ithaca, NY: Cornell University Press.

Lemos, Anabela. 2004. Interview with the author. February 5.

Lowe, Sarah. 2003. Toxic waste victory in Mozambique. *Horizons* (Oxfam), February.

Mangwiro, Charles. 1999. Obsolete pesticides leave Mozambicans with $600,000 problem. *African Eye News Service* (South Africa), July 22.

McCully, Patrick. 2001. *Silenced Rivers: The Ecology and Politics of Large Dams*. London: Zed Books.

Merchant, Carolyn. 1980. *The Death of Nature: Women, Ecology, and the Scientific Revolution*. San Francisco: Harper.

Moore, Donald, Jake Kosek, and Anand Pandian, eds. 2003. *Race, Nature, and the Politics of Difference*. Durham, NC: Duke University Press.

Mozambique activists win huge victory against toxic waste incineration. 2000. Coalition press release, October 5. http://www.ban.org.

Mozambique environmentalists defeat incinerator plan. 2000. Environment News Service (ENS), Maputo, Mozambique, October 13.

Neilsen, Poul. 1999. Letter to Livaningo. January.

Pellow, David N. 2007. *Resisting Global Toxics: Transnational Movements for Environmental Justice.* Cambridge, MA: MIT Press.

Puckett, Jim. 1998. Something rotten from Denmark: The incinerator "solution" to aid gone bad in Mozambique. *Multinational Monitor* 19, no. 12 (December): 24–26.

Rich nations gobbling resources at an unsustainable rate. 2004. Environment News Service (ENS), March 30.

SA dumping plan "trashed" by NYC. 1998. Africa News Service, January 8.

Smith, Andrea, 2005. *Conquest: Sexual Violence and American Indian Genocide.* Cambridge, MA: South End Press.

Smith, Ted, David A. Sonnenfeld, and David Naguib Pellow, eds. 2006. *Challenging the Chip: Labor Rights and Environmental Justice in the Global Electronics Industry.* Philadelphia: Temple University Press.

Speth, James Gustave. 2008. *The Bridge at the Edge of the World: Capitalism, the Environment, and Crossing from Crisis to Sustainability.* New Haven, CT: Yale University Press.

IV
Conclusion

12

Reflections on Environmental Inequality Beyond Borders

JoAnn Carmin and Julian Agyeman

The chapters in this book draw on diverse international case studies to illustrate how a globalized world is fundamentally altering the environmental justice terrain. Traditional studies of environmental justice examined the ways inequalities are generated and resolved within domestic contexts, paying particular attention to the distributional aspects of injustice and the need for recognition and participation (Schlosberg 2007; Schrader-Frechette 2002; Young 1990). More recently, scholars have drawn on theories of multiple spatialities of environmental justice and of multilevel governance and institutions (e.g., Walker 2010; Holifield, Porter, and Walker 2010; Pellow 2000; Sze and London 2008; Walker and Bulkeley 2006) to inform their assessments of the roots of environmental inequalities. Rather than hone in on a single strand of environmental justice scholarship, the authors in this book integrate traditional and emerging approaches. The result is that we not only learn how globalization is expanding and amplifying spatial injustice, but gain greater insight into the ways social, political, and economic institutions contribute to, reinforce, and have the potential to address and prevent inequalities.

Patterns of Environmental Inequality

Many of the points raised in the chapters in this book are aligned with themes that have come to characterize environmental justice scholarship. At the same time, the cases presented and arguments advanced extend our understanding of patterns of environmental inequality along three critical and interrelated dimensions. First, by taking global disparities as a starting point, and unpacking the ways they play out on the ground, many chapters offer nuanced perspectives on how inequalities within countries, as well as between rich and poor nations, are becoming further entrenched. While countries in the global South may benefit from the jobs and investments made by foreign companies and nations, many of these gains are modest at best. As the case of the Niger Delta suggests, investments can leave a legacy of environmental degradation and reinforce social and ethnic inequalities. Similarly, the case of the Hoodia illustrates how bioprospecting was pursued without consideration of local San values and not only affected land claims, but ignored existing social, ethnic, and cultural norms. Ultimately, this contributed to dissention, factions, and schisms within traditional communities. Further, the case of climate injustice in Durban demonstrates the presence of a fundamental irony. On the one hand, the global North is investing in green technology and promoting local development in the global South while, on the other hand, the North continues to engage in consumption patterns that are placing an extraordinary climate burden on this part of the world.

A second pattern, highlighted by Widener in chapter 8, is that inequalities are not limited to relations between the global North and South, but are taking place across developing nations. The extractive practices of multinational corporations, the siting of waste facilities, and reliance on inexpensive labor continue to promote environmental inequalities between developed and developing nations. However, the case of China provides an important counterpoint since it shows how the rise of nations committed to development, but not to international agreements, environmental quality, and human rights, is altering global dynamics. Rather than focus on how to develop in an environmentally sound fashion, many developing countries are seeking to provide goods and services at a rapid rate regardless of the environmental and social impacts. The result is that while some developed countries are striving to alter their behavior, some developing countries are perpetuating patterns of global environmental and social inequality.

Environmental justice scholarship often examines how corporations and governments are the culprits of inequalities. The cases presented in this book are no exception. Quite a few of the chapters draw on examples from extractive industries. Whether explicit or implicit, they demonstrate that remote demand leads corporations, and in some instances foreign governments, to initiate activities in distant places. Since many of the countries where extraction is taking place have rudimentary or no environmental and labor regulations, several of the chapters affirm long-standing patterns where corporate activities reinforce existing legacies of poverty and pollution.

While traditional pathways of inequality are explored, a third dimension highlighted by the chapters is that it is important to look beyond the "usual suspects" and understand how international foundations, conventions, and intergovernmental organizations can unintentionally lead to environmental inequalities. In particular, the authors challenge the notion that environmental inequality hinges solely on the distribution of environmental "bads" such as extraction and production. Instead, they demonstrate that funders seeking to promote environmental "goods," such as biodiversity, can do so in ways that inadvertently marginalize the needs of local populations. Similarly, we see that international conventions designed to protect the rights of indigenous peoples such as the San, as well as international treaty organizations and committees, can fail to protect people's health, support their local claims, and safeguard their cultural values.

Promoting Equity through Social and Institutional Change

As with most studies of environmental justice, this collection highlights the varied ways inequalities play out on the ground. While the contributions extend our understanding by showing how local actors are affected by global inequalities and how environmental injustices are being perpetuated, they also provide a more hopeful message. Although the chapters suggest that institutions are at the root of the problem, they also suggest that institutions have the potential to be part of the solution, particularly when engaged and prodded by nonstate actors, either directly or through their networks.

An argument reiterated in several of the chapters is that environmental and social change may be fostered through transparency, accountability, and the creation of learning mechanisms in both domestic and transnational arenas. The general view that has been advanced over the years is that altering the dynamics by which some groups, values, and views are given precedence over others can only be achieved through recognition of diversity and the creation of institutions that provide a means for different perspectives to be voiced (Young 1990, 1996; Schlosberg 2007). Consequently, most studies and writings focus on the role of law (e.g., Rechtschaffen and Gauna 2002) and the importance of democratic institutions and participatory process (e.g., Schrader-Frechette 2002; Schlosberg 2007). The contributors to this book recognize that democratic institutions and legal mechanisms are critical for reducing degradation, protecting human and ecosystem health, and achieving recognition and voice. At the same time, they point to the potential for addressing inequality through complementary systems of "soft law" (Vogel 2005) and multiparty forums. In particular, the authors emphasize the need for protocols that ensure transparency and procedures that will hold corporations and governments accountable for their actions. They also note that transparency and accountability require the development of mechanisms that ensure access to decision processes and communication among diverse actors so that information and ideas are exchanged and multiparty learning can take place.

A further argument advanced by many of the authors is that transnational nongovernmental and social movement organizations can promote equity and equality by influencing national and subnational decisions and institutions. Previous research has shown how the mobilization of civil society actors can raise awareness of inequalities and contribute to the development of new laws and policies, both through domestic initiatives (e.g., Bullard 1990; Tesh 2000) and the creation of ties to transnational actors (e.g., Keck and Sikkink 1998; Pellow 2007). In most chapters, we see that local actors around the world struggle to have their voices heard and have their claims recognized. By comparing resource extraction in different countries, Widener is able to demonstrate in chapter 8 that environmental inequalities not only continue unabated when there is limited government oversight and accountability, but when domestic nongovernmental organizations fail to coordinate their efforts and serve as watchdogs. In chapters 10 and 11 respectively, Hicks and Pellow extend these points by showing how the efficacy of local organizations can be contingent on the participatory norms within a given country. Drawing on ideas that are central to social movement scholarship (i.e., Keck and Sikkink 1998), they find that national context affects whether actors can be influential or whether they will be better able to achieve their goals when they enlist the support of transnational actors. Their cases further reveal that transnational actors do not simply complement the strengths or extend the capacities of local and national oppositional groups, but have the potential to redefine national and subnational political terrains in ways that alter political and social dynamics contributing to inequities, promote accountabilities, and foster new visions for social and environmental justice.

Conclusion

Overall, the chapters in this book suggest that individuals, communities, and countries will be more or less successful in preventing and coping with climate impacts, toxic exposures, and other inequalities according to their race, level of wealth, and access to social and political resources (Bullard and Wright 2009). Threats to local environmental quality and human health are amplified by globalization. At the same time, reversing the expansion and deepening of spatial inequalities requires connectivity and coordination that reaches from the local to the global. Through the course of this book, we see that domestic governments must not only establish and enforce laws that protect the environment and human rights, but also participate in international agreements that hold corporations and foreign governments accountable to global standards. While government action is essential, the achievement of spatial justice also appears to rest on the commitment of networked civil society actors to monitor the activities of intergovernmental organizations, national governments, and corporations and to ensure that the claims and concerns of local actors are recognized within countries as well as amplified beyond borders.

References

Bullard, Robert D. 1990. *Dumping in Dixie*. Boulder, CO: Westview Press.

Bullard, Robert D., and Beverly Wright. 2009. *Race, Place, and Environmental Justice After Hurricane Katrina: Struggles to Reclaim, Rebuild, and Revitalize New Orleans and the Gulf Coast*. Boulder, CO: Westview Press.

Holifield, Ryan, Michael Porter, and Gordon Walker. 2010. Introduction: Spaces of environmental justice—Frameworks for critical engagement. In R. Holifield, M. Porter, and G. Walker, eds., *Spaces of Environmental Justice*, 1–23. West Sussex: Wiley-Blackwell.

Keck, Margaret, and Kathryn Sikkink. 1998. *Activists beyond Borders: Trans-National Advocacy Networks in International Politics*. Ithaca, NY: Cornell University Press.

Pellow, David N. 2000. Environmental inequality formation. *American Behavioral Scientist* 43:581–601.

Pellow, David N. 2007. *Resisting Global Toxics: Transnational Movements for Environmental Justice*. Cambridge, MA: MIT Press.

Rechtschaffen, Clifford, and Eileen Gauna. 2002. *Environmental Justice: Law, Policy, and Regulation*. Durham, NC: Carolina Academic Press.

Schlosberg, David. 2007. *Defining Environmental Justice: Theories, Movements and Nature*. Oxford: Oxford University Press.

Schrader-Frechette, Kristen. 2002. *Environmental Justice: Creating Equality, Reclaiming Democracy*. New York: Oxford University Press.

Sze, Julie, and Jonathan K. London. 2008. Environmental justice at the crossroads. *Sociology Compass* 2(4):1331–1354.

Tesh, Sylvia N. 2000. *Uncertain Hazards: Environmental Activists and Scientific Proof*. Ithaca, NY: Cornell University Press.

Vogel, David. 2005. *The Market for Virtue: The Potential and Limits of Corporate Social Responsibility*. New York: Brookings Institution Press.

Walker, Gordon. 2010. Beyond Distribution and Proximity: Exploring the Multiple Spatialities of Environmental Justice. In R. Holifield, M. Porter, and G. Walker, eds., *Spaces of Environmental Justice*, 24–46. West Sussex: Wiley-Blackwell.

Walker, Gordon, and Harriet Bulkeley. 2006. Editorial—Geographies of environmental justice. *Geoforum* 37(5):655–659.

Young, Iris M. 1990. *Justice and the Politics of Difference*. Princeton, NJ: Princeton University Press.

Young, Iris M. 1996. Communication and the Other. In S. Benhabib, ed., *Democracy and Difference: Contesting the Boundaries of the Political*. Princeton, NJ: Princeton University Press.

About the Contributors

Mary A. Ackley is an Environment Officer for the United States Agency for International Development (USAID). She received her MS from the University of Vermont, where her thesis research focused on the perception of environmental and health risks in the mineral sector.

Julian Agyeman is Professor and Chair of Urban and Environmental Policy and Planning at Tufts University. His research interests sit at the nexus of environmental justice and sustainability, focusing on the possibility of a "just" sustainability.

Saleem H. Ali is Professor of Environmental Planning at the University of Vermont's Rubenstein School of Environment and Natural Resources and Director of the Institute for Environmental Diplomacy and Security at James Jeffords Center for Public Policy. His research focuses on the causes and consequences of environmental conflicts and how ecological factors can promote peace.

Alison Hope Alkon is Assistant Professor of Sociology at University of the Pacific in Stockton, California. Her research is located at the intersection of environmental sociology, social inequality, and food studies.

Isabelle Anguelovski is a doctoral candidate in the Department of Urban Studies and Planning at Massachusetts Institute of Technology. Her research is situated at the intersection of environmental justice, land policy, and urban planning, examining these issues in developing- and developed-country contexts.

Beth Schaefer Caniglia is Associate Professor of Sociology at Oklahoma State University. Her research focuses on environmental movements, organizations, and policymaking, including studies of the interaction of science, social movements, and public opinion.

JoAnn Carmin is Associate Professor of Environmental Policy and Planning in the Department of Urban Studies and Planning at Massachusetts Institute of Technology. She conducts research on civic engagement in environmental governance, environmental movements and organizations, and urban climate adaptation.

Barbara Hicks is Associate Professor of Political Science and Director of International Studies at New College of Florida. She writes on environmental movements and politics in Central and Eastern Europe.

Tammy L. Lewis is the Carol L. Zicklin Professor in the Honors Academy and Sociology Department at the City University of New York–Brooklyn College, where she conducts research and teaches in the areas of environmental sociology and transnational social movements, with a focus on Latin America.

David Naguib Pellow is Professor and Don A. Martindale Endowed Chair of Sociology at the University of Minnesota, where he teaches courses on social movements, environmental justice, globalization, immigration, and race and ethnicity.

Debra Roberts is Deputy Head of Environmental Planning and Climate Protection in eThekwini Municipality, South Africa. Her key responsibilities include overseeing the planning and protection of the city's natural resource base, ensuring that the environment is considered in all aspects of planning and development in the city, and directing and developing the Municipality's Climate Protection Programme.

Lisa A. Schweitzer is Associate Professor at the University of Southern California. Her research sits at the intersection of transportation, urban environments, and social justice, with a focus on the distribution of social and economic opportunities and the location of environmental hazards in the United States.

Max Stephenson Jr. currently serves as Director of the Virginia Tech Institute for Policy and Governance. He publishes in the areas of humanitarian relief and disaster mitigation, environmental politics and environmental justice, as well as governance and community change processes.

Saskia Vermeylen is a Lecturer in the Lancaster Environment Centre at Lancaster University. Her main area of interest is formal "Western" property law and how it subordinates different kinds of property law including customary law and informal law.

Gordon Walker is Chair of Environment, Risk and Justice in the Lancaster Environment Centre at Lancaster University. He conducts research on environmental justice in the United Kingdom and has studied the social dimensions of sustainable technologies, low carbon transitions, and risk management.

Patricia Widener is Assistant Professor of Sociology at Florida Atlantic University. In addition to extractive economies, oil contention, and environmental disasters, her research interests include the uncertain consumption of genetically modified foods.

Index

Urban and Industrial Environments

Series editor: Robert Gottlieb, Henry R. Luce Professor of Urban and Environmental Policy, Occidental College

Environmental Inequalities Beyond Borders

Urban and Industrial Environments

Series editor: Robert Gottlieb, Henry R. Luce Professor of Urban and Environmental Policy, Occidental College